CHRIST THE HEART OF CREATION

CHRIST THE HEART OF CREATION

Rowan Williams

BLOOMSBURY CONTINUUM
LONDON · NEW YORK · OXFORD · NEW DELHI · SYDNEY

BLOOMSBURY CONTINUUM
Bloomsbury Publishing Plc
50 Bedford Square, London, WC1B 3DP, UK

BLOOMSBURY, BLOOMSBURY CONTINUUM and the Diana logo are
trademarks of Bloomsbury Publishing Plc

First published in Great Britain 2018

A catalogue record for this book is available from the British Library

Library of Congress Cataloguing-in-Publication data has been applied for

ISBN: HB: 978-1-4729-4554-9; ePDF: 978-1-4729-4553-2;
ePub: 978-1-4729-4555-6

4 6 8 10 9 7 5 3

Typeset by Newgen KnowledgeWorks Pvt. Ltd., Chennai, India
Printed and bound in the U.S.A. by Berryville Graphics Inc., Berryville, Virginia

To find out more about our authors and books visit www.bloomsbury.com
and sign up for our newsletters

To commemorate the fiftieth anniversary of the death of Austin Marsden Farrer (1904–68), and in grateful and affectionate memory of John Bainbridge Webster (1955–2016).

CONTENTS

Acknowledgements

This book has had a somewhat prolonged gestation. I began teaching theology in Cambridge in the late seventies, at a time when the theological discussion of what could – must – be said about Jesus Christ was exceptionally lively and disputatious. Participation in the fortnightly Christology seminar and teaching for the special paper on modern Christology in the undergraduate theology course gave me a sense of the scope of contemporary debates; but my interest in the questions was further broadened by an invitation in the early eighties to write two long articles for the German theological reference work, the *Theologische Realenzyklopädie*, on the development of Christology in the early and mediaeval periods. Assembling material for this task allowed me to acquire some familiarity with the details of Byzantine and mediaeval treatments of the subject; and a good deal of what is in this book has its origins in that particular assignment, as well as in the continuing task of teaching the more modern material. When the electors to the Hulsean Lectureship in Cambridge did me the honour of inviting me to deliver a course of lectures in 2016, I was grateful for the opportunity of revisiting and updating notes and researches extending three decades and exploring in more depth an approach to traditional Christology whose roots are most especially to be found in my earlier reading of Thomas Aquinas. This book is for the most part a much expanded version of those lectures as delivered in the Divinity School at Cambridge during the Lent Term of 2016.

Some chapters or sections of chapters have been aired in other contexts. Parts of the introductory chapter were adapted for a De Lubac Lecture at St Louis University in 2017; the material in chapter 1.2 on John of Damascus was shared with Professor Graham Ward's seminar in Oxford in March 2018; ch.2.2 formed the substance of the Du Bose Lectures at the University of the South, Sewanee, in 2016 and a portion of it was read to the International Bonhoeffer Congress in Basel in the same year. The appendix on Wittgenstein as an unlikely and indirect exponent of classical Christology was originally a paper for the meeting of the British Wittgenstein Society in Leeds in 2016, and a shortened version was given as a lecture for the Theology Department of the University of Uppsala in 2017. I am grateful to the audiences at all these events, and to those who listened to and commented on the Cambridge lectures; in every instance, the questions and comments were of real value in polishing and improving the text. Continuing discussions with a variety of colleagues and students have been of great importance for me; Isidoros Katsos and Pui Ip in particular have sharpened my expression and enriched my perceptions in every conversation I have had with them, and my Cambridge colleagues Sarah Coakley, Ian McFarland and Catherine Pickstock have helped me in more ways than I can say by their scholarly and reflective labours. To my wife Jane my debt continues to grow daily.

Rowan Williams
Cambridge, Lent 2018

PREFACE

What I am trying to do in this book is to bring to light one aspect – a central and crucial aspect, I would argue – of how the Church's language about Jesus works; how it clarifies other areas of what Christians say and organizes other doctrines around itself. I believe that if we have a little more clarity about how this language works we may have a little more understanding of why it *dogma* is credible. If people take seriously doctrines such as the divinity of Christ, it is not primarily because they can treat them as if they were tidy conclusions to an argument, deductions from readily available evidence, but because – however obscurely they are grasped, however challenging the detail – they see that the language of doctrine holds together a set of intractably complex questions in a way that offers a coherent context for human living. They make sense, not first as an explanation of things but as a credible environment for action and imagination, a credible means of *connecting* narratives, practices, codes of behaviour; they offer a world to live in.

The reasons that might make us decide actually to live in that world, to *inhabit,* not just vaguely entertain, a scheme of language and imagery like the classical theologies of Christ's nature, will be as various as the histories of the people who make such a decision. Reflecting on the language of doctrine will not in itself do the job of persuading anyone to believe; what it may do is to give more depth and substance to imagining what it is like to believe and what new connections or possibilities are opened up by speaking and imagining like this.

So what is the aspect of this doctrinal tradition that I am inviting readers to think about here? This book argues that a very great deal of what has been said about Jesus across the centuries is shaped by a very particular concern, which has to do with how we think about the relation between God and what God has made. If people are driven to speak about Jesus as if divine freedom were fully at work in him, if they begin to speak about him as they speak about God, they are posing a serious intellectual challenge to themselves. If God is truly the source, the ground and the context of every limited, finite state of affairs, if God is the action or agency that makes everything else active, then God cannot be spoken of as one item in a list of the forces active in the world. God's action cannot be added to the action of some other agent in order to make a more effective force. And this also means that God's action is never in *competition* with any particular activity inside the universe.

How on earth, then, do we speak intelligibly about an individual bit of the universe – the human being called Jesus – as one in whom God is fully active, fully 'embodied' – incarnate, in the technical language of the Church? Is he an incomplete human being into whom God has entered to become a component part, replacing some aspect of his human nature? Is he a human individual upon whom God has such an unparalleled influence that he becomes a sort of channel for communicating divine truth or manifesting divine perfection?

The trouble with both of these models is that they presuppose that God is after all another item inside the universe: God can replace a missing bit of human nature and work as if divine action could supply a gap in human action. Or else, God is not capable of acting *in* but only *on* or *through* Jesus because where there is a complete human being, God can only act on it from outside. Early Christian thought wrestled at enormous length with versions of those two models and judged them inadequate: by the fifth Christian century, it was clear that speaking about Jesus in a way adequate to his role in Christian thinking and Christian worship must involve a different sort of model, in which the complete and unequivocal presence of divine action and human action inseparably united with one another was affirmed in a way that did not diminish the true and active presence of either and did not see them as related 'side by side', one of them influencing the other from outside.

And the point of this for the wider task of theology is that constructing this model was possible only on the strict assumption that divine and created action could never stand alongside each other as rivals (so that the more there is of one, the less there would be of the other). God makes the world to be *itself*, to have an integrity and completeness and goodness that is – by God's gift – its own. At the same time, God makes the world to be open to a relation with God's own infinite life that can enlarge and transfigure the created order without destroying it. The model developed in Christology is the model that clarifies all we say about God's relation with the world, the relation between infinite and finite, Creator and creation. The fullness and flourishing of creation is not something that has to be won at the Creator's expense; the outpouring of God's life into the world to fulfil the world's potential for joy and reconciliation does not entail an amputation of the full reality of the world's life. And all this is summed up in our belief in a Christ who is uninterruptedly living a creaturely, finite life on earth and at the same time living out of the depths of divine life and uninterruptedly enjoying the relation that eternally subsists between the divine Source or Father and the divine Word or Son.

It is in this sense that we can rightly speak of Jesus as *the heart of creation,* the one on whom all the patterns of finite existence converge to find their meaning. While the relation between Jesus and the eternal divine Word – the 'hypostatic union', which is an uninterrupted continuity of distinct, self-identifying, active life between the Word and Jesus – is unique, it can only be understood in connection to a general conception, a metaphysical model, of how the finite and the infinite relate to one another. And as the implications of what is said about Jesus become clearer and richer with the development of Christian discourse, this sense of what is involved in speaking of finite and infinite is in turn clarified and enriched.

This book is an attempt to trace something of this mutual illumination that connects Christology with the doctrine of creation. Elements in the traditional doctrinal picture that seem abstruse or over-complicated can make sense if understood in the light of a concern to leave no ambiguity at all about the non-competitive relation of Creator and creation. And – as later chapters in the book argue – clarity about this can play a vital role in clarifying certain themes in ethics and politics for the Christian. When we hear about the 'non-duality' of God and the world, we are probably inclined to think of textbook caricatures of Hindu or Buddhist cosmologies; but the Christological model requires us to think of non-duality in its proper sense: God and the world are not two things to be added together. Neither are they two things that are 'really' one thing. They exist in an asymmetrical relation in which one depends wholly on the other, yet is fully itself, made to be and to act according to its own logic and structure.

One writer who does not receive anything like an adequate treatment in this book, but who contributes some uniquely lucid insights on this, is the great fifteenth-century genius, Nicholas of Cusa, whose characterization of God as *non aliud* – 'not another thing' – in relation to the world expresses the heart of this point (he continues to influence contemporary theology in all sorts of ways, not least through the enthusiasm with which that phrase was taken up by the Swiss Catholic theologian, Hans Urs von Balthasar, one of the most independent and creative Catholic thinkers of the twentieth century). This *non aliud* principle, or what I have called – in what I know is a rather awkward phrase – 'non-dual non-identity', is at the heart of the relation between the infinite and the finite. And when this is clear, a number of recurrent tangles in Christian thought have some hope of being straightened out.

This hope of straightening out some tangles in the light of a clarified Christology is something that – as the opening chapter explains – I derive largely from the work of the subtlest and most eloquent Anglican thinker of the last century, Austin Farrer, who died just 50 years ago, and whose intellectual legacy is still being explored. My discussion here begins with a text of Farrer's, as a way of commemorating his anniversary, and also as a way of acknowledging an intellectual and spiritual debt that goes back a very long way indeed. But a good many other theologians have contributed to what is argued here, including some whom I have not directly discussed at great length in the body of the text. Thomas F. Torrance's writings on theology in general and Christology in particular had a very strong impact on my early reflections on the subject, and his little book on *Space, Time and Incarnation,* originally published in 1969, was the first text that enabled me to see clearly that the language of incarnation did not oblige you to think of an extra-terrestrial individual changing places in order to enter an alien world with its own self-contained spatial boundaries; rather, what the doctrine affirmed was a radical change of the relation between the world and its maker at a particular point in history, such that one element of that world was now uniquely the vehicle of the absolute creative freedom of God the Word. Leave behind a 'receptacle' view of space (in accordance with contemporary scientific understanding), Torrance argues, and the picture is substantially clarified.

More recently the exemplary precision and conceptual clarity of successive books by Kathryn Tanner on creation and on Christology (not least her 1988 study of *God and Creation in Christian Theology*) have helped me greatly in sharpening my own thinking on these subjects. The late and much-lamented John Webster wrote all too little on Christology, but what he did write was of characteristic authority and coherence, and the dedication of this book expresses my admiration for his contribution.

For many English-speaking theologians, the essays of Herbert McCabe, OP, have been models of sense, insight and economy of expression, and these too have been regularly at work in the background of this book. And finally, two pieces of very recent work – a long and fascinating essay by Paul DeHart of Vanderbilt University on the theological implications of some kinds of historical revisionism about the narratives of Jesus, and a highly original doctoral dissertation by Tim Boniface on Hans Frei and Dietrich Bonhoeffer, published as this book goes to press (*Jesus, Transcendence, and Generosity: Christology and Transcendence in Hans Frei and Dietrich Bonhoeffer*, Lanham, MD, Lexington Books/Fortress Academic 2018) – have helped to shape some of the final stages of writing. I mention them here because both deserve far fuller discussion.

This study is not meant as a comprehensive guide to Christologies ancient and modern, and there are obvious gaps in coverage. I have noted in passing that both Bonaventure and Nicholas of Cusa would merit much longer treatment. But the constraints of a relatively brief lecture series and of writing up those lectures in a limited time span have forced me to be selective. Similarly, the final chapter of the main text, in which I engage at some length with the thought of the Jesuit Erich Przywara, cries out for longer discussion of Hans Urs von Balthasar, for whom Przywara was a major influence, especially in his appropriation – mentioned above – of Nicholas of Cusa's *non aliud* language. But, on the principle that it may be more helpful to give more space to the less well-known writer, and also because Przywara's ideas relate so very closely to the main themes of this book, I have restricted reference to the Swiss theologian, confident that he will not lack for expositors and critics for the foreseeable future.

At times in the history of Christology, it is hard to see the wood for the trees, and I guess that there will be sections of this book which will have the same effect. The minute calibrations of vocabulary by a sixth-century Byzantine writer, the logical fishbones picked out in the language of *esse*, the 'act of being', in medieval scholasticism, the laboured discussions of merit and satisfaction, the textual complexities of Bonhoeffer or Przywara as they handle the legacy of German metaphysical debates, all these will seem a long way from a congregation singing 'Before the throne of God above' or 'Jesu, Lover of my soul' (or, for a Welsh Christian, '*Iesu, Iesu, 'rwyt ti'n ddigon*'); or from an Orthodox believer bowing to the ground before an icon of the saviour, or a pilgrim kissing the smooth, chilly stone in the basilica at Bethlehem where Mary is said to have given birth.

Yet these expressions of dramatic commitment to Jesus of Nazareth as the centre and animating power of Christian existence and prayer are precisely what generate the thickets of analysis and speculation that have grown up across the centuries. To *act* towards Jesus in this way continually presses on us the question of how we are to *speak* – *about* as well as *to* him. And, as this speaking develops and matures, it in turn generates – if it is doing its job – a deeper and steadier devotion. None of the writers discussed here thought that their conceptual labours were an end in themselves; all turned back day after day from speaking about to speaking to. I hope that this book will help readers sense the pressure that turns us back in that way to the Christ who is never a passive object to be discussed but who continues to put in question and to transfigure the lives of those who recognize him as the eternal Word made flesh.

Introduction: Beginning in the Middle (Ages): Aquinas's Christological Vision

1. Jesus Christ: Infinite Act and Finite Embodiment

When Austin Farrer delivered his Bampton Lectures, *The Glass of Vision*, at the University Church in Oxford in the autumn of 1948, they were recognized immediately by a wide variety of listeners as an unusually original and fertile series of explorations on the then unfrequented borderlands of philosophy and biblical hermeneutics. Building on the more extended and highly technical discussions he had undertaken a few years earlier in *Finite and Infinite*, they move from a treatment of the relation between natural and super-natural agency to a consideration of metaphor and analogy and a set of proposals as to how Scripture should be read – as well as incidentally sketching out a theology of grace. They remain one of his lasting achievements, probably more widely read than his more strictly metaphysical works, and recently republished in an anno-tated edition with a number of more recent essays commenting on their arguments.[1] And it is one of Farrer's decisive insights that provides the starting point for these chapters. Early in the lectures, Farrer in effect summarizes the metaphysical picture he had worked

---

1   Robert MacSwain, ed., *Scripture, Metaphysics and Poetry: Austin Farrer's* The Glass of Vision *with Critical Commentary*, Farnham: Ashgate, 2013.

out in his earlier writing, though with clarifications and modifications. We know from scrutinizing our own agency that there is a 'hierarchy' of sorts in our actions; some manifestly bring into play more resource, more innovative vision, more concentrated intelligence ('intelligence' of body as well as mind, as he significantly insists[2]); when we attempt to think of God, we are attempting to deploy and clarify a notion of agency that is unbrokenly using its entire resource, generating possibilities for every other conceivable agent and fully exercising an unlimited intelligence. As Farrer clearly says,[3] this means that infinite agency can never be prayed in aid to fill a gap in finite causal chains. What infinite agency causes simply *is* the system of secondary causality within which we finite agents act: we could not conceive infinite agency unless we lived in a world of finite causes and agencies that was for all practical purposes complete in its own terms. What it means for infinite causality/agency to be at work *is* that a system of finite causes is operating – not that a more impressive instance of finite causality is invoked to complete the picture. To use infinite agency to close a gap is to rob it of its infinite character.

Yet we speak theologically not only of the natural working of finite causes within the universe but of the 'supernatural' reality which is the life of finite agents transformed by or participating in the infinite. Does this not upset the balance and clarity of the basic model of finite and infinite? No, says Farrer, because we live not simply in a world of regular finite causes but in a world where the unique phenomenon of personal *will* characterizes certain of those finite agencies – will understood as the focal element in distinctively personal existence, that which brings into play the maximal resource of our created nature. And since – as we have seen – we conceive God as infinite personal will and intelligence, as the exercise of infinite resource fully and eternally present in every moment of its action, there exists in creation the possibility of relation between finite and infinite at a level other than that of universal causal activation. Personal relatedness between divine and human will unites divine life with the highest of the levels of finite agency; and this relation transformingly illuminates how human intelligence and love are rooted in infinite agency. This is something that in some degree

2   Ibid., p. 27.
3   Ibid., pp. 22–3.

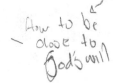
How to be close to God's will

can be intuited 'naturally' but must be anchored in a fuller awareness of the actual life of God as Trinity. What it promises is an unlimited and conscious growth into an enhancement of human intelligence and love in communion with God's infinite action.[4] Thus the world of interlocking finite causes is not closed in a mechanistic way: finite agencies may bring about effects greater than the sum of their parts through their relatedness to infinite act. As Farrer puts it,[5] God may bring about 'through second causes [i.e. finite causes] effects which do not arise from the natural powers of those causes'. Put slightly differently, this is a claim that under certain circumstances finite agency going about its business is open to possibilities in excess of its own immanent and predictable capacities, so that what an event or transaction in the sequence of finite causality makes possible is genuinely new, not capable of prediction from the analysis of habitual causal patterns alone. We have, says Farrer, some hint of this in the work of our own imagination as it transforms the givenness of the world; but properly *supernatural* activity in the world is discernible when we both recognize and act in tune with dimensions, purposes and possibilities in the world that are not simply obvious to the natural observer. And one significant form of this is what we call revelation. Revelation is something communicated from infinite agency or reality to the finite mind. But (in Farrer's picture) this is not a matter of God just interrupting the process of the world to 'insert' something alien into the gap; it happens as a result of what happens in the world of finite agents or substances, as these finite realities are modified in their relations to one another, drawn into newly meaningful shapes. There is no suspension or displacement of the stuff of the world, but that stuff is reorganized as if around a new magnetic point of focus. In the case of the central events of Christian revelation, in the specific shape of the life of Jesus, we come to grasp a new set of possibilities in talking about God: we come to acknowledge that 'in God there is an act of begotten and responsive love, that it is reciprocated, and that it is cemented by a Spirit mutually indwelling';[6] or that our human destiny is ultimately defined by incorporation into the

---

4   Ibid., pp. 33–4.
5   Ibid., p. 22.
6   Ibid., p. 34.

eternal act through the fellowship of Christ's Church; or that certain events may be rightly seen as examples of providential leading by God.

And here we come to the focal point of the argument. 'There is a sort of paradox involved in the very idea of a supernatural act', says Farrer.[7] The paradox is that for it to be a truly supernatural act, it cannot be simply another action standing alongside 'natural' acts. If it is really an action of another order, it must at the same time be genuinely the act of a finite, 'natural' agent, recognizably continuous with what that agent habitually does. If it is not this, it becomes something that *replaces* the natural act – which makes it simply another natural act, not a supernatural one. The key is the realization that, whereas the typical act of one sort of finite nature cannot coexist with the act of another kind of finite nature, this cannot apply in the case of infinity: we cannot say that the finite excludes the infinite *in the way* that one finite agency excludes another. Obviously (though Farrer does not elaborate the point at this stage), finitude and infinity are 'exclusive' in the sense that infinity is the absence of actual contingent limitation; but precisely because of this we have the paradox that the infinite cannot be 'excluded' from the finite in virtue of any specific property that is incompatible with some other specific property. So, Farrer concludes, 'in some true sense the creature and the Creator are both enacting the creature's life, though in different ways and at different depths'.[8] There is no sense in which infinite agency is a 'something' added to the sum total of finite causality; and so – assuming the fact of createdness as the mode of relation between finite and infinite – what the creature does is what the Creator is doing. Thus we can identify the creature *as creature* by saying, 'this action is not only the characteristic action of such and such a finite substance; it is also a distinctive mode in which the infinite causal action of the Creator is operative and knowable. It is an *asymmetrical* formulation, because we cannot claim that the Creator's act is only and exhaustively what the creature is doing, that it is defined by finite interactions. The Creator is that which activates a potentially unlimited set of modes in which finite agency is exercised, but is also simply what it eternally is.

7   Ibid., p. 35.
8   Ibid.

In the light of this clarification of the finite/infinite distinction, we can see that 'revelatory' action, including whatever events allow us a closer conscious share in infinite agency (in the love of the Trinity, to use the conventional theological phrasing), will be, not an interruption of the finite sequence, but a particular configuration of finite agency such that it communicates more than its own immanent content. And this recognition of duality in our apprehension of finite agency, seeing the finite as enacting the infinite without ceasing to be finite – and specifically seeing this at work in any finite agency that we identify as 'revealing' something of God not otherwise available to natural perception, holds the key to a range of theological puzzles. 'Upon this double personal agency in our one activity turns the verbally insoluble riddle of grace and freewill, or of Godhead and Manhood in Christ's One Person, or the efficacy of human prayer.'[9] In other words, Farrer is claiming that without a clear account of what we might call the logic of createdness, the most central elements of classical Christian theology will simply be a set of dead ends for thought.

Later in the lectures,[10] Farrer returns to the specific question of how this works in the case of incarnation. To speak of God's action in Jesus is to claim not merely that God brings about a particular historical result by means of natural agency – as a writer of Hebrew Scripture might claim is happening when King David defeats the Philistines – but that some result that is *not just another* episode in history is brought about through the historical doings of finite agency. The effect of Jesus' life, death and rising certainly includes historical matters – the existence of the Church, obviously, and all that goes with that. But the reconciliation of the world to God cannot be described as an episode in history among others; it is a change in what historical agents may hope for, think about and pray about. As such it is emphatically a 'supernatural' act, bringing about what no particular agency within creation could have done in virtue of its own immanent finite capacity. So when – as people who believe that the world has changed comprehensively because of him – we look for adequate language to tell the truth about Jesus, we shall need a model for the union of divine and human action in Christ that sees Christ as the historical and bodily *location* of unlimited active freedom,

9 Ibid., p. 36.
10 Ibid., pp. 91–2.

the place where God is active with an intensity that is nowhere else to be found. Here God's active freedom impinges on creation so as to bring about a change that is undoubtedly manifested in an historically tangible way (the risen Christ establishes the visible sacramental fellowship that will allow his life to be shared) but cannot be reduced to or identified with any specific historical outcome (as if we could conclude that God was at work because the effects of the life of Jesus were so obviously successful or spectacular). With this in mind, Farrer says, we embark on the search for clusters of metaphor in Scripture that point towards the presence of the unlimited within history, the search for a hermeneutic of scriptural imagery that allows us to have our imaginations enlarged in the direction of that which cannot finally be 'imaged' with any adequacy – the reality of an unlimited actuality that can be thought only in some sort of association with love and intelligence.

In the chapters that follow, I am trying to work with Farrer's central insight – but, so to speak, turning it around. Farrer uses a model of finite/infinite relation to illuminate a range of doctrinal questions;[11] my question is about how the evolution of doctrinal formulae itself prompts the clarification of that model. Chicken and egg, you may rightly say: the pressures that shape the language of traditional doctrine push forward an exploration of the metaphysical structure that alone will make sense of it. What this book addresses, therefore, is what it is about various approaches over the centuries to the doctrine of Christ – most particularly to the understanding of the person of Christ and the ascription to him of divinity and humanity together – that takes forward this exploration. That is to say, how does Christology itself generate a new and fuller grasp of the 'grammar' of createdness? Christology is not just one example of a theological theme or topic that is illuminated by a general metaphysical axiom about finite and infinite; it is, I shall argue, the major theological enterprise that itself shapes and clarifies that axiom. If it is doing its job carefully and consistently, Christology has a metaphysical implication, and what we shall see, I hope, in the discussion of assorted historical understandings of Christ's person is that the particular constraints that moulded doctrinal dispute in

<hr/>

11 For his own application of this to Christology, see especially the brief and profoundly original essay on 'Very God and Very Man', in the posthumous collection *Interpretation and Belief*, ed. Charles Conti, London: SPCK, 1976, pp. 126–37.

their context are bound in with these broader questions about the ontology of finite and infinite. To do justice to what Christology seeks to articulate presses us to work at the logic, or grammar, or however you want to put it, of speaking about God at all, speaking of infinite agency that is in some way characterized by what we would call intelligence and love – and also the logic of the language of 'creation', universal dependence. If we read the classical discussions of Christology with these issues in mind, we shall perhaps be less ready than some modern theologians to dismiss the vocabulary and the thought world worked out particularly in the intellectual trajectory that leads from the third- and fourth-century doctrinal debates to the extraordinary synthesis spelled out by Thomas Aquinas, and the refinements and revisions of this that eventually led to the Christologies of the Reformation era.

I have chosen to begin, unapologetically, by looking at that particular moment of synthesis in Aquinas's thought, seeing it as a watershed in the doctrinal story: I do not want to treat it as in every respect a timelessly true and adequate rendering of the Christological enterprise, but it does have a claim to be the point at which the broadest range of theoretical questions was brought into view and a robust and consistent vocabulary developed for integrating these questions. So often in this area of theology, later puzzles and apparent dead ends in doctrinal reflection can be transformed by a better understanding of what we discover that Aquinas has already discussed.

This means that I am not going to spend a great deal of time on those modern critiques of the classical framework that show a lack of awareness of exactly what was discussed in the development of that framework. Thus, the once popular complaint that claiming divinity and humanity to be equally predicable of Jesus Christ was simply to utter a contradiction (comparable to trying to describe a square circle[12]) ignores the absolutely basic point

---

12 A typical statement of this can be found in John Hick's essay, 'Jesus and the World's Religions', pp. 167–85 in John Hick, ed., *The Myth of God Incarnate*, London: SCM Press, 1977: the Chalcedonian formula 'remains a form of words without assignable meaning. For to say, without explanation, that the historical Jesus of Nazareth was also God is as devoid of meaning as to say that this circle drawn with pencil on paper is also a square' (p. 178). Not only the phrase 'without explanation' but the telling little word 'also' suggests a somewhat cavalier approach to what historic orthodoxy actually affirmed.

which Farrer was concerned to highlight: we are not talking of divinity and humanity as two *genera* alongside each other, so that the Christological claim is precisely *not* a claim that one subject possesses two kinds of (incompatible) defining natural qualities. Given that this point is taken completely for granted by every medieval theologian and is at least implicit in most later patristic writers, it is impossible to see the complaint as a new discovery, a new intellectual difficulty for an unexamined dogma. Slightly more serious are those modern reservations about the classical model which argue that, despite good intentions, the language used inexorably draws us towards a diminished account of the real finite humanity of Jesus. The traditional formula that 'there is no faith or hope' within the human subjectivity of Jesus (*nulla fides nec spes in Christo*) certainly suggests, at first glance, such a diminished picture, a humanity that is deprived of its particularity as a genuine subject of worldly experiences.[13] But, as we shall see, it is generally simply not the case that what the traditional formulations deny is the same as what defenders of the full humanity of Jesus want to affirm; there are certainly awkwardnesses in the classical language, as in the denial of faith and hope to Jesus, and we shall encounter assumptions that cannot easily be sustained in an intellectual framework in which psychological processes are very differently understood from the way they were approached in the thirteenth century. But a good many recent discussions and restatements of the

---

13   The discussion of whether we should ascribe faith and hope to Jesus (and the generally negative conclusion) goes back to Peter Lombard in the early twelfth century (*Liber Sententiarum* III.23, PL 191, 805–7). Aquinas deals with it in ST III.7. For a very useful and careful recent treatment of whether the incarnate Christ had faith, broadly defending the Thomist view, see Simon Francis Gaine, OP, *Did the Saviour See the Father? Christ, Salvation and the Vision of God*, London: Bloomsbury T&T Clark, 2015, Chapter 5. A common misunderstanding of the Byzantine view that the incarnate Christ is *anupostatos*, without a created hypostasis or principle of identification (see below, Chapter 1.2), sometimes leads people to suppose that classical orthodoxy thinks of Christ's humanity as 'impersonal' in the modern sense, as having no finite human individuality. Bonhoeffer, for example, in his Christology lectures (see below, Chapter 2.2), seems to understand the idea in this way and sees the Byzantine doctrine as 'an ultimately concealed form of docetism' (*Lectures on Christology*, in Clifford J. Green and Michael P. DeJonge, eds, *The Bonhoeffer Reader*, Minneapolis: Fortress Press, 2013, p. 291.

traditional language have argued that Aquinas's scheme still leaves room for an unambiguous affirmation of what we might call a three-dimensional psychological life in the incarnate Word, a life, that is, which grows and adjusts (and suffers) as ordinary finite human selves or subjects do.[14]

A more distinctively contemporary complaint, though, is that the dual-nature Christology of tradition is heavily shaped by the imperative to 'protect' the divine nature from suffering; and in a theological climate where divine impassibility is no longer taken for granted, where, indeed, some regard it as a positively wrong and damaging idea, there needs to be a stronger emphasis on the unity of Christ and the consequent direct involvement of God in the human suffering of Jesus. This is an issue we shall have to return to, but for now it is worth noting simply that the 'Farrer paradigm' does not entail a kind of quarantine-like isolation of the divine agent from what happens in and to Jesus – but it does entail a careful distinction between what can intelligibly be described as the experience of a finite subject and the imagining of a divine 'point of view'. The latter is something that can be conceived only in a complex metaphorical web of allusion or evocation, not as an object of direct speculation, since it is by definition not accessible to any finite subject. As Herbert McCabe spelled out in a characteristically lucid essay,[15] the classical theological and Christological scheme does not mean either that God stands aloof from the suffering of the human instrument he has assumed or any other human individual, or that his divine 'subjectivity' is somehow immersed in and identified with a human psyche, in an extreme instance of intersubjective empathy. The presence of God in or to the sufferings of Jesus of Nazareth is literally immeasurably more intimate than any intersubjective exchange of feeling; but this is not necessarily to qualify in any way what the doctrine of divine impassibility affirms, which is that God is not passive in relation to other agents on the same level, not part of an interactive system.

14 Gaine, op. cit., has some helpful reflections on this; and see also Sarah Coakley's contribution, 'Person of Christ', to The Cambridge Companion to the Summa Theologiae, ed. Philip McCosker and Denys Turner, Cambridge: Cambridge University Press, 2016, pp. 222–39, especially pp. 235–6, 238.

15 Herbert McCabe, OP, 'The Involvement of God', in God Matters, London: Mowbray, 1997, pp. 39–51, and cf. his review article, 'The Myth of God Incarnate' in the same collection, pp. 54–61, especially pp. 56–7.

These objections to the traditional structure of Christological thought bring into sharp focus some of the ways in which that structure has been misunderstood or imperfectly studied by some theologians. The result has been either a distancing from the classical formulations, or what could be called a remythologizing of Christology – a strongly narrative account of how a divine subject becomes a human subject, acquiring new 'experiences' in the process. Occasionally – by no means always – this has been allied with a strong emphasis on the theological significance of Jesus' masculinity, an issue that has obvious implications in contemporary discussions of gendered language about God and about the ordained ministry of women, but, whatever position is taken on such questions, it is something of an eccentricity to claim that there is a simple link between conservative stances in these areas and an orthodox Christology, when the Christology assumed is in fact at odds with the intellectual structure of mainstream teaching, Catholic and Protestant, on the person of Christ.[16] The doctrine of Christ's person as developed through the patristic and medieval periods represented a steady trajectory of pulling away from mythological accounts of incarnation as if it were an episode in the life of a heavenly subject; and this was in part because of the fundamental point we have seen emerging in this introductory discussion: the doctrine needs to be articulated in such a way that the grammar of our talk about God as such is not reduced to the level of language about some inhabitant, however exalted, of the universe. And I have already indicated that the question can be turned around so as to show how that 'grammar' is itself in several important respects shaped by the constraints of thinking consistently about Christ.

There is one last point to be noted by way of introduction. In the Reformation and post-Reformation theological world, the connection between the person of Christ and the work of Christ was more closely and explicitly drawn than had generally been the case before – although, as we shall see, Aquinas's scheme finds its completion in a detailed discussion of the Body of Christ. Some forms of modern theology – especially the thinking of Barth and Bonhoeffer, as we shall see in Chapter 2.2 – use the

---

16 Kathryn Tanner, *Christ the Key*, Cambridge: Cambridge University Press, 2010, has some judicious observations on this; see especially pp. 212–16.

Chalcedonian structure as a starting point for some very fresh and generative reflection on ethics and ecclesiology, arising out of their account of the way in which Christ's divine humanity works to secure salvation. In the course of the present discussion, we shall be looking at how these new insights can be located within the basic scheme that Farrer's metaphysic outlines. Understanding how Christ exists radically and exhaustively *for the other* can be seen as a natural development from the underlying grammar of our speech about divine action. If Christ is truly the embodiment of divine agency in a unique and unsurpassable sense, that agency has no element in it of ontological insecurity; it has literally nothing to defend. Thus a human agency that is characterized consistently by availability, *disponibilité*, for the other, a human agency that is identified as representative of the human other without reservation or restriction, is an entirely intelligible translation into human narrative and finite action of the undefended act of a God who cannot lose or lessen what is proper to divine life. Perhaps surprisingly, the classical structure turns out to be formative for a highly contemporary ethic and ecclesiology, especially in the hands of Bonhoeffer.

The main argument of these chapters, however, remains the claim that Christology, so far from requiring a rethinking of the classical account of divine perfections (impassibility, immutability and so on), actually provides the fullest possible rationale for them. And conversely, the classical modes of characterizing divine life, so far from being abstract and alien importations into a properly scriptural and/or experientially grounded theology, allow created existence its own integrity and dignity, and deliver us from a theology in which God is in danger of being seen simply as a very important or uniquely powerful agent in the universe competing with other agents in the universe for space or control. That God is in no imaginable sense the rival of humanity, that the relation between finite and infinite agency can never be one in which more of one means less of the other, and (crucially) that God can therefore have no 'interests' to defend over against the interest of the creatures God has made out of unconstrained and selfless love – all this is part of what makes the classical Christological synthesis still a spiritually and morally serious proposal for understanding what it is to be the object of creative and limitless generosity; or, in simple terms, for hearing the gospel.

2. Summarizing a Tradition: The Christology of Thomas Aquinas

Beginning a study like this with a discussion of a thirteenth-century theologian looks eccentric. But I have chosen to do this because Thomas Aquinas's account (especially as it is set out at the beginning of the Third Part of his *Summa Theologiae*[17]) of how we might find a consistent language to speak about the Incarnation is not only one of the first attempts at a completely comprehensive treatment of the topic, but, in its phrasing of questions about the subject, it also consistently directs us towards the fundamental point already emphasized: finite and infinite agency are not in rivalry. It is true that at first sight many of these questions seem almost absurdly recondite, discussing apparently wild counterfactuals. Is incarnation 'fitting' to God? Would it have been better for God to be incarnate from the beginning of creation? Could the second Person of the Trinity take human nature without involving the others Persons as well? Could the same divine Person be incarnate in a number of human individuals? Could more than one Person be incarnate? Does the Incarnation entail the assumption of a human mind? And so on. It is easy to make the mistake of thinking that this is a series of obsessively speculative debates, having little relevance to the central business of theological clarification. But a closer reading of these dense and abstract pages should make it clear that what is being undertaken is a massive grammatical clearing of the ground so that there is no room for any notion of incarnation as a heavenly individual 'turning into' an earthly one (and thus replacing some finite agency by a direct divine interruption).

To illustrate the point, we shall look briefly at a sequence of questions in this section of the *Summa*, III.iii.4, 5 and 6: 'Whether one Person can assume a created nature independently of another', 'Whether any divine Persons could have assumed human nature', and 'Whether several divine Persons could assume a nature that was numerically one'. Taken for granted throughout is a relatively simple formulation: the Incarnation is that divine action by which an individualized human substance is fully and inseparably united to the second Person of the Trinity ('assumed' by that Person, in St Thomas's preferred terminology). On the first of these questions, the problem that arises is that divine action is inseparably one, so that an act

---

17 III.i–xlix, especially i–ix.

involving any divine Person must be the act of them all; the entire nature of God subsists in each Person, so that there cannot be any account of incarnation that is not a statement about all three Persons. How then can we say that God the Son alone is incarnate? In response, Aquinas distinguishes[18] between the act of 'assumption' and the 'terminus' of that action: everything done by God is done inseparably by the Trinity; but what that action brings about is a state of affairs in which human nature is related to *the Person of the Son* – not to the divine nature in general. This helps us understand the following question, about whether any divine Person could be incarnate. Surely not, we might say, since the very shape of redemptive activity is to make us adopted sons and daughters of the eternal Father, to give our lives a 'filial' quality in their relation to God.[19] But Thomas's answer is, in effect, yes, of course, any divine Person could assume humanity, because anything that can be done by any one Person must be an aspect of divine capacity as such and thus common to all three Persons. If the divine action can unite humanity to the Son, it can unite humanity to the Father or the Spirit. But the fact that Christ as a matter of fact saves us by being the perfect exemplar of 'filiation', the condition of being a child of God, cannot be taken to imply that only the divine Son could bring about our adoption. In principle the Father, as the originating cause of the natural relationship that the divine Son has with him, could cause adoptive filiation to exist in us; or the Spirit, considered as the love between Father and Son, could do the same.[20] We cannot begin from the idea that for us to become children of God there must *necessarily* be a union of human nature with the Son. And so to the third question in this group, the answer has to be that indeed it would be possible for more than one divine Person to assume an individuated human nature. What makes the human nature of Jesus Christ a numerically single agent in the world is simply the normal set of natural qualities

---

18 III.iii.4c.

19 III.iii.5.2.

20 III.iii.5c and ad 2. As Dominic Legge, OP, argues in his lucid and wide-ranging recent monograph on *The Trinitarian Christology of St Thomas Aquinas*, Oxford: Oxford University Press, 2017 (pp. 125–7), a putative incarnation of the Father or the Spirit would have to look very different from the actual incarnation we are confronted with. He slightly underrates, I think, Aquinas's clarity about adoptive filiation being the goal, whichever divine person were to be incarnate.

in this particular contingent relation to one another that routinely serves to individuate a finite substance.[21] It is not that the human nature is individuated at this level by the direct presence of one divine Person. In God, three divine Persons constitute a single substantial agent; there is no objection in principle to thinking that the same might hold in respect of a single substantial human agent. But (and we shall be returning to this point) what is impossible is that the three Persons should assume a single pre-existing human *hypostasis* – that is, a pre-existing principle of agency determining the particular historical identity of the individuated nature.[22] Individuated nature is an abstract idea, and becomes concrete only when activated in the form of a self-continuous agent among agents. What the Incarnation cannot mean – whether it involves one divine Person or three – is that a divine hypostatic agency is added to or, worse, displaces, an existing finite principle of personal agency.

It needs to be said at once that all of this belongs to the realm of what we would call 'thought experiments': Aquinas is perfectly clear, only a few pages later on,[23] that it is more suitable or appropriate, *conveniens*, that the Son should be incarnate, since finite being itself in a sense images his eternal dependence on the Father: that we are destined by grace to be sons and daughters of God the Father does not indeed necessitate the Son's incarnation, but it is undoubtedly a more 'congruent' procedure that the divine Person to whom humanity is united should be the eternal paradigm of dependent love and filial relation. The point of the questions just discussed – and several more that need to be read in the same way – is to clarify what must *not* be said about the Incarnation. *The human life of Jesus is not an episode in the life of an eternal subject which changes its metaphysical location*; thus it is necessary to establish that there is no sense in which the Person of the divine Word is an enlarged version of finite individuality, such that the Incarnation would necessarily involve a negotiation for *Lebensraum* between two comparable individuals. The divine Word is not another (divine) instance of the sort of thing that the human individuality of Jesus exemplifies. These discussions are

---

21   III.iii.6c and ad 3.

22   Ibid., c: *esset tamen impossibile ut assumerent [sc. personae divinae] unam hypostasim vel unam personam humanam.*

23   III.iii.8.

meant to wean us away from imagining any kind of isomorphism between the two; and the extravagance of Aquinas's counterfactual proposals serves to underline the importance of getting this clear. If we fail to do so, as various details of his discussion imply, we shall end up with an unsustainable picture of God's nature. We may imagine it as an ensemble of three divine agents whose unity is subsequent to their distinctiveness; or we may confuse the eternal relation of the Word to the Father with the filial life of the Word on earth (as Son of Man, in St Thomas's terms) as though the former depended on the latter. Aquinas keeps two things firmly in view here – the necessity of affirming that the sonship of the Word is eternally and intrinsically an aspect of divine life; and the essential importance of understanding that the Persons of the Godhead are one in action. The former implies that the Trinitarian relationships are in no way constituted by events that take place in the world of finitude – another point to which we shall return in a later chapter. The latter challenges us to conceive of divine action as something radically different from the agency of individuals in a world of interacting individual substances: in one sense it is true to say that the human Jesus acts as such an individual; but the divine act by which his humanity is united to divinity is not another act in the same set or series.

Positively, what Aquinas has to say about the union is that (as we have already noted) it is a union at the level of hypostasis or, to use his preferred Latin term, *suppositum*. The 'supposit' is what can be said to 'have' a nature of this or that kind; it is that to which is ascribed such and such a kind: it provides the answer to the question of *which* individual of a certain nature is in question – and so in the human context, to the question, 'Who?' Talking about a supposit is talking about a reality that is more than the bare specification of what kind of thing is being spoken of; it is speaking of a particular subject of active existence (III.ii.2). To imagine that the Incarnation could be a union at the level of nature would make no sense: God is what God is, and that defining essence cannot be really or substantially united with any other kind of being. St Thomas goes through the various ways in which finite essences can be joined together to produce a new kind of thing, and has no difficulty in showing that none of these could possibly apply where one of the essences involved is perfect and unchangeable, and that the kind of union in which the essences are left unaffected and capable of continuing independent activity is not really a union in any interesting sense but at best an *ars*, the formal working together of the capacities of different natures (III.ii.1). Divinity and humanity together cannot *add up* to anything. But an individualized humanity united to a divine principle of distinct agency, what we could call an 'actualizing' presence united with it, poses no such problem.

And the result is what Thomas later describes as unity in *esse* – unity at the level of the distinctive act and mode of existing that belongs eternally to the divine Word. There is potential confusion in the fact that *esse*, like supposit, can sometimes be said to 'include' nature. And this means that we can say, from one point of view, that the eternal *esse* of the Word is unchangeably what it is, unaffected by its union with Jesus of Nazareth, and from another equally correct and valid point of view, that the *esse* of the Word 'includes' the active existence of the humanity that has been assumed (III. xvii.2). We shall return to the question of how *esse* is defined and used, but it is worth setting out at this stage the outline of what is being claimed and what is being ruled out, as well as one of the potential sources of unclarity in terminology. What Thomas's claim amounts to is that the 'act of being' in virtue of which the Word of God is the Word of God is the sole ground of the act of being in virtue of which Jesus of Nazareth is Jesus of Nazareth considered as an active finite agent; and the implication clearly is that there can be in Jesus no *finite* act of being in virtue of which he is who he is.

This is where difficulties arise for some who read Aquinas as implying that Jesus of Nazareth is deficient in finite 'integrity', so to speak, since there is no created *esse* in him. An immensely detailed and sophisticated recent study by Richard Cross[24] has argued strongly that Aquinas's position struggles unsuccessfully to avoid the implication of monophysitism – the belief that Christ has no *independent* human nature, but only one that is wholly absorbed into the divine. He notes the development from Aquinas's earlier Christology towards the slightly different styles of synthesis set out in the last year of Aquinas's life (when he had been immersing himself

---

24 Richard Cross, *The Metaphysics of the Incarnation: Thomas Aquinas to Duns Scotus*, Oxford: Oxford University Press, 2002. For a robust and nuanced Thomist account which responds to many of Cross's arguments, see now Michael J. Gorman, *Aquinas on the Metaphysics of the Hypostatic Union*, Cambridge: Cambridge University Press, 2017.

more fully in the writings of Cyril of Alexandria and John of Damascus and had absorbed the language and perspective of the Second Council of Constantinople[25]). Thomas in some of his earlier work uses the analogy of the union of a part with the whole to characterize the relation of humanity to the divine Person in Christ, but this creates major difficulties. It cannot be the case that the humanity of Jesus causes certain things to be true of the eternal Word *as such*, and Aquinas directly denies that this can be so.[26] Yet we should normally say that the existence of a part made certain things true about a whole of which it is a continuous or inseparable part. Aquinas at certain points defends the analogy, and even says that we can in a certain sense call humanity and divinity constitutive 'parts' of the supposit of the Word, on the grounds that a *part* of some subsistent agent does not contribute something extra to it or realize some potentiality in it; in technical terms, it is not an 'accident' in relation to the subsistent agent. In other words, the union of divinity and humanity in Jesus is more than just a coexistence of two self-subsisting agents (which would lead to the opposite heresy to monophysitism, the 'Nestorian' view of incarnation as two subsistent agents bound together in a single outward form in history). Thus Aquinas is bound to saying that the humanity of Jesus makes things true about the Word, even though it cannot make anything to be true of the Word in eternity; it makes things true about the Word's actual operation, we might say, even if it is not like the case of something acquiring an accidental modification, a new feature. But if a part of something is itself a substance in its own right, as obviously in the case of the humanity of Jesus, how can we construct a Christology on this basis without denying the integrity of the human individuality, and thus falling into something very like monophysitism?[27] The language of the single *esse* of the Word incarnate which Aquinas develops in the later works (in the *Summa* and in the short treatise of 1272, *de unione Verbi incarnati*) tries hard to avoid this problem, but – according to Cross – it does so only at the price of a lack of clarity

25 This point is made by A. Gaudel, 'La théologie de l' "*Assumptus Homo*"', Part II, *Revue des sciences religieuses* 17 (1932), pp. 214–34, especially pp. 225ff. Cf. Aaron Riches, *Ecce Homo: On the Divine Unity of Christ*, Grand Rapids, MI: Eerdmans, 2016, pp. 160–1.

26 See the texts cited in Cross, op. cit., p. 57.

27 Ibid., pp. 51–9.

in the terminology used. If Christ's humanity is a real (actual) individuated substance, it is capable of having its own *esse*: it is a real subject of agency, and Aquinas does not deny this. If (impossibly) the Word were to withdraw from Jesus of Nazareth, what would be left? For Thomas, there would have to be a new supposit supplied, since there was no prior substantive agent, no finite 'act of being' that had been replaced by the Person of the Word. But doesn't this imply that something is missing in the humanity assumed? That the human individuality of Jesus is ultimately not a real subject in the sense that all other human subjects are? If Jesus' humanity has no *esse* in itself, if what is assumed is only the sum total of the *conditions* for being a substantive agent, there is surely a problem; and Aquinas's ingenious attempts to find a way through by ascribing a 'secondary' *esse* to the human nature only muddy the waters.[28]

We shall come back shortly to look in more detail at these questions. Cross, a leading scholar on the thought of Duns Scotus, explores in depth the contrasting position of the Franciscan theologian, who emphasizes the implications of saying that Jesus of Nazareth, the human individual, is *aliquid* (something), just as the eternal Word is *aliquid* (indeed, Scotus seems to have held that we can also say that he is in some sense *aliquis*, someone).[29] Aquinas effectively grants, in his discussions in ST III.xvi, that the humanity of Jesus is a genuine created thing, a subject of predicates and an identifiable individual among other finite individuals; and the previous history of debate about Christology in the twelfth century had ruled that denying that the individual human nature of Jesus was *aliquid* was not theologically acceptable (the condemned opinion, that Jesus' humanity is 'nothing', is often referred to as 'nihilianism' or, less helpfully, 'nihilism'). But the Franciscan view from Scotus onwards is that we must go further and ascribe a created *esse* to Jesus, such that there is a true sense in which he is *a human agent*, a genuinely active individual substance in respect of other active finite substances, though dependent on the independent existence of the Word. Jesus does what he does as a finite subject, a psychological subject as we would say today, even if his 'subjectivity' (not the term a

28 Cross, op. cit., pp. 250–3.
29 Ibid., Chapter 5, especially pp. 128–33. On the use of *aliquis*, see Gaudel, op. cit., p. 231.

medieval would use, of course) is inseparably and permanently united to another subject, the Word of God. And in a concluding chapter to his book, Cross sets out to show how this can provide a positive agenda for modern Christology.[30] The Scotist view in principle takes away any problems about the individual consciousness of Jesus – a consciousness which is the genuine property of an actual individual, which is therefore the subject of the obviously finite acts of learning, knowing and understanding which we see in the Jesus of the Gospels, and the subject of the frustration that comes with lack of knowledge – arguably an intrinsic aspect of the human condition.

Claiming a genuine created centre of consciousness for the Word incarnate does not, of course, preclude that centre of consciousness being itself consciously experienced by a more comprehensive consciousness that is the divine Word's consciousness. If the Word is to save humanity by assuming genuine human experience, the Word must assume a subject characterized – like all of us – by limited knowledge and all that goes with it, even the ability to be mistaken.[31] Likewise, the Word must take on the experience of powerlessness and fear that belongs to humanity; this experience must be communicated to the Word in a manner that does not compromise the Word's eternal omniscience and omnipotence yet allows the Word to acquire a created awareness indirectly.[32] As Cross recognizes, this implies denying the notion that God is 'pure actuality' (i.e. that he is never in the position of having potentialities realized in his life): 'his immutability and impassibility should be understood respectively to man no more than imperishability and that nothing happens to him that he does not allow'.[33] And what the Scotist account of the Incarnation allows us to say is that the Word of God and the individual humanity of Jesus 'are two overlapping individuals'.[34] But they are not to be thought of as two realities that can be added together, so to speak, since the Word's individuality *embraces* that of the humanity and together they make up a unity that is 'not itself a person'

---

30 Ibid., pp. 311–24, especially pp. 317ff.
31 Ibid., pp. 315–16.
32 Ibid., pp. 319–23.
33 Ibid., p. 318.
34 Ibid., p. 322.

but is a real single but composite phenomenon. Scotus is clear[35] that to say that the Word and the humanity are both 'something' does not mean that there are two 'somethings' in Christ alongside each other. The Word supplies the humanity with nothing except the *negative* determination of not being part of or subject to any other finite agent – the negative determination that makes each of us an actual person.[36]

Cross presents his argument with admirable rigour; but his ultimate solution does not avoid all of the challenges he has himself identified, and some of his criticisms of Aquinas seem to miss Thomas's points. Cross defends the idea of a finite consciousness that somehow (it is not quite clear how) communicates information of a kind to an infinite consciousness: the infinite consciousness cannot literally share the actual ignorance experienced by that finite consciousness, but it can come to understand and embrace the frustration arising from it. But this raises some acute difficulties. As with any and every attempt to make sense of some sort of passibility in God, some kind of alteration or enhancement – such as learning by fresh experience – through the agency exercised by others, we are confronted with a cluster of paradoxes. If God 'experiences' exactly what a finite individual experiences, God must experience all that makes that individual experience the situation as they in fact do; but any finite individual experiences things precisely *as* finite – as having this history rather than that, this set of mental and emotional equipment rather than that. And if all that the claim means is that the Word is infallibly and completely 'aware' of what Jesus experiences, we should have to explain in what way this is different from the Word's knowledge as God of all true states of affairs. Again, to say that the Word experiences the *frustration* of ignorance but not the ignorance itself does not help: if we feel frustrated it is because ignorance means something or other for and to us, something that is rooted in our specific histories. If there is 'emotion' of some sort in the Word, it cannot be identical with what I as a finite subject feel. To say that the Word takes on a humanity

---

35 E.g., *Ordinatio* III.2.d6 qu.2 (*Beati Ioannis Duns Scoti ... Opera Omnia*, Vatican City 2006, Vol. 9, pp. 248–55), a careful discussion of the sense in which it can and cannot be said that there are two *aliqua* in Christ (and cf. pp. 260–3, as well as *Lectura* III.d11 qu.2, ed. cit., Vol. 20).

36 Cross, op. cit., p. 323.

equipped to feel all that we feel is simply to say that the Word assumes a genuine individuality; Cross is right about this, but I am less happy with his conclusion that this must mean a communication of the finite subject's experience to another terminus of experience. The telling phrase about 'two overlapping individuals' implies that the way the Word knows or understands is another instance of how subjects in general understand – so that the Word becomes another member of a class of knowing subjects. The language of two individuals unmistakeably suggests exactly what we have proposed that classical Christology sets out to dismantle: a picture of reality in which finite and infinite agencies operate in the same mode, the same metaphysical territory.

And it is not the case that Aquinas's scheme in any way precludes a genuine finite consciousness, including the consciousness of limit and pain, in Jesus.[37] Without going into detail, it is important to note that St Thomas undoubtedly grants that some kinds of ordinary learning processes go on in the human soul of Jesus.[38] He has qualms about ascribing real ignorance to Jesus (and Scotus would share such qualms), yet he has to conclude that the knowledge Jesus' soul possesses must come into his human awareness in the same way as happens in other human subjects. He is called *homo*, a human being, 'univocally' – that is, in the same sense as the term would have for other humans;[39] and so he can also be said to gain 'merit' by his actions as a creature,[40] winning for us the grace that he diffuses in his Body, the Church, since he has no need of it himself.[41] The limitless love that belongs to Jesus from the moment of his conception in the womb of Mary is actualized in the events of his life and death, but is in no way 'augmented' by these events;[42] yet it is only by the enactment of these, above all the death on the cross, that his love, now embodied in the world, can release the grace we need. *Limitless* love has to become actively real in our world through *limited* human action, including suffering. Aquinas's commitment

---

37   See above, n. 14, for recent treatments of this by Gaine and Coakley.

38   ST III.xii.1–4.

39   ST III.11.5c: *Christus dicitur homo univoce cum aliis hominibus.*

40   *Comm.Sent.* III.19A.1.

41   ST III.viii.1, xlviii.1.

42   ST III.xlviii.1.

to the single *esse* of the incarnate Word does not therefore seem to qualify his affirmation of the truly earthly and historical nature of the incarnate activity of Christ or of the fact that what we habitually say about human processes, including mental or even emotional processes, must apply in his case.

In short, though this is to compress unmercifully a very wide-ranging and technical discussion between advocates of the two systems, it is not obvious that Aquinas's scheme sets up difficulties that only a Scotist alternative can resolve; and in relation to the argument that is being pursued in these pages, it is Aquinas who seems clearer about the incommensurability of human individuality and divine personal *esse*, clearer about the fact that the Word and the human Jesus cannot be seen as two *instances* of anything (even granted, with Scotus, that they are not two instances on the same level). We shall be coming back shortly to an examination of the use of *esse* in a bit more detail. But it is perhaps worth spending a little time looking briefly at what Aquinas's usage was meant to guard against or rule out in the discussions of the generations immediately before him. He inherits a map of the Christological territory that was shaped by the twelfth-century summary of Christological models provided in Peter Lombard's *Sentences*, a summary behind which stand several decades of spirited debate.[43] Lombard begins from a simple question: Christian faith claims that 'God became human': does this mean that God thus becomes something he was not already, something other than his divine self, a new *aliquid*? There are three ways of answering this, says Lombard. We might say that there is a created substance, a human individual (*homo*), which at the point of the conception in the womb of Mary is assumed into union with the Word, so that we can also say that the Word is now what he was not before. Lombard is not happy with this, because it suggests that the Word whose substance is divine can become a substance that is not divine, which implies a difference between God and God's 'essence', God's defining form of being. This would mean that a divine Person could somehow change its definition, acquiring a second set of defining attributes, though

---

43 Peter Lombard, *Liber Sententiarum* III contains his substantive discussion of Christology; see III.6.1.37 for his account of the three main ways of answering the question of whether God becomes *aliquid*, 'something' that he was not before.

the divine nature itself cannot change – which is obviously a confused position. A second option focuses on the meaning of the words 'subsist' and 'subsistence': the Word continues to subsist as God, unchanged, but comes simultaneously to subsist as a human individual, being essentially unchanged by its union with a created soul and body. Lombard prefers a third approach, less likely to compromise or confuse our discourse about divine unchangeability: we could say that the Word in the Incarnation is in a state of 'having' a human being (*habens hominem*), rather like an individual putting on a coat or otherwise acquiring a characteristic which does not affect who or what they are. This *habitus* theory allows us to hold on to the unchanging nature of God and specifically of God the Word, but it also involves making a clear distinction between two things – the relation of the Word to its divine nature and the relation of the Word to the human nature it assumes. The former is intrinsic and necessary, such that the Word is inconceivable unless understood as wholly identical with the essence of God; the latter is more like an 'accidental' relation, something that comes to be true in a limited sense or for a limited period without affecting the subject.

The problem with it is that it makes the humanity assumed dangerously like an assemblage of qualities with no identity as a finite reality. Lombard's eagerness to distance himself from the language of the humanity as a *homo assumptus*, a complete individual entering into union with the Word, leads him to a theory that risks evacuating the humanity of its coherence as a genuine *item* in the created world. As noted earlier, theologies that understated or diminished the substantive reality of Jesus' humanity were condemned: in 1170, Pope Alexander III ruled against the teaching that Christ's humanity was *nihil*, nothing in itself, and reaffirmed that it must be *aliquid*. And although Peter Lombard himself did not go so far as this, the *habitus* theory was seen as inadequate to the logic of the basic Christian proposition that God became *homo*, a human being like others. Some form or other of the 'subsistence' approach outlined in the previous paragraph was thus the only really viable option left. The questions that were around in the twelfth century frequently turn on what it is that gives unity or cohesion to Christ's humanity. Hugh of St Victor, earlier in the century, had proposed that the presence of the Word brought about the existence of a human individual, uniting body and soul at the same time as uniting that body and soul with the Word.[44] But Gilbert Porreta, perhaps the most complex and sophisticated mind in twelfth-century French theology, had objected that this would imply that there was nothing for the Word to be united with if the ground of the created individuality of Jesus was simply the act of the Word. There must be a sense in which we can say that the humanity of Jesus is a *res*, a thing in itself: it does not become a finite substance simply in virtue of the Incarnation.

Gilbert proposed another model, in which there is indeed a substantive finite reality assumed by the Word but unified in virtue of its completeness in all that constitutes a human agent. However, the unique distinguishing personal characteristic or property of the eternal Word, the unique fact of 'filiation', being the Son of the Father, is communicated to the finite substance so that all its *actual* life is determined by and pervaded by this divine personal property. It is true to say that the humanity becomes a subsistent reality because of the union with the Word, but this means simply that it becomes an actual and active substance in the world rather than a static and abstractly conceived individual, 'frozen' in time as the sum of necessary human characteristics but as yet not a truly existing agent. The Word's eternal 'way of being God', as God the Son, structures and actualizes the agency of this real finite substance; nothing is changed in the Word's way of being God, and nothing changes in respect of the essence of God. And Gilbert is also clear that there is no question of a divine subsistent taking over or replacing a created one, since the relation between the divine Person and the divine nature is not like that between a finite substance and a finite nature: that is to say, the Word and the individual humanity are not two of any kind.[45]

With Gilbert's view (of which Lombard's second option is a rather unsatisfactory version), we are on the way to Aquinas's synthesis. Gilbert, in essence, locates the crucial aspect of the union at the level of what makes

44 See, for example, *de sacramentis* II.1, PL176, 393D–399B.

45 For Gilbert's texts, see the citations in Lauge Olaf Nielsen, *Theology and Philosophy in the Twelfth Century: A Study of Gilbert Porreta's Thinking and the Theological Expositions of the Doctrine of the Incarnation during the Period 1130–1180*, Leiden: Brill, 1982, especially pp. 163–89. This work is an invaluable source for the study of early medieval Christology.

the Word to be the Word or Son, the *proprietas personalis*: this – because it is not the same as the definition of the divine essence – is communicable to and in finite agency, and when so communicated, without reserve or interruption, constitutes a finite agent as a perfect finite exemplification of 'being the child of the divine Father'. And this allows us to say that it is indeed the Word that makes the humanity what it is, in the sense that it makes it to be the *way* it actively is (not in the sense that it makes it to be the *sort* of thing it is, a human individual in the abstract). As we shall see, Gilbert's account echoes some of the themes we find in earlier Greek Christian thought, though it is unlikely that he was aware of these affinities. Aquinas, who in his last year of activity is self-consciously trying to accommodate the Greek patristic legacy, makes the connections more directly.

The twelfth-century discussion is fascinating and thorough, and even a brief survey of some of its themes indicates what Aquinas was attempting to navigate in his development of the 'subsistence' model by way of an extended use of the idea of a single *esse* in Christ. He knows that there are three positions that have to be avoided. A simple *homo assumptus* scheme will not deliver an adequate account of the radical dependence of the humanity on the divine Person, and will create unmanageable complications if it is so phrased as to imply that the Word becomes the subject of two sets of predicates (since the Word's relation to the divine essence is not that of an individual to a genus). Equally, the notion that the Word is what individuates the human nature of Jesus, which would otherwise be a set of unconnected constituent parts, cannot do justice to the basic doctrinal position that there is a real something for the Word to be united to, and that the individual humanity is in the case of Jesus exactly what it is in the case of the rest of humankind. Nor will it do to say that the humanity is an 'accident', the contingent condition of a subject which remains the same in essence: this fails in two directions, in not giving the humanity an integrity of its own but also in not presenting the union with the Word as truly formative of the actual human identity. Aquinas's refinement of *esse* language is an attempt to fend off all these tempting but unsatisfactory views; it allows him to insist very clearly on the point that the Word is not an individual instance of divinity in the way that Jesus is an instance of humanity, and so to deny that there is any isomorphism between the divine supposit and what we normally understand by human individuality.

So, to connect this with our opening discussion, what Aquinas achieves, more successfully than any previous theologian (and more successfully than most later ones too, given the awkwardness of Scotus's language about Word and human being as *aliquid* in much the same sense), is to develop a vocabulary in which the union of divine and human in Jesus is in no way the fusion of two comparable metaphysical subjects. The emphasis is on the act of being by which the Word is what it eternally is as divine Person; an act of being which 'enacts' its personal distinctiveness by comprehensively shaping the finite actions of a human subject in such a way that the real and concrete distinctiveness of that subject cannot be spoken of without reference to the Word. Finite agency becomes a real communication of more than it is (abstractly considered) in itself; so that Aquinas is spelling out pretty much what Farrer is describing as the characteristic relation of finite and infinite agency.

3. The Unity of Christ

So how are we to understand the proposition that Christ's unity is the unity of a single *esse*? Michael Gorman wisely observes[46] that in considering Aquinas's views about *esse* we need to keep in view what specific questions he is trying to deal with: 'Until it becomes clear what question or questions Aquinas is asking, there is no point in attempting to say what his answer or answers might be.' And there is one basic clarification that has to be made at the outset: *esse* is *not* the name of some kind of thing; it is simply the verb 'to be,' and it has in Latin all the looseness of those words in English. Insofar as Aquinas is giving it any extra precision in his discussion, it is in stressing that *esse* designates not just existing in the most general sense (just 'being there'), but *active* existence. Yet even with this specification, the term can still cover a broad range of meanings. Obviously the broadest and simplest sense of the verb 'to be' is indeed 'just being there'; but nothing is 'just there' unless it is some *sort* of thing. *Esse* means *active* existence, and so denotes all that is involved in actively being the particular kind of substance that a thing is, the kind of impact its presence makes in the world as it really is. However, the meaning of the word does not coincide with *essentia*, which is the word for

46 Op. cit., pp. 101–2.

[handwritten note: Without God there is a natural inclination to bad things in some individuals.]

what defines a particular kind of substance in a general way, as an abstraction; what *esse* designates is the actual *presence in the world* of this particular sort of thing. Thus the 'essence' of a horse is the ensemble of qualities we use to define what counts, generally, as a horse; if all these things are present, we identify something as a horse rather than as a cat or a koala bear. The *esse* of a horse is the perceptible activity, the *fact* that doing-what-horses-do is, in this or that specific situation, an element of the actual universe we inhabit. This is admittedly a rather difficult distinction to clarify adequately, but it is a significant one, as we shall see later. And then, finally, *esse* is applied to actual individuals in the world; just as nothing is 'just there', so too nothing is there as just a *kind* of thing – any old horse, any old human. Being there in the world is being this or that distinct subject, *this* horse, *this* human, since only in this particular identifying context can we speak of active being.

To spell this out in a different idiom, we could say that there are in this context three ways of answering the question of 'what there is', what we mean by saying something exists. The first is to do with whether we can in general expect to see a thing around in the world we are familiar with; so that we may expect to see dogs around but not (with apologies to J. K. Rowling) hippogriffs or unicorns. Dogs 'exist' as unicorns do not. The second is to do with whether such and such a specified phenomenon can be identified as an actual case of some existing form of being: that's a dog, not a fox or a footstool; or, that's a live dog, not a stuffed one; there is an actually existing and acting dog here. The third is about recognizing this live and active phenomenon as identical with the active phenomenon we have encountered elsewhere; that's Fido, not Spot or Rover; this dog can be identified as having a unique history, a unique set of specifying relations and so on (Mrs Abercrombie's dog, not Mr Prichard's; the one that bit the postman, not the one that had first prize in the sheepdog trials). As Aquinas wrestles with how to define *esse*, a wrestling that persisted through his working life, these are the three elements that are gradually coming into clearer and clearer focus.

It is the third sense of *esse* that is obviously the most comprehensive, designating as it does the concrete and continuous agent in the world, the particular acting subject with a unique history; and this helps us see why Aquinas connects *esse* in this sense with two other important words, *subsistentia* and *suppositum*. In the actual world of changes and transactions between particular subjects or agents, the reference of *esse* language is the fact of something's subsisting as an active and unique substance, being the subject of particular predicates, descriptions and narratives. Its meaning thus coincides with the basic condition or ground of a distinct set of qualities, descriptions and so on – what is 'supposed' as the ultimate agency that gives coherence to this set of characteristics and activities. So, with any particular individual, we can say that they 'are', that they 'have esse' (not in fact a very helpful way of speaking), in virtue of 'being there otherwise than potentially', in virtue of exercising a particular kind of agency (that appropriate to the essence they instantiate), and in virtue of being a unique and distinct subject. The *esse* of Socrates is not something Socrates 'has' in anything like the sense in which Socrates has two ears, a bald head, a bad cold or a sense of humour (all of these in turn require rather different senses of the word 'has'): the *esse* of Socrates is the active presence of this individual, distinguishable in a range of ways from other subjects as a coherent and continuous subject for discourse.

Esse as *suppositum* – as the ground or condition taken for granted when we are talking about a continuous and active subject – is clearly the most comprehensive sense of the word. We could rightly say that speaking of Socrates only in terms of what makes him human would be a *partial* way of speaking about him; it might successfully distinguish Socrates the philosopher from – say – a whimsical philosopher's pet cat called Socrates, but it would not tell us what is most distinctive and important about Socrates. There is thus a sense – but one that needs careful handling – in which we could say that *esse*-in-general (being actively there) and the *esse* of being this thing rather than that (being the specific subsisting agent that is Socrates) were 'parts' of a whole which was constituted by talking about Socrates in his full historical individuality. But what makes this a bit awkward is that we clearly cannot speak of Socrates as if he could be dissolved into components – being-in-general, being human and being Socrates, with the last of these understood as the sum of the other two plus a mysterious something else.[47] The part–whole language is at best a useful framework for understanding the difference between a comprehensive and a less comprehensive description

47 See, for example, Gorman, op. cit., p. 109: 'essence and existence are not two little things that get cobbled together to make a big thing'.

We are thought as being as God's image, composed of soul (God Father), spirit (God Spirit), and body (God made man). All existing from the beginning. *A word made flesh?*

INTRODUCTION   29   *Body is limited as the disobedia and sin put it far from God.*

of what exists indivisibly in the real world. This may help us to understand why Aquinas (despite what seem to be reservations in some of his work) offers the part–whole structure as a way of speaking about the Incarnation, and what he does and does not mean by it. At ST III.xvii.2, he stresses that nothing is or can be added to the *esse* of being the divine Word by the human nature in which the Word is incarnate;[48] the relation between them is like that between a complex whole and subsidiary elements of it that do not in themselves have the character of being subjects of active predication (even if they can be said to 'have' *esse* in that they are actively involved in a distinct individual life; they are an element of 'that by which' this individual is actively present in the world). Thus Aquinas[49] says that 'being embodied' or 'being ensouled' only make sense as part of what 'being Socrates' means: we cannot talk about an unspecified 'embodiedness' or 'being embodied' that is a subject in its own right.

So if we now apply this to the question of the Incarnation, we have a pattern something like this. The *esse* of the divine Word as such, as the second Person of the eternal Trinity, is what it is in virtue of its eternal relation to God the Father – an eternal living-out of divine life in the mode of 'filiation', the eternal self-sufficient life that is God's realizing itself as 'Son', as the divine life receiving divine life as eternal gift and eternally giving it in return. Nothing can add to or subtract from this; so far as it goes, *it is a complete account of what it is to be the divine Word*. But when we speak theologically of the divine Word, we do not and cannot speak simply of this eternal subject; we speak of what the divine Word has actually done in this world and of how we have learned to identify the divine Word in action within human history. Aquinas expresses this in III.ii.4 by speaking of *alia et alia ratio subsistendi*, 'two different senses of subsisting'.[50] When we are speaking in these terms, it should be clear that we cannot appropriately or adequately

48 *non adveniat ei [sc. Filio Dei] novum esse personale, sed solum nova habitudo esse personalis praeexistentis ad naturam humanam.* No different way of 'personal' being is added to the Word, but only a new 'habitude' or relatedness entered into by a pre-existing personal *esse*, which now has the additional role of activating this human nature, not only of being eternally itself.

49 ST III.xvii.2c.

50 See Aaron Riches, *Ecce Homo: On the Divine Unity of Christ*, pp. 174–5, for a clear discussion of this passage and its rather complex relation with Aquinas's probably earlier

identify the divine Word without speaking of Jesus of Nazareth: the human agent we identify as Jesus is an inseparable part of our theological discourse about the Word, to the extent that we should never have learned to speak plainly about the Word's activity, or to associate ourselves in faith with the Word's activity, independently of Jesus. Talking about the *esse* of the Word *as active in creation and history* requires reference to this individuated human nature, active in its own created mode. But – and here is the salient and controversial point – this human individuality, while in all respects complete as such, is not, in the perspective of theological discourse, an independent subject or supposit. It is what it is as a human, historical fact, simply and entirely as that which is activated by the Word and through which the Word historically communicates. On the (impossible) supposition that the Word were removed from the human identity of Jesus (a regular medieval thought experiment), it would 'acquire' a finite human *esse*: it would be what it was independently of the Word's subsistent being, and its own identity would no longer be fundamentally constituted by its being the vehicle of the Word's action and communication; thus it would evidently be a new and different *esse*, since it would no longer *mean* what it formerly did as the embodiment of eternal filiation in human shape. Its *esse* would now be – like other human individualities – bound in with the agency of a finite supposit; its ultimate coherence would no longer be inseparable from the eternal *esse* of the Word. But as it is, the content of 'being Jesus of Nazareth' is grounded in and determined by the *esse* that is 'being the eternal Word'. Even though the historical *esse* that is Jesus' human identity of course includes things that do not and cannot belong to the *esse* of the Word as such (the eternal action of the Word cannot be specified as *necessarily involving* what is contingently true about Jesus), the conclusion has to be that nothing can be said of Jesus of

account of the question in his *de unione*. Gorman (op. cit., Chapter 5) argues that the *de unione* passage, which allows that the human nature of Christ has a certain kind of *esse* in itself, avoids a pitfall in the ST argument. Saying that the humanity of Jesus is 'actuated' by the divine *esse* of the Word is problematic because in a strict sense only the divine essence can be actuated by divine *esse*: and Aquinas cannot mean that the human essence and the divine are identical. But I think that the key issue is the difference, implied but not fully stated in Aquinas, between the actuating of the human essence as *human* and its actuation as *this* human substance.

Nazareth that is not in a strict sense spoken 'about' the Word of God, considered as the final ground or condition of the historical identity of Jesus.

Richard Cross has argued, as we saw earlier, that all this makes Aquinas practically a monophysite – that is, someone who denies that the human individuality of Jesus is a proper subject of predication in itself and who thus absorbs the human nature indistinguishably into the divine so as to produce a compound neither properly divine nor properly human. But – although I disagree with Cross only with some trepidation – I am not sure that he has done justice to Aquinas's final position, as expressed in the *Summa*. We have already noted some of the ways in which his preferred Scotist account creates problems for the grammar of divinity itself and for the understanding of what divine Persons are and are not. But I am not convinced in any event that his reading of Aquinas is always fair. Thus in III. xvi.5, a text Cross alludes to in order to make his point about 'monophysite' implications,[51] what Aquinas actually says is that the name 'Christ' designates both 'the anointing divinity and the anointed humanity'. One subject is referred to by this name, but it is clear that this subject is not simply the divine Word existing from eternity. The subject would have to be specified – say – as 'the agent of human salvation', who is indeed substantively the divine Word but – *as* agent of our salvation – is correctly identified in terms of what identifies the human individual Jesus, including those things that identify Jesus as this human individual rather than that. Jesus is recognizable humanly by being the son of Mary, born on such and such a date, characterized by a particular eye colour and so on. But this cannot mean that what it is to be the eternal Word of God can be picked out by reference to parentage or eye colour. So to say, as Aquinas does, that the humanity of Jesus is one with the *esse* of the Word and has no *esse* apart from that divine personal *esse* is simply to make the point that the active human presence of Jesus in the world is indistinguishable from the active presence of the eternal Word in the world. Talking about Socrates is ultimately the same thing as talking about Socrates' history, what Socrates does, even if identifying Socrates does not mean spelling out all of this history. There are of course plenty of ways of identifying Socrates that do not require us to specify everything he does; for that matter, there are contexts where we

---

51 Cross, op. cit., pp. 59–60, especially p. 59, n. 33.

can identify Socrates without mentioning any particular thing he does (we know this is a bust of Socrates not Aristotle, because we know from other sources what Socrates is meant to look like). But an *adequate* account of what we mean by 'Socrates' in our ongoing speech practices is one in which various localized or close-focused ways of speaking about him are placed in the context of a comprehensive discourse about his entire life and action. The analogy is not perfect, and Aquinas does not think it is, but it allows us to grasp something about his conviction as to what most needs saying in our theology of the Incarnation: that there is no gap between the active, specific presence of Jesus in human history and the active, specific presence of the divine Word.

The somewhat paradoxical implication of this, though, is that we do not need to find some sort of absence in the human constitution of Jesus into which the Word can be inserted. To use an image I have sketched elsewhere, the human life of Jesus – which is, for Aquinas, unequivocally 'a created something'[52] – is a 'performance', an acting-out, of the life of the divine Word that is remotely comparable to the performance of a musical score in an actual concert. It is an unbroken exemplification in human terms of what it is to be wholly living out a life of filiation to the eternal Father. For it to be this, *it must be the action of a human agent*, since any interruption of this exemplification of divine filiation would destroy the point of living it out in a non-divine medium (we may recall here Farrer's account of the paradox of supernatural action). Just as a translation which left difficult words in the original would not count as a successful translation, so the human enactment of the life of the eternal Word must be the unbroken performance of a fully and recognizably human life. If some phase or aspect of human agency could not 'carry' the presence of filial divine life, that aspect of human life would not be transfigured and re-created by the presence of the Creator. It would show us, so to speak, a word or phrase left 'untranslated', as if a writer had concluded that something in the original was simply too complex for any possible words in the language of the translation. And we should thus be left with the dualist structure which Aquinas is consistently setting out to subvert: a structure in which divine agency competed with created agency, occasionally displacing it in order to remedy its inadequacies. The single *esse*

52   ST III.ii.7, xvi.8 and 10.

model with which Aquinas works is designed to give us a coherent way of speaking about an uninterrupted created agency which is at the same time in every respect activated, made actually present in the world by the eternal action of the Word.

In this light, the tortuous discussions to which Aquinas subjects his readers of whether the Word could be incarnate in several human individuals, whether all three Persons of the Trinity could be incarnate, whether the incarnate Word was capable of surprise or fear and so on, should all be read in the context of one basic concern. The Incarnation cannot involve any relation between creative and created agency that posits them working 'alongside' each other as elements in the world's process. As Aquinas makes plain,[53] Christ's human nature, the human essence he instantiates, is *perfecta*, complete in every respect; as we might put it, it has integrity as an account of the sort of being he is in his earthly life. If there is indeed one *esse* in the incarnate, there cannot be any interruption in its incarnate activity. So far from implying a monophysite schema, the single *esse* model insists upon the integrity of the human nature. As we shall see in the next chapter, it can be argued that, throughout the entire history of Christology, an increasing precision about what complete humanity means goes hand in hand with a comparable precision as to what complete divinity means in Christ; Aquinas's formulation stands at the end of a long and careful process of conceptual refinement. Precisely because we have to affirm the unbroken completeness of the human activity, we have to acknowledge that, whatever the role of the divine Word as such, it cannot be as a supplement to a defective human identity or an agency that occasionally interrupts it.

Scotists like Richard Cross, who are rightly eager to affirm that the humanity of Jesus is genuinely an individual created substance in some sense, have argued that Aquinas's final version of the single *esse* model compromises both the divinity and the humanity; and Cross notes, quite properly,[54] that Aquinas had, in the short treatise *de unione*, allowed a 'secondary *esse*' to the humanity, perhaps suggesting that he himself had doubts about the viability of the single *esse* structure. However, I would read Aquinas's text rather differently from the way Cross proposes. What Aquinas says is that the *esse*

53 E.g., III.xviii.1.
54 Op. cit., p. 63.

of the human life of Jesus *belongs* to the one supposit of the eternal Word; Cross paraphrases this by saying that 'if a nature is a truth-maker, then it must communicate *esse* to its *suppositum*', and asks how this is different from claiming that the human nature 'activates a passive potency' in the supposit. 'Activating a passive potency' means that the Word would eternally have the capacity to become something different from or to acquire something additional to its eternal identity – a notion that Aquinas consistently denies, for the obvious reason that this would subject the Word to finite agency and compromise its definition as eternally, changelessly, purely active. But the implication that Cross claims to identify is not so clear. Aquinas always recognized that there was a sense in which the *entire* agency of the Word, in eternity and in time, could be spoken of as one reality, which had its unity in the unity of the divine Word: in this connection, the humanity of Jesus is instrumental to the Word, but could not be said to 'contribute' to the defining *esse* of the Word, only to what can truly be said of the Word in action, the agency of our redemption, which is not the actualizing of some potential in God but the temporal expression of God's eternal purpose. It is the case that the life of Jesus makes certain things true about the activity of the Word in history; it is not the case that the life of Jesus makes certain things true about the way divine life is lived in the mode of filiation. In his full discussion of the unity of *esse* question in ST III.xviii.2, Aquinas explicitly distinguishes between the way in which we ascribe *esse* to a nature and the way in which we ascribe it to a hypostasis or supposit, a specific active element in the world. Talking of *esse* in respect of nature is talking about the way in which an identifiable present and active reality is 'characterized'; the nature is *that in virtue of which it is the sort of thing it is*, the features that make us rightly conclude that this object satisfies the conditions for being identified as this *sort* of object. In this context it is wrong to say that nature 'has' *esse*: what is being asserted is that the abstract notion of a definable sort of existence is present as a, or the, formative principle of an active subject. But when we speak about personal or hypostatic *esse*, we speak of *what* or *who* it is that is identified as an active subject. Many things may be true of such a subject, and would be part of what I earlier called a comprehensive account of it, but they add nothing to that basic identification. What would otherwise be the *esse* of a human individual's existence is united to the personal *esse* of the Word, the Word's way of being God. Just as in ordinary discourse we could loosely say that being the person of Socrates 'includes' being bald or witty or short, so in our theological language we can say that being the person of the Word 'includes' being human; but just as baldness or wit do not tell us who Socrates is, what ultimately makes Socrates who he is or what enables us decisively to pick out Socrates from others (and not knowing that Socrates was bald would not make it impossible to offer some credible identification of Socrates), so with the humanity of Christ.[55] Talking about Socrates at all must involve, implicitly, all that necessarily belongs to talking about a human individual (being embodied, for example); but you could not say that *any* talking about Socrates would have to involve mention of his baldness. Likewise with Christ: any talking about Christ our saviour would have to involve talking about what it is to be the Word of God, but the Word of God is not identified *as such* by the humanity it takes on. The *esse* of that humanity is not other than the identifying act of being that is the Word's existence, but it contributes nothing extra to that identifying *esse*. This does not mean (to make the point once again) that we can as a matter of fact talk about the Word of God independently of the incarnate Christ – simply that we come to recognize in the incarnate Christ the personal direct and directive presence of the divine Word as supposit of this human individual; and this obliges us to recognize that our language about the Word will have to go beyond talking about Jesus of Nazareth as a human individual alone.

4. Transforming Humanity: Christ as the Ground of Communion

To most modern readers, all this is likely to come across at first sight as a set of rebarbative technicalities, as distant as could be from the proclamation of Christ as Lord and saviour. But I hope that by now we are able to see how

---

55 Gorman, op. cit., p. 117, speaks about this as a distinction between 'unqualified' and 'qualified' existence, but is concerned that Aquinas's examples of qualified existence are instances of accidents, qualities predicated of a subject, rather than anything that could be regarded as a subject in its own right. Hence his sympathy for the Aquinas of the *de unione* in his attempt to find an acceptable way of saying that the human nature of Christ has *some* kind of *esse*, as it clearly cannot be a sort of accidental determination if it really is *aliquid*.

the discussion is moulded by a couple of fundamental underlying concerns about how we do justice to the fact that we are trying to speak intelligibly about what *God* does – that is, about infinite action, not another instance of the kind of agency we regularly encounter within the interactive universe. It is essential to be clear that the presence of the divine Word in and as the active historical presence of Jesus of Nazareth is not the intrusion into the world of a rival isomorphic personal agency alongside or instead of a particular finite agency. Belief in the Incarnation is the belief that the specific concrete and historical agent that is Jesus of Nazareth simply *is* the act of God the Word in a unique sense, quite distinct from the way in which divine agency is *universally* the ultimate activator of any and every finite substance. Aquinas's preferred idiom for this is in terms of thinking about the act of God the Word at two levels – the eternal and the definitive life of the Word in relation to the eternal Father, the life we recognize and specify as that of the Son of the eternal Father, and the life of the Word considered as the activating principle in the life of Jesus. From the latter point of view, we can reasonably speak of a *sort* of duality in active existence, *esse*: there is a genuine distinction between what is said about the act of being that is Jesus as a finite agent and the act of being that is the second Person of the Trinity in eternal bliss. Jesus of Nazareth is not the second Person of the Trinity in the sense that Mary Ann Evans is George Eliot (the same individual under a different designation for certain temporary purposes). But to say this is not to say that there are then two 'acts' alongside each other, let alone two 'overlapping individuals'. While it is true that for all practical purposes in our conceptuality the existence of Jesus 'counts' as a real form of subsistence in the world, it is not one element in a partnership between two such subsistents, since it is what/who it is solely in virtue of its being 'supposited' by the Word.

To say this is to say what Aquinas and those who have followed him (including, as we have seen, Farrer) have said about the relation of finite and infinite: they do not 'add up'. God and the world are not two *of* anything; and so likewise, the Word and Jesus are not two of anything. Similarly, the world is not a component part of God, nor God a component part of the world; and Jesus is not a part of the divine life, nor the Word an element in the composition of Jesus. Analogies here are going to be very imperfect, but we might think of a situation in which we could hear a succession of distant noises and gradually come to recognize them as forming a tune played by a band in a neighbouring street. What we have recognized is not an extra item in the sum total of sense data (we may recognize the tune without actually hearing any more notes), but an organizing formal principle that connects the data. And we would not say that the data we had initially encountered were *as physical data* 'parts' of the tune in a straightforward sense; the tune exists prior to these enactments of its form. It is a shaky comparison, but at least gives some sense of how we can intelligibly speak of apprehending a form of agency that is not reducible to a set of discrete data, that is not a something alongside those data that could be added to it as an extra item, and that is not composed of the data we apprehend in the sense that a house is composed of bricks, or even in the sense that water is composed of hydrogen and oxygen. To recognize something as enacting and embodying a formal unity does not mean that we come to see that unity as built up by the specific phenomena we are currently experiencing; but it does entail seeing those phenomena as given intelligible connection by something whose integrity and substantiality are independent of this enactment, yet which is not simply another determinate thing in a list of things.

As we shall see later in this book when we discuss the development of Christological terminology in the Byzantine period, there is in earlier essays in Christology a steady trajectory towards Aquinas's formulation, as theologians increasingly recognize the necessity of creating a conceptual structure that will allow genuine finite substantiality to the humanity of Jesus while maintaining the immutability of the divine Person. There is one *hypostasis, suppositum* or *esse* in Jesus in the sense that there are not two rival agents involved. In regard to the divinity and humanity existing in Christ, it cannot be that the more there is of one, the less there is of the other. But it is true that the single principle or supposit can be spoken of both 'abstractly' as the unchanging act of God the Word, and historically as the act of Jesus of Nazareth in the totality of which the Word is uniquely active in the world. The *esse* we apprehend is therefore describable as 'composite' in the very loose sense that it can be spoken of both in itself *and* as the ultimate 'organizing' principle of a finite set of phenomena (the humanity of Jesus) – or better as that which establishes the most comprehensive unity, meaning and communicative content of that set of phenomena.

Uniquely in the case of Jesus of Nazareth, this is a meaning that ultimately transforms all other finite meanings, transforms the significance and communicative capacity of every other finite agent. And this is itself a consequence of the unique relation between the Word and the phenomena of Jesus' human existence. As we shall see in discussions later in this book, what is claimed about Jesus is that, in virtue of his union with the Word, the relations in which he stands or which he creates through his human agency are in principle capable of being extended without limit in the created world. The relations in which human individuals are routinely involved are limited in the sense that both the extent and the effect of contact with other human subjects is constrained by the location of any one individual in their material and cultural context. But when we are trying to understand what might be entailed in the claim that this particular individual is the embodiment of a divine subsistent agency, it emerges that this kind of constraint cannot apply in any straightforward way. The Word, the divine suppositum, is the agency whereby the created order is sustained in coherence: it is thus related to every form of finite agency as that which draws it towards harmony, internal and external.[56] So what specifically, through the fact of union in *esse*, gives the humanity of Jesus its distinct finite character, its own internal coherence and continuity of purpose, is identical with that which gives *all* things their cohesion – a theme already strongly marked in Christian Scripture (as in, for example, Colossians 1.15–20, as well as the prologue to the Fourth Gospel). The life that lives in Jesus is the active source of all relations in the finite world; so it is natural that, in its human embodiment, it is creative of unrestricted relation in the human world – and indeed beyond, if we take seriously Paul's meditations in Romans 8 on the dependence of the entire creation on the reconciling process that occurs in the death and resurrection of Jesus. For Jesus of Nazareth to be Jesus of Nazareth is also for him to be the unique embodiment in the finite world of an agency that holds the diversity of creation in unified tension; where he is active creation itself is brought closer to its ideal convergence. So too,

56 This is very well explored in Legge, *Trinitarian Christology*, Chapter 3, especially pp. 67– 82. See, for example, p. 72, 'The incarnation is ordered not only to the satisfaction for sin ... but also to the restoration of the whole order of creation'; Aquinas's understanding of the Word as the animating centre of all finite intelligibility and interdependence is a theme that deserves much more discussion, and is another of those elements of his Christology which root him deeply in the patristic and Byzantine theological world.

when he establishes relations between himself and other human agents, something more is happening than the simple connection of individuals that would be the case in other situations. The human person engaged in relation by Jesus is connected to the Word of God in and through that relation – and, depending on the condition and orientation of that person, such a connection may bring both promise and judgement, a consistent theme in St John's Gospel. But for those whose relation with Jesus is one of loving trust and 'alignment' of will or desire, the effect is what the New Testament calls incorporation into the identity of Jesus – becoming a member of the 'Body' of Christ. The relation in which we stand is no longer that of individual to individual; our human identity shares the direction of the Word's own agency, and the Word's relation with the Father.

So at one obvious level, the effect of Jesus' relation with other humans has an *effect* radically different from the effect of routine human relations. Other human agents are affiliated to and aligned with the relation of Jesus and the Word of God to the Father in so direct and intimate a way that they can be spoken of as derivative embodiments of the Word within creation – or more accurately, as involved in a *communal* embodiment of the Word in the Body of Christ (in the next chapter, we shall see how Augustine in particular helps to clarify this aspect of the overall theological argument). And then, at a slightly different level and partly because of what we have just outlined, we can speak of the human identity of Jesus as free to initiate relations with those who are in fact distant in time and space from the circumstances of his human life in this world. As the incarnation of the Word, as an active human individual united with the Word in an unparalleled way, his agency is inseparable from the universal work of the Word: in Aquinas's terminology,[57] Christ's human actions are the 'instruments' of his divine agency. This is not to say that the work of the Word within creation *depends* on the action of Jesus of Nazareth; only that, wherever the one is, the other is there also, whether visibly or invisibly. This is why Jesus of Nazareth can be proclaimed as embodying universal hope, not a culture-specific or temporary message. Putting it schematically: because Jesus is uniquely united in *esse* with the Word, Jesus is Head of the Body which is the Church; because he is Head of the Body, his action as a human agent is

57 E.g., ST III.viii.1 ad 1.

not confined in the way that any other human agent's is, but is the vehicle of the Word's universal action; and because this is so, it is in relation to him that any and all may find their fulfilment and salvation.

Thus the theological structure we have been considering, in which the key concept is the unity of *esse*, active subsistence, between Jesus and the Word, becomes the ground for a theology of mission which is not simply the proclamation of a system that is universally true but more fundamentally the proclamation of an agent whose liberty to engage in potentially transforming relation with any human subject is absolute. The union of the human individuality we call Jesus with the suppositum that is the Word's eternity means that Jesus is both truly a human individual in the sense that no element is missing in his reality as an historical agent, *and* that the word 'individual' is ultimately an inadequate designation for him, since the extent and effect of his agency is unconfined by the ordinary limits of historical action on the part of a single subject. We shall be returning later in this book to some of the ways in which this cluster of ideas affected debates especially in the Reformation era and afterwards; but for Aquinas, the 'Headship' of Christ – that is, his directive and creative effect through those united with him in faith and sacramental community – can be understood only through the basic model he has developed of the non-competitive relationship of human identity and divine subsistence, and its implications for what we can say about the identity of Jesus. And the obvious question is how far his complex account represents, if not an inevitable, at least an intelligible development from the initial events in which the Christian community came into being around what was believed to be the continuing presence of Jesus of Nazareth. It is to this that we turn next.

PART ONE

1.1

FORMULATING THE QUESTION: FROM PAUL TO AUGUSTINE

1. New Testament Origins: History, Faith and Narrative

The beginnings of Christology pose a problem rather like the classical paradox associated with the Stoic philosopher Zeno. If an arrow is fired, it has to cover half of its trajectory before it completes its flight; and before that it has to complete a quarter, and so on in ever-diminishing fractions, until the conclusion must be drawn that it could never have started moving at all. Yet in the world we know, arrows regularly fly and reach their targets. There is a style of discussion around Christian origins which is a bit reminiscent of Zeno's imagined questioner: how does Christian thinking about Jesus begin its trajectory and then arrive at what the New Testament (let alone later Christian doctrine) actually says? Should we not be trying to reconstruct a line of reasoning, starting with the establishable facts about Jesus of Nazareth, so that we can judge whether the confession of Jesus as Lord and God is a justified place to end up? The tempting route is to look for 'evidence' that can be reconstructed from the canonical (or frequently, these days, the non-canonical) text, so that we can assess the Bible's developed language about Jesus against the truth that can be reconstructed. But of course, the

43

very enterprise of tracing this development begs a number of questions. To start with, in what sense could belief in Christ's divinity be simply a conclusion drawn from evidence? And is the evidence restricted to facts about Jesus or does it include the earliest stages of interpretation? Exactly how do we agree on solid criteria for what counts as clear historical data here, data completely untouched by the processes of transmission and interpretation? A great deal of recent biblical scholarship, more acutely aware than before of the theological agenda of what may once have seemed simple narratives, is commendably cautious about drawing unsupportable historical conclusions from theologically inflected narratives, and effectively leaves the arrow on the string, registering warnings about any attempts to connect history and theology in illegitimate and indefensible ways. New Testament study for most of the past century at least has steadily dismantled the old polarity of a 'Jesus of history' over against a 'Christ of faith', a polarity which tended to presuppose the possibility of reconstructing a Jesus who is, as it were, seen from nowhere, whose reliably established sayings and doings can act as a check against speculative irresponsibility. But it has also moved on from the powerful and influential resolution of the issue associated above all with the school of Rudolf Bultmann, a theology focused on the sheer fact of 'proclamation', independently of any resort to historical narrative.[1] Bultmann's approach is bound in as much with Heideggerian philosophy and with a Lutheran understanding of the relative importance of human imagining or arguing on the one hand and divine manifestation in freedom on the other as it is with strict considerations of literary history: Christology for Bultmann is most emphatically not and cannot be about anything for which we could supply 'evidence'. But subsequent scholarship has been uneasy with the philosophical over-determination of his readings; and theologians have

---

1   For a manageable introduction to Bultmann's thought, his brief *Jesus Christ and Mythology*, London: SCM, 1960, is a good place to start. Gareth Jones, *Bultmann: Towards a Critical Theology*, Cambridge: Polity Press, 1991, especially Chapter 2, remains valuable. On recent and new approaches to the 'Quest for the Historical Jesus', see N. T. Wright's wonderfully vivid survey in the first three chapters of *Jesus and the Victory of God*, SPCK, 1996. A different approach, more systematically distanced from any attempts at historical reconstruction, is found in Luke Timothy Johnson, *The Real Jesus: The Misguided Quest for the Historical Jesus and the Truth of the Traditional Gospels*, San Francisco: HarperCollins, 1997.

not been comfortable with the reduction of Christology to the bare event of proclamation, the Word uttered out of an impenetrable historical silence and darkness. Surely theology claims something more, something about an embodied *narrative* that displays God's action rather than a naked demand for the obedience of faith? Yet the question also remains of whether it is possible to identify anything of such an embodied narrative that could be scrutinized independently of the further narrative of how it was repeatedly told.

While the naïveté of many earlier discussions in this area has been thoroughly chastened in more recent decades, there remains a nagging question. Is there *any* sense in which the believer of today can trace or reconstruct or even just imagine whatever it was that prompted the trajectory of theological reflection that leads eventually to something like the Third Part of Thomas's *Summa*? There are two immediate problems with saying yes to this. One is more pragmatic: if Christian faith does indeed relate to an historical personage, its authenticity cannot rest upon some kind of supposedly objective view of its central figure, as it is in the nature of human and historical individuals that they are not available for inspection outside their own time and place. In the nineteenth century, Kierkegaard's tortuous and mischievous discussions of the supposed (but illusory) advantage of the follower contemporary with the incarnate one and the 'follower at second hand'[2] represent the most sophisticated version of this point: he notes that contemporary as well as 'second hand' follower alike have to *learn* their knowledge of the saviour as an historical figure, and that it is a mistake to think that we can arrive at some kind of perspective-free (un-learned) vision of primary 'evidence' for ascribing divinity to Jesus. The second point is more fundamental still: how could we specify what counted as evidence that would justify us in giving divine worship to a human being? as if the confession of faith were a highly likely solution to a troubling problem of *explanation*. Evidence is gathered so that we can make informed judgements; we know what it would be to ask for evidence of an historical event, or what would count towards, say, establishing that such and such a text was the work of this author rather than that. In term of Christian origins, we could in principle recognize evidence for whether or not the tomb of Jesus was empty (though in fact we simply do not have enough collateral material to say a great deal about this as a purely historical

2   See below, pp. 265–6.

issue), and we could come to a reasonably likely conclusion as to whether St Paul wrote the letters to Timothy and Titus in the New Testament. But this notion of evidence does not fit well with the question of whether we should believe in the resurrection of Jesus or in the inspiration of 1 Timothy; even more so with the confession of Jesus as Lord and God. We may reasonably say that certain putative facts about Jesus would (at least) pose a serious problem for such a confession – a high likelihood that the crucifixion never happened, or that Jesus systematically infringed the Ten Commandments[3] or that he was not Jewish – facts that would make plain nonsense of the claims made for him. Some – especially N. T. Wright – would go further and say that we would need a good deal more in the way of positive historical anchorage to talk sensibly about Christology – a high probability that Jesus foresaw his death and ascribed certain meanings to it, or that his words and practice implicitly claimed a particular kind of authority to re-draw the boundaries of God's people or to effect God's forgiveness or to anticipate God's judgement. Questions like these, capable in principle of being settled by historical evidence, though in practice persistently eluding settlement, are important because claims or commitments are being made which would be vacuous if these things were not approximately as the biblical narrative suggests; we simply would not be interested in these features of the narrative above others unless they had some relation with existing commitments of devotion and reflection. The arrow has left the bow.

This is why our discussion here will not try to ground Christological thinking *primarily* on any reconstruction of Jesus' historical mission. Questions about this have a crucial place, as has already been granted; but our first meeting with Jesus of Nazareth on the page of human record is with a figure already heavily interpreted, the object of a level of commitment that is – to put it mildly – unusual. The datum we work with is the Jesus

---

3   Jesus as exemplary transgressor is a theme that William Blake mischievously develops in *The Everlasting Gospel*: the Jesus of the New Testament narrative is anything but an exemplar of conventional restraint and humility or even chastity (William Blake, *The Complete Poems*, ed. W. H. Stevenson, London: Longmans, 3rd edition, 2007, pp. 900–9). For an attempt to relate this to a wider theological perspective, see Rowan Williams, '"The human form divine": Radicalism and Orthodoxy in William Blake', in Zoe Bennett and David B. Gowler, eds, *Radical Christian Voices and Practice: Essays in Honour of Christopher Rowland*, Oxford: Oxford University Press, 2012, pp. 151–64.

who is presented, 'narrated', in the Christian Scriptures – not as a way of blocking out critical enquiry but as a way of recognizing clearly that the task of Christology is not to advance supposedly neutral evidence in order to justify a conclusion. Whatever is going on in the confession of Jesus of Nazareth as Lord and God, it is not an attempt to deduce some obscure extra fact about an historical figure that will explain or illuminate their life as chronicled – and so render the narrative in which this is presented to us essentially redundant, or at any rate superseded.[4]

In a sense, then, the whole enterprise of Christology begins with problems of *language*: with the fact that, a couple of decades after the execution of Jesus of Nazareth, what was being said about him by some of his followers showed signs of exceptional linguistic eccentricity. The earliest surviving written sentences to have 'Jesus' or 'Christ'/'the anointed', or 'the Lord Jesus' as their subject, the sentences written about him by Paul of Tarsus, exhibit a bewildering variety of register or idiom within a very brief space. We may move rapidly from sentences of a kind that could apply to any member of the human race to other sentences stating or implying things that could not normally be said of a human subject. If we look at Paul's meditations in 1 Corinthians 11 on the Lord's Supper, the communal meal of the Christian community, we can see him moving from a fairly straightforwardly descriptive mode – 'The Lord Jesus ... took bread, and when he had given thanks, he broke it' (1 Cor. 11.23–24) – to something dramatically different, only a few

4   One of the most influential discussions of this in twentieth-century theology is the work of Hans Frei, especially *The Identity of Jesus Christ: The Hermeneutical Bases of Dogmatic Theology*, Philadelphia: Fortress Press, 1975. Frei's central argument is that in reading the Gospels we have to accept that Jesus is who the Gospels say he is – that is to say, we have to read this character, Jesus, *as he is identified by the text*, not as a version of some imagined more 'accurate' or even innocent account. For a sympathetic and particularly insightful discussion of Frei's approach, see Paul J. DeHart, *The Trial of the Witnesses: The Rise and Decline of Postliberal Theology*, Oxford: Blackwell, 2006, Chapter 3, especially pp. 128–42. The recently published collections of some of Frei's drafts, letters and otherwise unpublished lectures, incidentally, make it clear that Austin Farrer was a thinker he greatly admired; there is work to do on the continuities here. See Hans W. Frei (ed. Mike Higton and Mark Alan Bowald), *Reading Faithfully*, Vol. II: *Writing from the Archives: Theology and Hermeneutics*, Vol. II: *Writing from the Archives: Frei's Theological Background*, Cambridge, James Clarke and Co., 2017.

How is the transition between body and spirit.
Has Paul discussed the role of Jesus as being
not only Son of God but God made man or Flesh?

48   CHRIST THE HEART OF CREATION

lines later. 'Christ', 'the Anointed' (a term with obvious royal associations in the Jewish context), already identified with Jesus, is said to have a 'body' that must be spiritually discerned; failure to discern it has grave consequences for the well-being of body and soul. Less than a page further on (1 Cor. 12.12–27), this 'body' appears as some kind of organism in which individual believers are elements. 'Christ', 'the Anointed', is a word for what holds together believers in a collective identity, a word for the ground of their association with Jesus through the agency of the 'Spirit'. A few chapters later (1 Cor. 15), 'Christ' is the subject of a brief narrative declaring that he died and was buried and appeared after his death to his followers: he is preparing to return to the world as a prelude to defeating all forms of finite authority and delivering up a pacified and restored creation to God. And at the very beginning of the letter in which these well-known passages appear, we are told that 'the Anointed Jesus' is presently active in preserving believers in their loyalty to him until he is manifest again in the world (1 Cor. 1.7–8) and is identical with the power and wisdom of God (1 Cor. 1.24). Elsewhere he is said to be 'alive' in Paul himself (Gal. 2.20); he has been declared to be God's Son (Rom. 1.4) and is the medium through which restored relation with God is bestowed on human beings (Rom. 3.22). He has died and he cannot die again (Rom. 6.9); he prays for us before the throne of God (Rom. 8.34), and it is a present fact that he loves us (Rom. 8.35, 39; cf. Gal. 2.20 for the same in the past tense).

Examples could be multiplied, but the point is clear: the range of activity ascribed to Jesus in Paul's writing alone is well beyond what is normally ascribable to a human individual – and, even more tantalizingly, the very identity of Jesus is reimagined and redescribed as that which grounds the collective identity of the community. In a recent essay on the work of Christ in the New Testament,[5] Michael J. Gorman lists ten functions or activities connected with the figure of Christ, ten ways in which Jesus is described as introducing characteristically divine activity into the historical world. Without reproducing the entire list, we can note that what is said of this

5   Michael J. Gorman, 'The Work of Christ in the New Testament', in Francesca Aran Murphy and Troy A. Stefano, eds, *The Oxford Handbook of Christology*, Oxford: Oxford University Press, 2015, pp. 72–86, especially pp. 76–83 (this is, by the way, a different Michael J. Gorman from the Thomist scholar mentioned in the first chapter).

human figure includes being the ultimate agent of divine judgement in and for the world, being the one who puts divine rule or authority into effect, both in his actual historical ministry (through healing, exorcism and so on) and when he returns at the end of all things, bestowing or releasing the divine Spirit and re-creating the divinely called and constituted human community, relating to the body of believers as God relates to Israel. Where his activity is recognized, there is 'new creation' (2 Cor. 5.17): his active presence is associated with an entirely new frame of reference for perceiving human agency and human hope. And there are enigmatic passages (2 Cor. 8.9, Phil 2. 6–8) implying that Jesus' human life on earth is a deliberately willed self-identifying with the poverty or shame of human existence on the part of an agent whose existence does not begin with his earthly conception. In addition to what Gorman notes, we could add (thinking back to the first examples we listed earlier of linguistic novelty where Jesus is concerned) that Jesus is spoken of as present in a distinctive way in the ceremony of the Lord's Supper, as the one who invites and also judges in that context and also as the common food that unites the guests. All the questions of Christology across the centuries begin with this deeply problematic and unusual set of linguistic habits in the earliest Christian communities – habits visible of course in New Testament writers other than Paul (especially John), habits that have to do with the community's worship as well as its reflection and teaching. We are presented in the language of these communities with a subject (a created substance, in the later idiom of the Thomist language we began with), of whom things are predicated that are not routinely predicable of created substances or subjects; a subject who is identified not simply and exhaustively by the means we use in order to identify other finite subjects, but with reference to other relations and attributes that take us beyond the range of 'normal' identifying characteristics for a human being.

New Testament scholarship has for the most part moved away in recent decades from the era when the problem seemed to be how a blameless Galilean rabbi got into bad company and acquired an embarrassing cluster of metaphysical or mythological attributes.[6] Since the 1970s, there has been

6   Though something like this is still argued with formidable learning and skill by the late Geza Vermes; see, for example, *The Authentic Gospel of Jesus*, London: Allen Lane/

a more and more systematic study of the intellectual and imaginative Jewish worlds of Jesus' day, and a recognition that, within that world, there was nothing all that remarkable about a certain merging of human figures with agents in or from Heaven.[7] The great heavenly mediators of God's action, the great angelic figures in whom divine presence and power reside, and the saints and intercessors of revealed history appear in profusion in the literature of the time – Michael, Moses, Enoch, Melchizedek and so on. There was nothing unusual in the idea that such heavenly agents might be manifest in history. It does not seem to have been so unthinkable that significant leaders of the present could be identified with heavenly powers; throwaway lines in the New Testament itself (as in Acts 5.36 and 8.10) suggest as much and the same possibility is borne out by the evidence of apocalyptic and rabbinic speculation. It is borne out *negatively* by the strong reaction found in rabbinical literature after the first Christian century against the language of heavenly mediators, angelic high priests and so on.[8] In other words, talking about Jesus in ways that exceed the compass of habitual speech about a human individual would not in itself have been so extraordinary at the time; to this extent at least, the bewildering shifts of register in Paul's language would have been odd but probably not that odd for Jewish readers.

The interesting problem is subtly different. Given that Paul and other Christian writers seem to have had the option of identifying Jesus of Nazareth as the earthly embodiment – and concealment – of a distinct individual heavenly power of some kind (the Archangel Michael, Melchizedek as a quasi-angelic high priest, the ascended Enoch or Elijah), it is still striking that this is never allowed to obscure the prosaic particularity of the

Penguin, 2003, and *Christian Beginnings: From Nazareth to Nicaea, AD 30–325*, London: Allen Lane/Penguin, 2012.

7   Among the copious literature in this field, reference may be made to Christopher Rowland's ground-breaking *The Open Heaven: A Study of Apocalyptic in Judaism and Early Christianity*, London: SPCK, 1982; William Horbury, *Jewish Messianism and the Cult of Christ*, London: SCM Press, 1998; and some of the essays in Jacob Neusner, William S. Green and Ernest Frerichs, eds, *Judaisms and their Messiahs at the Turn of the Christian Era*, Cambridge: Cambridge University Press, 1987, especially those by John J. Collins, Shemaryahu Talmon and J. H. Charlesworth.

8   The classic study is still Alan. F. Segal, *Two Powers in Heaven: Early Rabbinic Reports about Christianity and Gnosticism*, Leiden: Brill, 1978; 2nd edition, 2002.

narratives about Jesus as human agent and human sufferer and the focus on Jesus as a continuous human subject, born, maturing, dying. The central importance of the Temple in the Jewish world of this period and the immensely rich complex of imagery connected with it and its liturgy has been studied more intensively than ever in recent decades, and it is quite clear that a Jesus who was understood as restoring the access of God's people to God's full presence would readily be described in the language of priesthood and associated with mediatorial figures in the heavenly court or sanctuary. In Christian liturgy and Christian apocalyptic, these associations are long-lived and fruitful.[9] Yet despite the ascription of supernatural power and pre-existence to the agency that is manifested in and as Jesus (and indeed also concealed or disguised in Jesus; the theme of the hiddenness of heavenly power or agency appears in, for example, 2 Cor. 2.8), the narratives of everyday encounter in Galilee persist, and there is no attempt to qualify or soften the embarrassment of Jesus' judicial murder. On the contrary, this event, scandalous in different ways for Jews and non-Jews alike, becomes a paradoxical reinforcement for the credibility of Paul's message, and is picked up in John's Gospel to affirm that Jesus' extremity of human suffering is simultaneously a revelation of divine glory (e.g., John 12.23–33, 13.31–32). The apparent weakness or implausibility of a proclamation that has at its centre an executed criminal is used as a kind of demonstration of divine power: since this proclamation has no obvious human force or successfulness to commend it, it must be God alone who makes it credible (1 Cor. 1.18–2.5). And the apparent passivity of Jesus as victim of human violence is turned around so that it appears as the supreme manifestation of divine initiative: God 'gives' Jesus to be a victim (e.g., Rom. 3.25, 8.32; 2 Cor. 5.21), but Jesus equally and freely gives himself (Gal. 2.20), accepting his death as a vocation in obedience to God, so that his own willed and chosen powerlessness may be transparent to God's act and power. God's calling of Jesus to his task, Jesus' acceptance of what that task entails, and the actual collision between the divine will and the diabolical rejection of it in the crucifixion are all inseparably bound up together – and bound up with what

9   See particularly the work of Margaret Barker; e.g., *The Great High Priest: The Temple Roots of Christian Liturgy*, Edinburgh: T&T Clark, 2003, and *Temple Theology: An Introduction*, London: SPCK, 2004.

the resurrection of Jesus means – in Paul's account of how Jesus changes our human situation once and for all.

The point is that the identity of Jesus as human sufferer and the further identity of that suffering with the divine action are never eclipsed in the language of Christian Scripture. The narrative of Jesus is never presented simply as that of a divine or quasi-divine agent temporarily manifest or at least temporarily active on earth. The conceptual and imaginative challenge of Jesus' suffering and death continues to unsettle the language of Jesus as straightforwardly the manifestation of a heavenly power or personage. And part of what we see in the early development of Christological language up to the end of the second century, and indeed beyond, is a continued unsettlement in which the strong pressure to accept a 'heavenly power' model is repeatedly resisted in the name, initially, of the need to affirm without ambiguity the vulnerability of Jesus to suffering – a theme, for example, stressed very insistently in Ignatius of Antioch at the start of the second century.[10] This unsettlement is one of the factors which generate the long argument of Christological discussion and prevent it being abortively resolved by appeal to a narrative of the descent and return of a heavenly mediator: the actuality of worldly failure and death refuses to be ignored. But the other factor is a further trajectory of reflection which Paul sets in motion: in what is probably his most unusual idiom or idea, he speaks about actions, perceptions and the lives of individuals as being 'in Christ'. Without going into the enormous scholarly literature about the roots of this way of speaking,[11] it seems likely that one significant source for the language is in the idea that you can say that someone is 'in' an ancestor. The writer of the Letter to the Hebrews famously argues that when Abraham pays his tribute to Melchizedek, the patriarch Levi is 'in' Abraham's loins (Heb. 7.9–10): Abraham is the ultimate source of Levi's life and so

See For suffering references.

10 See, for example, Ignatius's Letter to the Smyrnaeans IV.

11 For a recent collection of perspectives on the question, see Michael. J. Thate, Kevin J. Vanhoozer and Constantine R. Campbell, eds, 'In Christ' in Paul: Explorations in Paul's Theology of Union and Participation, Tübingen: Mohr Siebeck, 2014, especially the essay by Campbell on 'Metaphor, Reality, and Union with Christ', pp. 61–86; also Grant Macaskill, Union with Christ in the New Testament, Oxford: Oxford University Press, 2013.

contains his descendant's identity in potential. This is what is behind Paul's argument that 'in' Adam all have died (1 Cor. 15.22), and that – quoting Genesis – 'in' Isaac Abraham's children are to be reckoned (Rom. 9.7). God's promise to Abraham is that 'in' him all nations will be blessed (Gal. 3.8, echoing Gen. 12.3, 18.18, 22.18), presumably by their affiliation to or alliance with his descendants. Against this background, when Paul speaks of being 'in' Christ, it is hard to avoid the implication that he sees Jesus as being as much the source of a single community of kinship as Adam or Abraham – the source of a new *human* kinship (as in Adam) and the source of a *specific* kinship among those who have received God's promise (as in Abraham). To be affiliated with Jesus, then, is something like being a 'descendant' of Jesus, deriving your own identity and the conditions and constraints of community membership from this common source.[12] But the analogy does not stop there: to be 'in' such an ancestor is to be able to claim that what he is doing *you* are doing. You occupy the same space, stand in the same relations (as with Levi paying tribute to Melchizedek 'in' Abraham). And in Paul's frame of reference, this means that aspects of Jesus' activity, in time and beyond, can be reckoned as *our* activity – most dramatically that the prayer Jesus offers, 'Abba, Father', is ours (Rom 8.15, Gal. 4.6). Our trust in God (our 'faith') is in some sense the same trust as Abraham's, since we are spiritually Abraham's kin, Abraham's progeny (Rom. 4.16–17); but the association we have as 'kindred' or 'progeny' of Jesus is even more radical an identification, since it allows us to be described as children, not merely of Abraham but of *God*, sharing the relation of Jesus to the God he prays to as 'Abba'. And – crucially – unlike Abraham, Jesus is still the *active* subject of diverse present verbs; he is alive to pray and to bestow grace on behalf of the Father and so forth, not just an ancestor – a chronologically remote source of kinship – but a contemporary, a current and direct source of life, action and corporate connectedness. It is worth noting too that speaking of Jesus as still or continuously active in this way

12 The model of Jesus as an 'ancestor' has been taken up enthusiastically in some modern African theologies, e.g., Kwame Bediako, *Jesus in African Culture: A Ghanaian Perspective*, Accra: Assempa Publishers, 1990; cf. the older study by John S. Mbiti, 'Some African Concepts of Christology', in G. F. Vicedom, ed., *Christ and the Younger Churches*, London: SPCK, 1972, pp. 51–62.

takes for granted that he is not literally and physically a passive object in the world – a dead body: his corporate or inclusive role is inseparable from the conviction that he is not in his tomb, and the heart of Paul's theology of the resurrection is not so much the overcoming of death for this human individual as the expansion of the effect of Jesus' actual bodily life to include the life of the believing community and, ultimately, the cosmos itself (putting 1 Cor. 15 alongside Rom. 8).[13]

So what Paul's Christology assumes is a complex of ideas which have yet to be assembled systematically but which pull insistently away from the simple model of the manifesting of an angelic or supernatural individual on earth. First, it is essential to recognize that what is 'manifested' is not a superhuman agency in any straightforward sense, since it is vulnerable to struggle and pain and shares the condition of ordinary human subjects in that respect (the point is underlined even more starkly in the Letter to the Hebrews, especially Chapters 2 and 5), being to all appearances passive in the hands of human power. And second, it is essential that the identity of Jesus Christ is understood as generating a 'lineage' a communal identity, that allows its members to see themselves as gifted with the same mode of activity that belongs to their 'ancestor', so that his acts can be attributed to them as securely as Abraham's act can be attributed to Levi or as the blessedness of Abraham can be ascribed to the covenant people. And while the primary sense of the 'ancestor' analogy (if that is indeed part of what being 'in' Christ means) is clearly receding fast in Paul's usage, as the idiom simply becomes more pervasive and self-explanatory, what survives is the focal conviction of action shared between Jesus and the community of which he is the fountainhead.[14]

The implication of these two points is that several possible accounts of Jesus Christ are shown to be inadequate. There is no literary evidence that at some primitive point the 'Jesus movement' was focused simply upon the

---

13 I have attempted to trace some of these connections in *Resurrection: Interpreting the Easter Gospel*, London: Darton, Longman & Todd, 1982; 2nd edition, 2002, Chapter 5.
14 See, for example, the essays by Susan Eastman, Isaac Augustine Morales, OP, and Joshua W. Jipp in Thate, Vanhoozer and Campbell, op. cit.; also Peter-Ben Smit, *Paradigms of Being in Christ: A Study of the Epistle to the Philippians*, London: Bloomsbury, 2013, Chapter 3.

memory of Jesus as charismatic teacher and healer and no more.[15] Nor is there literary evidence of a transitional stage at which reflection on Jesus as teacher and example was beginning to be elaborated by way of speculative identifications with heavenly figures: in the New Testament we seem to be always well past any such point. And the speculations that are taking shape in Paul do not represent just a version of Jesus as embodied angel or re-embodied patriarch: Jesus' actual human history matters too much, including the theological trauma of his trial and execution. His identity cannot be translated without remainder into that of an apocalyptic or mediatorial figure simply visiting the earth to manifest divine secrets; what such a model would leave out is the central role played in Paul's identification of Jesus by his crucifixion. We could come at the question in another way by saying that, for Paul and other New Testament writers, Jesus cannot be spoken of simply as an individual in the past. He is not only currently active, but the 'kinship group' of which he is the common and defining 'ancestor' is here and now open to his agency and growing into a different kind of existence as a result of that agency, which is 'appropriated' to its human members, in the sense that what they do and say in the name or *persona* of Jesus counts as done or said by Jesus. Jesus' human narrative identity, including his death, is understood as divine action – not a witness to or promise of divine action but *that action itself*; it is *as* human passivity, freely accepted, that his death becomes divine agency. We need, though, to state this with care: Jesus *acts* so as to become passive, accepts his suffering as a free choice; we are not saying that Jesus must be unequivocally passive because God's action could only occur in him if he ceased to be humanly active. The point is rather that the presence of divine action is not to be correlated with an inflation or reinforcement of human action to a degree of superhuman invulnerability and triumph; instead it is coincident with a human act of self-surrender, which requires human decision, human resource and steadiness of purpose and so on – hence Paul's arguments at the start of 1 Corinthians (1.18–2.5) about the fallacy of assimilating divine wisdom or power to a maximal version of created capacity. The

---

15 The position associated with the North America 'Jesus Seminar' scholars; for an accessible and forceful summary, see Robert W. Funk, *A Credible Jesus: Fragments of a Vision*, Santa Rosa: Polebridge Press, 2002.

central claim Paul makes is not that divine action entails an evacuation of human freedom, but that the particular kind of human freedom that in some sense releases divine action to transform the created world is an act of full openness to divine purpose and divine love. As we shall see in a later chapter,[16] the significance of what is (following Phil. 2.7) regularly called the *kenōsis*, the self-emptying of Christ is not that it involves a sort of collision between divine action and human action, such that one or the other element must be denied, qualified or diminished, but that a certain mode of finite life (self-sacrifice, other-directed love) is so attuned to the eternal mode of divine action that it becomes the occasion and vehicle of that infinite agency within the finite world.

→ We can think here in 2 aspects. Certainly, we should talk about deny passions, and other bad things coming from the north of men. Using the body, for bad purposes

2. From Paul to Nicaea: The Logos and the Flesh

To see Paul's Christology in these terms is to begin to see some of the lines of continuity I have suggested between the developed discussion we find in the Middle Ages and the origins of Christological language. If this reading of Paul is accurate, there is already a refusal to treat the specific humanity of Jesus as episodic, accidental or incomplete; already a conviction that the humanity *in its entirety* is the form taken by the act of God in history; already the acknowledgement of divine action here and now exercised by Jesus and participated in by those whom he calls into community – the theology of Jesus as Head of the Body which we have seen to be so significant for Aquinas.[17] But, as Christology develops in the first Christian centuries, there is not a steady trajectory in the direction of the developed account; it is more a story of a series of local conceptual difficulties, whose piecemeal solutions cumulatively pose the radical questions of the fifth century and afterwards. This has something to do with what we have already referred to in the Jewish context, the availability of apparently tidier conceptual frameworks for identifying Jesus. These frameworks are from time to time tried out and elaborated by Christian thinkers. As various models are tried and discarded, various options for resolving the basic linguistic tensions

16 Below, Chapter 2.2.
17 Above, pp. 39–40.

Second, we should not get in the assumption that our suffering is something we can manage but something allowed by God.

with which we began in this chapter become unusable; new structures and conceptualities have to be created.

Central to the entire development of early Christian theology was the range of schemes utilizing the notion of *logos*. In Stoic thought, the word designated – roughly – the pattern of interconnection in the universe, the ideal state of harmony or balance among the forces at work in the world.[18] Not a personified agent in any way for Stoic philosophers, it acquired rather different associations in the hands of some religious philosophers around the turn of the millennium, especially Philo of Alexandria, for whom the word designated a kind of mediating power in Heaven, transmitting to the finite universe the ordering and governing power of God.[19] For Philo, this power can be described as an 'archangel', a heavenly high priest and so on, though there is a good deal of debate about how far he really thought of his *logos* as an actual person in Heaven and how far he was deliberately using the currently available Jewish language about heavenly mediators as a metaphor for the way in which God's action is distributed and 'applied' within the universe.[20] But the structure Philo creates is undoubtedly one which offered rich possibilities to Christian thinkers, since it seemed to point to a uniquely powerful heavenly personage who could without too much difficulty be identified with the power that is embodied in Jesus. Whether or not the writer of the Fourth Gospel knew Philo directly (not all that likely[21]), the language of *logos* becoming flesh in Jesus provided a very

18 *Logos* is the creative fire which animates everything and periodically destroys and restores everything. The rationality of the human thinker is a response to this active flow of kindling life in all things. But it is important to remember that this remains for the Stoics a *physical* principle, in contrast to the use later made of it by Jewish and Christian thinkers.

19 On Philo, see S. Sandmel, *Philo of Alexandria: An Introduction*, Oxford: Oxford University Press, 1979; more recently, F. Alesse, *Philo of Alexandria and Post-Aristotelian Philosophy*, Leiden: Brill, 2008. On Philo's doctrine of the Logos, see also Rowan Williams, *Arius: Heresy and Tradition*, London: SCM Press, 2009 (second edition), pp. 117–24.

20 Williams, op. cit., p. 118, with references to the scholarly literature.

21 Nothing in St John's Gospel suggests the detailed cosmology of Philo or even the use of allegorical readings of Hebrew Scripture to establish the existence of a semi-divine intermediary principle. For a slightly more positive assessment, see Ruth Edwards,

resourceful model for most early Christian theologians, one which did not commit them to a too strongly mythological world of archangelic priests, but which did anchor the identity of Jesus firmly in the heavenly places and allowed him to be presented as unquestionably embodying the 'power and wisdom' of God, as Paul had expressed it. God's own life is thought of as diffusing itself through a derivative or secondary divine power (the expression *deuteros theos*, 'a second God', originates with Philo[22]), and this is identified as what becomes enfleshed in Jesus of Nazareth.

The most sophisticated version of this model is developed by Origen in the third century.[23] For Origen, the Logos is the life of God 'condensed' or 'concentrated' into a form that can be communicated to the finite universe. The supreme God, unchangeable, immaterial and perfect, must – so to speak – pass the light of his purity and simplicity through a prism, whereby his single, indivisible life becomes the source of the multiple manifestations of life that constitute the world of intelligible reality. The Logos is, from one point of view, the first step away from absolute divine plenitude; from another, the necessary moment in which God generates a mode of divine life that can actually be shared with finite existents.[24] Prescinding for a moment from the detail of this, what matters for our present discussion is that Origen uses this starting point to elaborate a theory about the constitution of Christ that – just as much as Philo's general cosmological model – shapes all later treatments, both positively and negatively. In broad outline, Origen argues that all human subjects begin as individual minds (*noes*) united in the Logos

Discovering John: Content, Interpretation, Reception, London: SPCK, 2014 (second edition).

22 Williams, op. cit., p. 118; the phrase can be found in Philo's *Questions on Genesis*, II.62 (text in the Loeb Classical Library, ed. and trans. Ralph Marcus, Cambridge, MA: Harvard University Press, 1953. It is later used by Origen in, for example, *contra Celsum* V.39.

23 Among recent works, Mark Edwards, *Catholicity and Heresy in the Early Church*, London: Ashgate, 2009, deserves mention. See also Williams, op. cit., pp. 131–43, and John Behr, *Formation of Christian Theology*, Vol. 1: *The Way to Nicaea*, Crestwood, NY: St Vladimir's Seminary Press, 2001, pp. 163–206, especially pp. 184–91.

24 The key texts are in the first books of Origen's *Commentary on John*; a useful translation is that by Ronald Heine in the Fathers of the Church series, Washington, DC: Catholic University of America Press, 1989.

and sharing the Logos's contemplative gaze towards God; but, turning in on themselves, they fall away from this condition. To prevent their complete dissolution or degradation, God clothes them in flesh so that they have an opportunity to recover their strength and freedom by subduing the flesh and ordering its activities and desires according to true understanding (the word 'reason' for this is not very helpful to a modern Western mind; to be *logikos* is to have the deep harmonious understanding that is supremely at work in *the* Logos). One of the created spirits never falls away from its contemplative dignity and stability, however; it remains bound to the eternal Logos, and so there is no necessity for its embodiment. But this means that if it freely accepts embodiment, it can open up to other, fallen, spirits the recovery of their full freedom. So the incarnation of the Logos means that this finite spirit united to the Logos becomes embodied both to show that finite spirit is fully capable of living in the flesh without being subordinated to it and to clear away the obstacles that embodied spirits have put in the way of the action of the Logos, so that all may realize their union with this eternal act of freedom, bliss, understanding and adoration.[25]

So for Origen, Jesus is what happens when a created spirit united with eternal Logos unites in turn with the vulnerable, 'passible' flesh of an ordinary human being.[26] The invulnerable and stable *nous* that is one with the Logos is the medium by which the Logos can unite with the body and also with the unstable world of fallen spirits. The goal of this process is that we are restored to our proper place and function as contemplators of God's eternal being and truth. Origen is careful to minimize what might be called the mythological residue, the language of a heavenly entity descending to earth. The Logos as such does not descend or change in any way; the pre-existent spirit that will be the spirit of Jesus can be said to 'descend', but only in the same sense that spirits in general can be said to descend into their

---

25 See, for example, the *Commentary on John* I.24–7; Behr, op. cit., pp. 169–84, is a clear and reliable summary.

26 Behr, op. cit., pp. 197–200; on Origen's doctrine of the incarnation, see, for a very brief survey, Rowan Williams, 'Origen on the Soul of Jesus', *Origeniana Tertia*, ed. Richard Hanson and Henri Crouzel, Rome: Edizioni dell'Ateneo, 1985, pp. 131–7, and also Nicholas Madden, 'An Aspect of Origen's Christology', in Thomas Finan and Vincent Twomey, eds, *Studies in Patristic Christology*, Dublin: Four Courts Press, 1998, pp. 23–36.

bodies – the difference being that this descent is not an emergency provision resulting from falling away from God. Jesus is thus on earth a formally complete human individual, with the same constituent parts as all other humans – contemplative *nous*, responsive and instinctual 'soul' (*psuché*) and passible, mutable body.

Origen's significance in the history of the development of Christology is partly to do with his clarity about this formal human completeness: the saviour is, for him, indisputably a complete finite agent in the same sense that other finite agents are. It is important not to be distracted by the fact that what Origen believed constituted a complete finite agent was, by later theological standards, rather eccentric; the stark disjunction between the essential, pre-existing life of the finite spirit and the contingent, damage-limiting reality of embodiment brings its own problems, as the thinkers and polemicists of the fourth to sixth centuries did not fail to point out,[27] but Origen had understood that a fundamental implication of the Christian narrative was the impossibility of treating the historical person of the saviour as a mere passive vehicle for direct divine activity. Without the reality of a created *nous* in Jesus, the restoration of the right relationship between spirit and body would have to be something externally imposed by God's will, not a reworking from within of the possibilities of finite existence. And the basic model proposed by Origen for the nature of the Logos's unity with the created *nous* of Jesus is one of perfect and unbroken unity in act – the act of contemplating the Father. It is a way of underlining the absolute and definitive priority of the eternal act that belongs to the Logos without sacrificing the integrity of a finite act which actualizes this prior reality within the world's processes. In this way, Origen's scheme can be understood as a step away from an unexamined mythological model in which the heavenly simply *is* the sole real agent, filling in a gap in the continuities of the world.

But the weight of unfinished business in Origen's theology became a more and more severe pressure on Christian reflection in the later third and early fourth century, contributing to the major theological crisis which dominated the fourth century. The eternal Logos eternally contemplates

---

27 See Elizabeth A. Clark, *The Origenist Controversy: The Cultural Construction of an Early Christian Debate*, Princeton: Princeton University Press, 1992, Chapter 3.

the Father; but does this mean that in some sense the Logos is the *recipient* as well as the agent of divine activity, that the Logos is acted upon *before* it or he acts? And if the Logos is acted upon by God before it or he exercises divine agency towards the creation, does this not put the Logos ultimately closer to creation than Creator, with the Father alone bring *entirely* active, exercising true and unqualified divinity? Origen himself seems to have expressed different views on this at different stages of his career, though the exact meaning of his language is still hotly debated;[28] but a very robust doctrine of the unbroken continuity of divine life between its source in the Father and its expression in the Logos means that it is not seen by him as a fatal contradiction or aporia. However, a philosophical climate in which the radical difference between divine self-subsistence or simplicity and finite passivity and conditionedness is more sharply defined will be less accommodating and more anxious.[29] Origen still inhabits an intellectual world where it is possible to think of 'being' as distributed hierarchically and univocally: it is realized at different levels in different intensities. Absent this, and the ascription of divinity to the Logos must be analogical: the Logos cannot be described as divine in the same sense in which divinity is ascribed to the Father.

This seems to have been the conclusion reached by the Alexandrian priest Arius at the beginning of the fourth century.[30] He is strongly critical of any language implying that there are two co-ordinate subjects possessing divine life, and equally of any suggestion that talking about the Logos is simply personifying an internal characteristic of the Father. The only remaining option, as he sees it, is to make it clear that the Logos is a created substance, endowed by the true God with as much dignity and liberty as a creature can carry, so as to be able to convey the divine purpose to a creation that the Father as such is too exalted to reach directly. And although reconstructing Arius's views is an uncertain affair, it was certainly

---

28 Williams, *Arius*, pp. 140–3.

29 Ibid., pp. 176, 231–2.

30 On the trajectory from Origen to Arius, see (apart from Williams, op. cit.) above all the first chapter of Lewis Ayres's magisterial *Nicaea and Its Legacy: An Approach to Fourth-Century Trinitarian Theology*, Oxford: Oxford University Press, 2006 (second edition).

true that some of his contemporaries thought he was also claiming that the Logos directly took the place of a human *nous* in Jesus;[31] if so, this would be a completely natural deduction from his general repudiation of Origen's metaphysics. Since the New Testament undeniably presents Jesus as 'troubled in spirit', as subject to psychic as well as physical suffering and change, this becomes another important component in the argument that the Logos cannot be God in the strict sense. The subject of Jesus' inner pain or doubt must be something that is finite and vulnerable; and in the absence of Origen's mediating pre-existent spirit, this is either a straightforward human mind or the heavenly but non-divine subjectivity of the Word. The former was evidently a view that Arius rejected. And his conclusion that the Logos was a figure rather like the great angelic mediators of Jewish and Jewish–Christian speculation seems to have been reinforced by liturgical habits of speaking of the Logos as leading the praises of the heavenly court or temple. We have noted how important the imagery of Temple worship was in the first days of Christian reflection and worship, and the idea that human worship was 'carried' into the sanctuary of Heaven by the Logos was unmistakeably current in Alexandrian circles. Arius had some plausible grounds for seeing his synthesis as holding together many venerable traditions of exegesis and liturgy, in which the Logos was the supremely graced and gifted mediator between God and creation.[32] He certainly has no interest in ascribing to Jesus an ordinary human subjectivity, as this would nullify the central theological claim that the Word took flesh in Jesus. Origen had already noted the problem in affirming that Jesus truly suffered, and for him the presence of the created *nous* in Jesus had averted a conceptual crisis. Arius offers the more economical, but, as it turned out, far more problematic, solution that the Logos could not be divine in the full and proper sense.

The details of the fourth-century debate need not be set out in full here. But in terms of the developing logic of talking about Christ, this debate has a decisive and slightly paradoxical effect. The majority of the Church

---

31   See R. P. C. Hanson, *The Search for the Christian Doctrine of God: The Arian Controversy 318–381*, Edinburgh: T&T Clark, 1988, p. 83.

32   On the liturgical background, see Rowan Williams, 'Angels Unawares: Heavenly Liturgy and Earthly Theology in Alexandria', *Studia Patristica* XXX, pp. 50–363.

finally rejected Arius's solution and repudiated any suggestion that the divinity of the Logos was in any sense inferior to or different from that of the Father: Father and Son – and, as was clarified gradually in the fourth century, Holy Spirit also – lived one and the same life, exercised one and the same activity, enjoyed one and the same unchangeable and impassible (i.e., purely active, unconditioned) nature. Qualifying the divinity of the eternal Word could not now be a solution to the question of how we could think about the suffering of the incarnate Word. And the unmistakeable implication of this is that there is no way in which the Word can be fitted into a gap within the constitution of the human individual Jesus. If Jesus suffers, it is a human self that suffers. This means that *it is the affirmation of unequivocal divinity for the Logos that mandates the affirmation of unequivocal humanity for Jesus.* The solution to the conundrum of their unity cannot be found by blurring the definition of either element. And this is not a matter of some abstract intellectual concern to preserve pre-Christian or sub-Christian doctrines of divinity or humanity (as is occasionally argued); it is most immediately the result of detailed arguments over the exegesis of key scriptural texts,[33] and the conclusion that they require these two affirmations in full rigour.

But this further means that theology has taken a very decisive step away from any residual idea that divine nature or agency is a vastly magnified version of finite agency. The divinity that is now ascribed unequivocally to the Word is the pure agency that cannot be conceived as sharing any logical space with conditioned, reactive or interactive agencies such as inhabit the finite world. We are, undeniably, left with the major issue of how to speak about the relations of Father, Son and Spirit as somehow reciprocal and mutually defining without making them instances of the sort of interaction of finite agents that we are familiar with; and this occupies a good deal of theological energy up to and beyond the Middle Ages, gradually settling into the notion of an absolute simultaneity of relationship, which simply is the eternal and necessary actualization of what it is to be divine (i.e. there

---

33 On the centrality of exegesis in patristic debate, see Frances Young, *Biblical Exegesis and the Formation of Christian Culture,* Cambridge: Cambridge University Press, 1997, and also *God's Presence: A Contemporary Recapitulation of Early Christianity,* Cambridge: Cambridge University Press, 2013, Chapter 1.

are no partial initiatives and responses in divine life, no developments, no divinity that is not unequivocally a pattern of relation and no divine act that is not equally the act of all the divine subsistents). But within the more specific area of Christology, the long-term effect of the fourth-century controversies is to lay out the grammar of the relation between finite and infinite with a conceptual clarity that had not been seen before. Divine life is indeed (as Arius would have agreed) utterly beyond the narrative of stimulus and response, the interweaving of action and passivity. As such, it cannot stand alongside finite action as another part of the picture – an enlarged version of finite freedom with the most egregious limitations stripped away. It will resist any claim to exhaustive conceptualization; the Platonic language about the divine as 'beyond being'[34] will increasingly be naturalized into Christian usage. This leaves the way clear to an unambiguous assertion of complete humanity in Christ, since there is no need to leave a space in Christ for divinity to fill. In a way, there are two paradoxes here. As we have just seen, the more clear theology becomes about the full divinity of Christ, the more space there is for acknowledging his humanity. But also, the more clear the doctrinal formulae become which set out what must be affirmed about divine action, the more it is plain that finite conceptualities will be inadequate to characterize divine life, and a discipline of negation will increasingly apply. Doctrinal clarity in this area, so far from implying arrogant claims to know what it is like to be divine, has the effect precisely of making it necessary to speak of God's nature in apophatic formulations. Christology, we could say, has forced the issue for Christian theology of recognizing fully what it means to acknowledge the sheer radical otherness of God; the very discourse that declares God's direct engagement with and communication through the finite world is what most plainly compels us to insist on God's transcendence of the categories of the finite and thus – the recurring theme of these chapters – the essentially non-competitive character of the juxtaposition of divine and created. To trace the evolution of the theological problem through the thickets of fourth-century controversy is to see something of how Christology becomes the means of clarifying what finitude itself means.

---

34 *epekeina tēs ousias* (Plato, *Republic* 509b8).

3. Towards Chalcedon

The point just outlined about how finite and infinite can and cannot be juxtaposed did not immediately clarify issues in Christology, however. The clear separation of divine self-subsistence and finite life of all kinds led some of the theologians of the fourth and fifth centuries to argue for the necessity of there being two 'subjects' in Christ, one capable of suffering and one not; even for ascribing certain actions of Jesus to a finite subject and others to an infinite. What had been a rhetorical way of underlining the paradox of divine and human agency at work in a single human individual came closer to being a full-blown disjunction of personal agents. And one implication of this was that the union between the Word and the human individuality of Jesus was understood by these theologians as an intense and unbroken instance of the prophetic 'indwelling' of a human person by the divine.[35] The quite understandable reluctance to reopen the question of attributing suffering to the Logos led to an insistence that, if the Logos was indeed to be spoken of as unequivocally divine, there must be a complete human individual to whom the suffering can be attributed 'alongside' the divine indwelling Word. Against this, other theologians attempted to find a vocabulary for distinguishing the divine and human agencies without introducing two distinct subjects: divinity and humanity are sometimes presented as two sets of qualities ascribable to a single subject, and there is the beginning of a theme that will be of some significance for later Christological developments, the idea that each 'nature' becomes, through their union in Christ, capable of being described in terms of the attributes of the other. But this needs the further qualifications that (i) it is the single divine subject, the Word, who brings about this exchange of predicates, and (ii) while the humanity is substantially changed by the exchange, the divinity is not. This latter point is crucial for the overall model being used, as without it we should be back with the familiar problem of the Logos being passive in respect to other agencies. Since there is no way in which passivity can be ascribed to God, the only way in which the exchange of properties can make sense is if the unbroken and unqualified agency of God acts upon the

---

35 The best recent introduction can be found in John Behr, *The Case Against Diodore and Theodore: Texts and Their Contexts*, Oxford: Oxford University Press, 2011, pp. 5–28.

humanity to create actual new possibilities for it, while itself permitting a qualified use of human predicates to be ascribed to the Word in its action to bring this about. The exact status and significance of this kind of approach remains disputed even in modern debates, as will appear later on.[36]

The heart of the tension between these diverse styles of Christological language in the bitter debates leading up to the Council of Chalcedon in 451 is to do with whether in Christ we are looking at one or two centres or termini of action. The 'dualist' view, normally associated with the theologians of Western Syria and Asia Minor, assumes that the only way of avoiding a re-mythologized discourse about the Logos as exposed to direct limitation and suffering is to posit a human individuality that is strictly comparable to our own in its independence and completeness. It builds on the important fourth-century dispute involving Apollinaris of Laodicaea, in which Apollinaris's denial of an independent spiritual subject, a finite *nous*, in Jesus was finally and emphatically rejected by more or less all parties in the continuing theological debate. If the purpose of the Incarnation was the comprehensive re-creation of human nature from within, it would make no sense to suppose that some aspect of human nature was ignored in this process, with a divine 'supplement' provided.[37] For the more dualist theologians, this mandated a vocabulary of two active substances coinciding in one phenomenon, Jesus Christ, within the finite world. But the awkward language of certain acts of Christ being attributable to divinity rather than humanity in effect led back to the same difficulty – as if the humanity had to be interrupted and supplemented by a divine activity that suspended the finite element in the union. Opponents of the dualist model – their most eloquent representative being Cyril of Alexandria[38] – insisted that theology should have no truck with anything

36 Below, Chapter 1.2, especially the discussion of the work of Christopher Beeley.

37 This is what is crystallized in the famous dictum of Gregory of Nazianzus that 'what has not been assumed has not been healed' (*to gar aproslēpton atherapeuton*, Gregory, *ep*. 51, to Cledonius).

38 A collection of pertinent texts in Lionel R. Wickham, ed. and trans., *Cyril of Alexandria: Selected Letters*, Oxford: Oxford University Press, 1983; for a general introduction to Cyril (more sympathetic than most), see John McGuckin, *Saint Cyril of Alexandria and the Christological Controversy*, Crestwood, NY: St Vladimir's Seminary Press, 2004, especially Chapter 3.

implying 'two Christs' (a formula which was often used as a sort of short-hand in early Christian theology for Gnostic disjunctions between heavenly and earthly forms of the Redeemer).[39] While Jesus Christ possessed all that would be needed to 'count' as human, lacking no element in the human composition, this integral human reality had to be understood as entirely and directly activated by one divine agent, the Word. It is as if the complete set of human elements making up the distinct individuality of Jesus remains only *potentially* real unless and until activated by the eternally subsisting reality of the Logos. We can see very clearly here the origins of the medieval discussions summarized in our first chapter. In other words, for Jesus to be *actually* and concretely *human* he must be taken by the Word as a vehicle or instrument for *divine* action; the ensemble of human elements must be 'assumed', in the later Latin vocabulary of the scholastic theologians – *proslēpton* in the Greek of the Fathers.

The very fragile settlement brokered at Chalcedon – which we shall be examining at more length in the next chapter – attempted to combine the favourite phrases of both schools, but was widely regarded as having given too much ground to the dualists, in that it underlined the claim that neither divinity nor humanity changed their fundamental definition in the Incarnation, and drew back from presenting the incarnate Christ as a reality in which the two natures perfectly *converged* rather than just coinciding. The definition certainly insisted on a single hypostasis, a single active subsistent as the ultimate source of action in Christ, but retained a hint of the dualist idiom by which the union was to be seen as a sort of external appearance in which two independent substances were simultaneously at work. Rigorist Cyrillines, of whom there was no shortage, concluded that the formula gave too little room for affirming that the two natures, the two clusters of essential defining qualities, were activated or realized by a single subject. Since hypostasis at this date is primarily the term that is used to designate Persons of the Trinity, its use in the Christological context is not immediately clear. Cyril had insisted that the union of divinity and humanity in Christ was *kath' hupostasin* – something at the level of substantive reality rather than a

---

39 See, for example, Rowan Williams, 'Defining Heresy', in Alan Kreider, ed., *The Origins of Christendom in the West*, Edinburgh: T&T Clark, 2001, pp. 313–35, especially pp. 332–4.

mere appearance.[40] This turn of phrase may originally have meant no more than an insistence that the union was not a merely theoretical matter; *kata monen ten theorian*[41] gradually became a positive formula to denote 'what there is one of' in the union that takes place in the Incarnation. Cyril also stored up much later controversy by using the word *phusis*, 'nature', for the same purpose, although this word was understood by some as meaning the same as 'essence', *ousia*. For him, it is a way of stressing the concrete and lasting character of the unity between the two essences, divine and human; but it could be and was read as ascribing to Jesus a 'nature' that was neither divine nor human but a unique compound. One of the major tasks of post-Chalcedonian theology was to sharpen up the terminological resources needed to clarify positions. What might it mean to say that a full human individuality, such as all now agreed must be recognized in Jesus Christ, was 'assumed' by the agency of the divine Word in such a way as neither to interrupt or diminish the human nor to compromise or reduce the divine? Chalcedon – notoriously – offered a neat outline of the agenda rather than a full resolution. So far from being a sign of theology's capitulation to an alien intellectual technology, it signalled the beginning of a distinctively theological attempt to develop a language for identity, individual and generic, and to provide a systematic set of protocols for understanding the biblical record so as to avoid what I earlier called a remythologizing of language about Christ – as if Christ were a heavenly individual spending a section of his ongoing life on earth.

It may be helpful to note once again that the patristic anxiety about compromising the unchangeability or impassibility of God was not an abstract concern for a kind of metaphysical correctness. The controversies of the second Christian century in particular had focused on questions posed by the varied accounts of the origin of the universe advanced in the texts and communities we now call 'Gnostic'. Sophisticated and elaborate narratives of how the universe unfolds out of primordial unity and purity towards its present compromised or unenlightened condition had often presented the origins of finite reality as grounded in a sort of self-separation

---

40 See Wickham, *Cyril of Alexandria*, pp. 4–5, n. 6, on the fact that the phrase does not at this point have anything like the technical sense of denoting a specific kind of union.

41 See the Second Letter to Succensus, Wickham, op. cit., pp. 92–3.

of divine life into its constituent qualities – most dramatically in the story of divine 'Sophia', Wisdom, fallen from Heaven and imprisoned in the material order. Other, more polarized, versions of the story posited an act of cosmic rebellion against the true God, with an inferior deity claiming through false revelations to be the ultimate truth.[42] In reaction to these and similar schemes, what became the mainstream of Christian thinking insisted on the absolute and indivisible unity of God and the voluntary character of creation: affirming the unity of the Creator implied that creation itself was a coherent system designed by God, rather than an increasingly dysfunctional emanation from the divine, a dissolution of divine integrity in the plurality and conflict of material being. In effect, the opposition to Gnostic cosmologies (or what Christian polemicists understood to be Gnostic cosmologies) is the beginning and the condition of the clarificatory process that is developing in the Christological controversies of later centuries: God's absolute independence of any narrative of change, necessary emanation, division and so on is inseparable from the defence of the idea of a creation that is unified and good in itself. The logic of creation requires God to be God as much as it requires creation to be finite; without a clear assertion that God cannot be conceived as passive or divisible, we are left with various versions of a universe in which divine and finite being are in some sense understood as univocally related, in such a way that the divine self-subsistence and liberty are put in question.

Christian theologians show a high degree of neuralgia around these questions in the fourth and fifth centuries, and both sides in the Christological debate are preoccupied with the same cluster of problems. The 'dualists' of Western Syria see in the Cyrilline position a return to fundamental ontological confusion, with a divine Logos passive in the face of suffering, and thus vulnerable to change. The Cyrillines see in their opponents a dividing of Christ which echoes a Gnostic disdain for the material and contingent world as something with which the divine cannot be directly in touch. What emerges gradually in the wake of Chalcedon is a structure of ideas

---

42   Alastair H. B. Logan, *Gnostic Truth and Christian Heresy: A Study in the History of Gnosticism*, Edinburgh: T&T Clark, 1996, is a comprehensive overview of various systems; Chapter 3 is particularly relevant. See also Christoph Markschies, *Gnosis: An Introduction*, London and New York: T&T Clark, 2003, Chapters 3 and 4.

that steadily purges the language of incarnation of any residual implication of two *objects*, divinity and humanity, that have to be accommodated in a single space, and develops models for thinking through a mode of unity that is not simply absorption or fusion. This will certainly entail a continuing insistence that the divine Word has to be understood as unchanged in the context of the new relation to finite being which constitutes the incarnate identity; not because of philosophical fastidiousness, but so as to preserve the very idea of the integrity of the finite order, in which God's action works not by displacing but by intensifying from within the capacity of created agency. In a universe that does not consist of impermeable fixed substances but is a system of interacting finite processes, it is possible to imagine such processes developing in various levels of openness to the fundamental infinite initiative upon which they depend, without being bound to a model of Creator and creation as related in a way comparable to mutually exclusive atomistic subjects (this was the point made by Austin Farrer in the passage quoted at the start of this book). What we are seeing in theology after Chalcedon is the search for more and more adequate ways of speaking about this.

4. A Latin Voice: Augustine on the Unity of Christ

Alongside the controversies that racked the Eastern Mediterranean world during the fourth and fifth centuries, the world of Latin theology saw its own significant developments, above all in the thought of Augustine of Hippo. He wrote no substantial systematic treatise on Christology; he will have known next to nothing of the debates accelerating in the East (he has a very limited knowledge of Greek), and he died before the fifth-century councils had issued their determinations. However, the vocabulary and conceptual structure he uses in discussing the person and work of Christ exhibit many of the same tensions and resolutions as the theology of the contemporary Greek-speaking churches.[43] The distinctive language he opts for in fact offers a valuable complement to the Eastern discussions, in that

---

43 The major study remains Tarsicius van Bavel, *Recherches sur la Christologie de saint Augustin. L'humain et le divin d'après saint Augustin*, Freibourg: Editions Universitaires, 1954.

he shows a strong interest in broadly *linguistic* considerations, exploring the phenomenon of the incarnate Christ in terms of what would be meant by thinking of the Word speaking in, as and through the humanity of Jesus: the Incarnation is seen in significant part as the event in which a finite phenomenon, Jesus' humanity, becomes wholly a vehicle of *communication* for the divine Word. And this basic model helps Augustine to develop a theology of 'the whole Christ', *totus Christus*, which allows for a sophisticated account of how we both combine and distinguish between speaking of the Word in its eternal selfhood, the Word incarnate in Jesus and the Word considered as the actively unifying principle of the believing community's life.

Augustine regularly uses the word *persona* to denote 'what there is one of' in Christ. Although it normally renders the Greek *prosopon*, Augustine's usage does not carry the problematic associations which this word acquires in the East, where it tends to designate the visible and tangible unity possessed by Jesus Christ as a phenomenon in this world. In contrast to this, Augustine understands *persona* as pointing to the source of what is said and done in Christ and also to the role of human subject which Christ enacts. On the one hand: the incarnate Christ can be said to 'sustain the role' (*agere personam*) of eternal Wisdom.[44] When Christ speaks, he speaks with and for eternal Wisdom, stands for that Wisdom and enacts its actions in what he communicates. On the other: the Word 'acts a human individual'.[45] Eternal Wisdom takes on the role of a human speaker – an idea that is of great importance for Augustine's reading of the Psalms. In his earliest writing on the subject, he is inclined to use *persona* simply to designate the speaker of a particular biblical text: when Christ says certain things indicating weakness or limitation, we ascribe it to the *persona hominis* or *carnis*.[46] But as his thought matures, it is clear that he has come to see *persona* as always designating the ultimate source of communication and of action in general: the Word may speak in the role of a human individual or indeed on behalf of the whole human race in its solidarity, but remains ultimately the sole *speaker*, the one who in speaking both divinely and humanly takes responsibility, as

---

44 See, for example, *exp. Gal.*27, *de agone Christi* 20, 22.

45 *agere hominem* (which we could also render as 'actuates a human being'), as in *de div. qu.*83.

46 *en.Ps.*56.

we might say, for both the divine and the human. What unites the divine and the human in Christ is *unitas personae*:[47] one agent is activating both 'natures'.

This way of thinking about the unity of Christ helpfully cuts across some of the metaphysical tangles gradually resolving themselves in the East, though it still stands in need of clarification to avoid any implication that the humanity is a passive instrument without its own created fullness and appropriate power of finite initiative. He never questions the formal completeness of Jesus' humanity and affirms it explicitly and forcefully;[48] but the question of what kind of actual unified substance the incarnate Word is remains a matter he does not directly address, and the language of *persona* can leave a vague sense in the superficial reader that the Word's agency in Jesus is simply the adoption of a mode of speaking rather than a substantial solidarity. In fact, however, the discourses on the Psalms make it very clear that a lot more than this is being claimed. The ability of the Word to speak in Christ for humanity, especially for humanity in its need, guilt, degradation and poverty, is an ability that presupposes a genuine identification: Christ truly stands in the place of sinful humanity, freely and deliberately taking on the consequences of its fallenness so that he can give voice to its need in the presence of the Father. Because he actually occupies a place within human history and suffers in his own particular humanity, it should be plain that his voicing of human distress is a function of the reality of his fleshly condition. As in later Christology, he is free to make his own the condition of the rest of suffering humanity because his own humanity, fully united with the Word, is not confined or limited in its charity by sin.[49]

Following other writers, he makes use of the analogy of the union between soul and body.[50] The substances of soul and body are naturally and

47 *ep.* 137.

48 Ibid.

49 See, for example, *enchiridion* 12.40. The theme of Christ assuming the voice of suffering and sinful humanity is a constant one in the *enarrationes in Psalmos*; see Michael Cameron, *Christ Meets Me Everywhere: Augustine's Early Figurative Exegesis*, Oxford: Oxford University Press, 2012, especially Chapter 6, and, by the same author, the article on the *enarrationes* in Allan D. Fitzgerald, ed., *Augustine Through the Ages: An Encyclopaedia*, Grand Rapids, MI: Eerdmans, 1999, pp. 290–6.

50 See, for example, *ep.* 137.9, *tr. Ioh.* 19.15.

irreducibly distinct: in a lesser way, we could say that they reflect the distinction of divinity and humanity in that they do not occupy the same logical space (more of one does not mean less of the other); in the union that is the human constitution, they remain the *sort* of thing they are, even though we can quite uncontroversially speak of them as inseparably united and as a single locus of action and predication. They cannot be separated out as two subjects; what one does, the other does. Augustine is in no doubt about the fact that the Word in the union is not changed and does not become capable of suffering *as* divine Word. He is clear about the presence of a created soul in Jesus[51] and clear that it is this that is the subject of suffering and not the eternal Word. Yet this does not mean that we should not say that the Word is the person who suffers when Jesus suffers – suffering in and through the human nature in its completeness. There is a latish letter of Augustine's appended to a treatise in which the Gaulish monk Leporius sets out a recantation of his earlier views about Christ, views which show a strongly dualist tendency and an anxiety about ascribing passibility to the Word as incarnate:[52] Augustine is sympathetic to Leporius's qualms (putting them down to *pius timor*, 'devout misgivings'), but it is clear that in helping to shape Leporius's new confession of faith, he has insisted on the unity of the ultimate subject in Jesus, and also on the asymmetry between the divine agency and the created, in that the latter changes radically as a result of the union, while the former does not. Leporius evidently borrows Augustine's own favoured phrasing when he asserts that there is one *persona* in Christ, 'embracing' the Word and the individuated humanity; but the unity of this *persona* resides in the unity of the eternal and unchanging subsistent who is the Word.[53]

Later controversies cast their shadow before them: Augustine anticipates Aquinas's attempts to find a way of saying that the unity of the Word can be considered from more than one perspective. It is unambiguously clear that the eternal Word is complete as a divine subsistent; nothing can be added to this reality, nothing can qualify it in what it is; yet we may also

51 E.g., *de fide et symbol* IV.8.
52 *libellus emendationis*, sent to the bishops of Gaul with a covering letter from Augustine (*ep.* 219).
53 *libellus* 3.

rightly say that the Word exists *as* the unifying and identifying ground of an individual human existence. It is this double conviction that Aquinas seeks to crystallize in his language about a sort of composite *esse* in the incarnate Word; Augustine, less systematic, leaves us to work out how the single speaking subject who is the eternal Word can 'personate' human nature, give it voice, enact its conditions and reshape them, without in any way whatsoever ceasing to be what it eternally and 'necessarily' is, the pure agency of God subsisting as Son. But, like Aquinas, Augustine also turns for elucidation to Paul's language about Christ existing in and as the Body that is the community of believers. Augustine is the first to use the expression *totus Christus*, 'the complete Christ', to denote the complex unity that is not only the Word and Jesus but Jesus and the members of his Body, understood as making up together a single *persona*, a single acting and speaking subject. It is a theme developed far more intensely by Augustine than by his Eastern contemporaries, and its significance in shaping the idea of a single but composite subsistent life for the Word incarnate has not always been given its due credit. Tarsicius van Bavel, in a lucid digest of Augustine's teaching on this topic,[54] cites Sermon 341 as a focal text: here Augustine says that 'Christ' has three meanings, referring to the eternal and pre-existent Word, to the incarnate figure of the redeemer and mediator, and to the 'whole Christ', head and body. It is echoed in Sermon 133.8, where the same language of 'the whole Christ, head and Body' (*totus Christus, caput et corpus*) is used; and given a slightly different twist in the Discourses on John (*tr. Ioh.* 21.8.), where Augustine speaks of 'the whole human individual, he and we' (*totus homo, ille et nos*). The human collectivity that is the Church is one *homo* with Jesus and so fully one with the Word, who – as the same treatise on John has already spelled out (21.7) – may be said to 'learn' and grow in his human members. Jesus is the *persona* who utters the words that Christians speak – a theme that pervades Augustine's discourses on the Psalms – so that human words, even words of pain or doubt or rebellion, are adopted as his in order that they can be transformed; and in an analogous way the Word is the *persona* of Jesus, taking on, becoming 'answerable' for, the human words, acts

---

54 Tarsicius van Bavel, OSA, 'The Concept of the "Whole Christ"', in Tarsicius van Bavel and Bernard Bruning, eds, *Saint Augustine*, Brussels and Heverlee: Mercatorfonds/ Augustinian Historical Institute, 2007, pp. 263–71.

and sufferings of Jesus. As Augustine insists in, for example, his *enarratio* on Psalm 142, Christ cannot be separated from the Body he has chosen; we cannot, so to speak, *add* the Body to Christ, any more than we can add Jesus to the Word. Such language would be a serious category mistake. For Augustine, the assumption of humanity by the Word provides us with a way in to thinking about the unity of believers with Christ in terms of unity *in act*, such that we are spared the intractable problems of negotiating the relative 'space' to be occupied by different partners in a relationship of finite substances.

To pursue Christological reflection along these lines is to develop the implications of precisely the linguistic oddities of Christian Scripture with which we began this chapter. Jesus Christ is spoken of and identified in terms not only of historical actions performed by a recognizable human individual but also of a continuing activity in the community that is established in the wake of the Paschal events. His continuing activity within the community – as Aquinas will further clarify – is a function of the fact that this activity is ultimately not merely that of an individual in human history. Who he 'ultimately' is is something specified by his relation to the Father, the relation which is eternally exemplified by the Word. Because his identity is thus anchored beyond the human world, it is in essence radically unlike all familiar forms of finite identity – even when it does indeed meet the requirements of ordinary human identifiability (we know roughly what would count as criteria for identifying Jesus of Nazareth as an historical character, what would distinguish him from Peter, Judas and Mary). The identity of the Word includes this routine historical identity but is not confined by it; thus the ever-widening net of relations in which Jesus is the decisive factor in determining the relation of other individuals to God the Father is taken into the identity of the Word – in the sense that the answer to the questions, 'Who is now causing and defining the relation of these lives with the Father? Who is acting and speaking in those relations so as to give them their distinctive character?' is 'Jesus Christ'.

John Webster, in an all-too-brief article on 'Prolegomena to Christology', sums this up with typical economy and eloquence: '[Christ's] identity', he writes, 'is not located in a temporally remote sphere, nor is it "finished" in the sense that it can be docketed as a closed, achieved reality which does not initiate active encounter with us ... [T]he trajectory of Jesus Christ's identity stretches inexorably into the present, his past being gathered into his present identity as one who cannot truthfully be spoken of only in the past tense.'[55] In another essay, he takes issue with the Lutheran theologian Robert Jensen for blurring the distinction between Christ and his Body (not least with the startling claim that 'the church is the risen Christ's Ego', which is certainly not what any reader of Augustine or Aquinas would conclude),[56] and makes the helpful stipulation[57] that 'the notion of *totus Christus* ... will be impermissible if it elides the distinction between Christ and the objects of his mercy'. Yet, granting the force and rightness of these caveats, the unity of Head and Body has about it enough that is analogic-ally parallel to the unity of Word and humanity (as a unity of complete asymmetrical dependence) to allow us to say that, just as the recogniz-ability of the Word in history is bound to the humanity of Jesus, so the recognizability of Jesus in the world is bound to the visible community *insofar as it is constituted by turning and returning to the foundational and sustaining act of Christ.* And to allow this is – crucially – to introduce into the Church a principle of radical relativization of any claims it may make for itself and of radical Christ-centred judgement on its current life. Later in this book,[58] we shall be looking at the way in which Dietrich Bonhoeffer argues, in effect, that the identity of Jesus is so wholly bound up with his act of taking responsibility for the welfare of the other and the reconcili-ation of the other with God that we cannot think his identity without this defining 'for the other' character; and so if the Christian life is a matter of letting Christ be formed in the community that bears his name, the Church too must be distinctive in its character as existing for the other, for the world's reconciliation with God. The Word which engages with the world in the incarnate form of Jesus continues to seek embodiment in the community (one of Bonhoeffer's most regular emphases, from his ear-liest work as a theologian), and the eternal character of the Word itself in

---

55 John Webster, 'Prolegomena to Christology: Four Theses', *Confessing God: Essays in Christian Dogmatics II*, London: T&T Clark, 2005, pp. 131–49, quotation from p. 131.

56 Ibid., pp. 163–4; for further discussion of Robert Jensen, see below, pp. 158–160.

57 Ibid., p. 174.

58 Below, Chapter 2.2.

relation to the Father thus imprints itself on humanity and speaks and acts for God's promise in the world.

Relating this back to Augustine's discussion, we can see the parallel between Bonhoeffer's stress on how God in Christ takes responsibility for and represents the human condition and Augustine's understanding of *unitas personae*, the one voice that gives voice to the human community in its collective need. For both thinkers, there is an analogy between the way in which the Word unites with Jesus in a union without confusion or separation (to borrow the language of Chalcedon) and the way in which Jesus unites with the believing community. The Word is identified in principle quite independently of Jesus in the sense that nothing in human history makes the Word to be anything that the Word is not eternally. Likewise, Jesus is identified historically quite independently of the history of his followers in the sense that his followers depend wholly on his incarnate life for their life as his Body, as inhabitants of the new creation. Yet a complete account of the Word and a consideration of how in fact the Word is made known in the world would need to refer to Jesus of Nazareth; and a complete account of Jesus of Nazareth would need to refer to his Body. If Paul and Augustine are right, it is as true to say of Jesus that he is never without the Church as it is to say of the Word that it is never without Jesus. And for both Bonhoeffer and Augustine, this emphatically does not mean that there is anything but a wholly one-sided relation between Word and Jesus and Jesus and Church. The Church may be 'Christ existing as community', in Bonhoeffer's phrase,[59] but this cannot mean that the existence of the community simply *is* the presence of Christ. The community is what it is in virtue of the inexhaustible act of God summoning, judging and sustaining it – just as the life of Jesus is not simply 'the same thing as' the life of the Word, since it is what it is because of the inexhaustible action that pervades and structures it.

---

59 Developed in his 1927 doctoral dissertation, *Sanctorum Communio: A Theological Study of the Sociology of the Church*, Volume 1 of the collected English edition of his works, ed. Clifford J. Green, trans. Reinhard Krauss and Nancy Lukens, Minneapolis: Fortress Press, 2009. Bonhoeffer is self-consciously picking up and reshaping Hegel's language about 'God existing as community'.

Thus a theology of the Body of Christ should help us see something of what it is to think – as Thomas does more abstractly and generally – what it is to associate the divine Word with a set of contingent attributes and historical propositions. We do so with good reason and on firm theological grounds: no one, no ultimate source of communicative action, other than the divine Word is at work in Jesus and the Church in its reality as Christ's Body, and so it is right to say that the Word was born and was crucified; but this does not mean that the ordinary mechanics of human action are suspended or interrupted, as if the fact that the Word was born means that a human individual was *not* or that the Word was bound to put aside the human particularity of Jesus in order to perform divine acts. And so in the Church, to say that the identity of the Church is the identity of Jesus Christ, or that Christ exists as Christian community, does not mean that no individual Christian acts out of their own finite resource and reflection, or that the Church is a place where directly divine 'Christ-shaped' action alternates with merely human processes. Where the Church is itself, finite action is conformed to and woven into the eternal initiative of the Word through union with Jesus Christ in the Spirit; but since the Church is not united with Jesus Christ in precisely the same sense as Jesus is united with the Word, the transparency of finite action to divine in the body of believers is irregular and episodic – apart from those actions where the Church does *nothing but* declare its identity in Christ (in the sacraments and in obedient attention to Scripture). Yet we can say of the Church as we say about Jesus Christ that what it exists to embody and communicate, what in other words it *means*, is simply the Word. Augustine's emphasis on the *persona* as focus of unity opens up a train of thought about unity in active communication – in the conformity of the vehicle to the content of what is being shared by God. In the context of anxieties about how divine and human relate and coincide in Jesus, this is significantly useful in helping to clear away any residue of the covertly materialist assumptions that set the two side by side in the same ontological framework.

In any attempt to understand how Western theology handles the themes and legacy of Chalcedon, it is important to recognize that Augustine's thought, especially in relation to the *totus Christus* idea, provides a resource for addressing from a rather different perspective some of the themes that become central to the Byzantine writers we shall be looking at in the next chapter. Aquinas on Head and Body reflects this supplementary Augustinian legacy. Augustine's theology of the one *persona* and the whole Christ, Head and Body, offers a more obviously exegetical way in to what both the Byzantines and Aquinas are trying to say about the tangled question of the double or even triple identity of the Word – as eternal, as incarnate and as the unifying principle of the believing community. If we are wedded to an idea of Jesus Christ as simply an historical individual, even an historical individual in whom the divine Word was uniquely present, we miss an essential element in the Christological project.

What this chapter has sought to show is that there is indeed a continuity between the first attempts by St Paul to think through the mystery of Christ's person and the distinctive emphases of the medieval synthesis of Aquinas, and that Augustine's exegetical approach is a significant line of connection between them. Paul, as we began by noting, uses of Jesus Christ a range of language that is unmistakeably eccentric as an account of any 'individual' (even an individual descending from Heaven) especially in his repeated affirmations – never fully explained or glossed – that 'Christ' is a reality in whom or in which others live. For this to be stated intelligibly, the relatively simple proposition that Jesus of Nazareth is the uniquely uninterrupted vehicle of the Word's action needs to be both clarified and elaborated. First, we need to be clear that the Word's union with the humanity of Jesus, the union in virtue of which the whole of Jesus' specific historical identity becomes the vehicle of God's action, transforms that historical identity, so that it is not only generative of a new community but is abidingly active within that community – working through the community's members to realize the divine will, but also calling those members to repentance and transformation, since their transparency to the divine will is imperfect. Following on from this, we need an account of the identity of the Word that will allow us to see the Word as not a superior kind of 'heavenly individual' (ruling this out was the effect of the condemnation of Arius in the fourth century) but – well, what? Augustine famously offers the phrase 'subsistent relation',[60] which underlies Aquinas's Trinitarian theology, but it is not a term that is instantly intelligible. In connection with Christology, however,

60 See Lewis Ayres, *Augustine and the Trinity*, Cambridge: Cambridge University Press, 2010, pp. 268–72.

we can begin to see how its meaning can be filled out. The humanly specific life of Jesus is given its definitive shape by its union with divine action; but what it is united with is that divine action which is derived from and responsive to the fundamental self-giving or self-bestowing of the divine source. It is, as we have noted already, divine act as *filial*. As such, it defies categorization as some sort of individual in any sense that would apply to finite reality; yet we may call it 'personal' in the sense that it is a unique form of agency eternally realizing the love and intelligence that is God. And also as such it is something *communicable* to finite reality, something that is capable of living in and through a finite medium. In its definitive presence in the humanity of Jesus, it realizes a unique form of union, a full and uninterrupted alignment of life and effect. Because of that effect within the finite world, made possible by the character of the eternal Word, the relation to Jesus of those who believe in him and affiliate with his community is more than the relation of an individual to other individuals. And so we arrive at the problem to which Aquinas's model of *esse* seeks to provide a solution: the Word is one in *esse*, whether in eternity, in Galilee or in the Eucharist at the parish church and in the believer's prayer and service, precisely because the Word is *unconditioned divine agency in its filial exercise* – not a subject among other subjects. It is the ground of unlimited saving relation among finite beings (ultimately both human and non-human). But in affirming this, there is no suggestion that the humanity of Jesus becomes merely instrumental or abstract, some sort of temporary vehicle to bring about the effect that is the ecclesial community. Jesus remains inseparably the recognizable voice and active presence of the Word in human history; Christian devotion never reaches the point at which reference to this human focus becomes dispensable. There are serious debates to be had as to how far we can go in seeing the action of the Word as being real in the world and in human lives independently of a *conscious* acknowledgement of the Word incarnate (we shall be discussing later how these debates develop in the Reformation period and after), but such debates cannot obscure the fact that *talking* about the Word's filial existence *vis-à-vis* the Father (the *pros ton theon*, 'in relation to the Father', of John 1.1) will always entail reference to the enacting of this filial identity in Jesus.

This point bears indirectly on another topic that needs to be mentioned briefly before moving on, and that is the relation between what has been said about the role of the Word and the theology of the Holy Spirit. Christian Scripture – especially, once again, Paul and John – frequently suggests a model in which the Spirit is the agent that *connects* the agency and prayer of the believer with the agency of the Word, primarily of course the agency of Word uniquely embodied in Jesus. Indeed, it could be said that the definition of the Spirit's distinctive role in much of the New Testament is that it is the divine action which consolidates the community's identity as inhabited and formed by Jesus Christ – initially by being 'poured out' in baptism (1 Cor. 12.13; cf. John 7.37–39), then by shaping the virtues of the community and the interweaving of distinct gifts and vocations in the community (Rom. 12.3–7, 1 Cor. 12), and by sharpening discernment among believers through the gift of 'truthful' life, life within the reality of the Word's relation with the Father (John 15.26–16.15). Perhaps its most significant expression is in enabling the believer to pray to the Father as Jesus did (Rom. 8.14–17, Gal. 4.6). Setting this in the context of the understanding of Christ outlined in New Testament and early Christian reflection, as we have surveyed it in this chapter, we could say that the importance of this dimension is to underline the recognition that the relation which comes into existence between Christ and the believer is neither something 'automatic', as if Christ's active identity simply spread outwards from its historical centre, nor something created by human choice, by the believer simply deciding to be affiliated with Jesus. This relation is as much the product of divine agency as the agency that shapes the human life of the incarnate Word and constitutes this human life as the form for the lives of believers, but is not reducible to the identity of the Word because it acts to bring human beings – and indeed the whole world they inhabit – into *relation* with the Word. By creating this connection with the Word, it makes possible in all the innumerable histories of human subjects that diverse participation in and reflection of the eternal life of divine filiation. And by moving within the entire created process to bring the Word to birth (the 'overshadowing' of the Spirit spoken of in the account of the annunciation to Mary, understood in the light of the whole history of the Spirit's connection-making in creation), the Spirit both prepares for the Word's incarnation and connects the incarnate Word with the human order and the created order more generally in the 'new creation'.

The significance of this in the context of the overall argument is that the connection between the agency of the believer and that of the divine

Word can in no sense be an example of the connections that can be made *between finite agencies by finite causes*. The processes of the world work by the unfolding of connections – straightforward causal chains, the emergent properties of complex substances, the elusive and surprising connections between intelligent agents that we call culture and language, and so on. What unites believers to the act and being of the Word is not a matter of one substance acting on another, nor the production of a new kind of composite agency in the world – nor *simply* a new set of linguistic habits (however telling these may be in understanding the scope of what is being affirmed, as in the case of the language of Paul or John). Christ as incarnate Word does not 'exercise an influence' on finite agents like that of ordinary finite causal agencies, nor does he introduce extra causal factors into the finite world or simply initiate a tradition of teaching and speculation; as we noted at the beginning of the first chapter, the effect of Jesus' life is both historical, in the sense that there comes to be a community with certain distinguishing marks, and theological, initiating a new set of human possibilities, a new creation (2 Cor. 5.17). The theological claim is that in the movement – the 'culture' if you will – that has its traceable historical roots in Jesus of Nazareth a connection is made between human subjects and the divine Word that is not just a matter of historical continuity or mental sympathy or affinity; and if so, it makes sense to say that this too is divine agency, suffusing and not displacing finite connectedness, but an agency that is not that of the Word, nor that of the Word's eternal Source. In this way, the Christological insistence on the non-rivalry of finite and infinite lays the foundation for the theological recognition of a further term of divine agency; Trinitarian reflection is born from Christology, as is regularly recognized, but it turns out to be another fruit of the same fundamental grammar of finite and infinite when we pursue the implications of the claim that believers are united with the Word incarnate by means other than subjective assent and social bonds. In the terminology associated with Augustine's theology of the Spirit, we recognize that the love uniting Christians is the bond of love uniting Father and Son; the gift (*donum*) bestowed on believers is the gift exchanged between Father and Son.[61]

---

61 Augustine, *de trinitate* V.xv/16–xvi/17, XV.xviii/32–xix/37.

The theological exploration of Jesus' identity, the recognition of the reality described as Christ's Body and the ascription to the Holy Spirit of the links between these two are themes that are already developed in the pages of Christian Scripture. But tracing the evolution of Christological language in the early Church up to and including Augustine has shown us that, as each of these sets of insights makes an increasingly insistent impact on both the others, the theological agenda inevitably moves towards that clarifying of the grammar of God as Creator which we have seen as central to developed Christological reflection. The discussion of this, directly and indirectly, in the Byzantine period provides the bridge which links the first centuries with the medieval synthesis; but to understand the issues that arise in this period – roughly from the late fifth to the eighth century – we must first return briefly to the Council of Chalcedon's attempt to define a vocabulary for any adequately recognizable discussion of Christ's identity.

1.2

Refining the Vocabulary: The Contribution of Early Byzantine Theology

1. Chalcedon and its Aftermath

After the great doctrinal crises of the fourth century there was, as we have seen, less and less room for any compromise about what has necessarily to be ascribed to God in terms of changelessness or freedom from suffering; and the last chapter has suggested that this is a good deal more than a sort of anxiety to preserve metaphysical proprieties. The classical negatives about divine nature, the insistence on what cannot in any circumstances be predicated of God, are meant to clarify the impossibility of representing God and God's action as any kind of circumscribed presence within the world, and thus the impossibility of representing the divine in Jesus as a complementary or additional item in the composition of his identity. The formula emerging from the Council of Chalcedon,[1] insisting on the

---

1 Text in Jaroslav Pelikan and Valerie Hotchkiss, eds, *Creeds and Confessions of Faith in the Christian Tradition*, Vol. 1: *Early, Eastern and Mediaeval*, New Haven and London: Yale University Press, 2003, pp. 174–81, especially p. 181.

completeness or 'perfection' of both natures in Christ ('One and the same, complete as regards divinity and complete as regards humanity'), achieves a balance of sorts with its repeated use of 'one and the same' (*heis kai ho autos*), as if to underline that the two 'natures' or *ousiai*, 'essences', cannot be added to one another. There is one subject of whom the totality of unequivocal divine attributes may be predicated and who also unequivocally fulfils all the conditions for being a member of the human race. But in phrasing the definition so as to safeguard the integrity of each nature, the language of some sort of duality of agency was inevitably used – though not quite as bluntly as it had been in the Synodical Letter of Pope Leo (the 'Tome of Leo') written a couple of years before Chalcedon in response to the earlier stages of the controversy that led directly to the Council. Leo had spoken[2] of a duality of *forma*, and, in a famously controversial passage, described how each *forma* in Christ 'acts' (*agit*) according to its own nature, divinity producing miracles, humanity undergoing suffering. For most of those present at Chalcedon, such language was uncomfortably close to the formulations preferred by the Syrian theologians of the generation before, and the Council's agreed formula gave no hostages to fortune on this. But its clear affirmation of two essences, unmixed and unchanging, in Christ still proved too close for comfort to Syrian dualism in the eyes of a substantial party in the Eastern Church. And there are contemporary scholars who consider that the formula is indeed a capitulation to the anxieties of 'Antiochene' theology about preserving the metaphysical attributes of God. In the words of Christopher Beeley, in a notable and controversial study of patristic Christology, *The Unity of Christ*, 'the council does not define Christ primarily as the divine Son of God, who in the divine economy assumed human existence (or nature) for our salvation'.[3] The formula seems to begin from the one *incarnate* Christ whose hypostasis is operative in two self-contained and independent natural modes – 'acknowledged *in* two natures', as the text has it.

There is indeed – as has already been indicated in the preceding chapter – a problem in Chalcedon's language to the extent that it implies that there is a single hypostasis which relates *in the same way* to two sets

2   Ibid., p. 117.
3   Christopher A. Beeley, *The Unity of Christ: Continuity and Conflict in Patristic Tradition*, New Haven and London: Yale University Press, 2012, p. 282.

of attributes – which is the implication of saying, as the formula does, that Christ is of one essence (*homoousios*) with the Father as regards his divinity and of one essence with us as regards his humanity. The difficulty is that, taken at face value, this would mean either that the hypostasis somehow pre-exists both 'natures' or at least is independent of them in some sense, or that two abstract sets of attributes somehow come together to be unified in one agent. On either account, we are left with (to put it mildly) some logically uncomfortable elements – an abstract individuality that has no essential definition or an abstractly definable nature with no instantiation. Beeley is right to note that Pope Leo's language about nature or *forma* as itself 'acting' in some sense is unhelpful; and the model of the one hypostasis exercising two sorts of natural agency takes us straight back to the difficulties of treating divine and human nature as comparable, coexistent clusters of predicates attaching to an individual. The first major caution that must be entered about Chalcedon's language is the reminder that if we are serious about the difference between God and creation, we must think of the divine subsistents not as separate instances of a generic divine nature,[4] but as fully and interdependently realizing a divine life which cannot be thought of apart from its interrelated eternal action as Trinity. The divine hypostasis of the Word is not one of three examples of divinity – a point already emerging in the more sophisticated treatments of Trinitarian theology in the fourth century; it is part of what it intrinsically is *to be God* that the divine life is lived in the eternal mode (an unsatisfactory word) of filiation, as in the eternal mode of active origination or of 'proceeding'. A full Christian account of what it is to be God would include the familiar quasi-grammatical aspects of unchangeability or freedom from suffering – but would have to include also the stipulation that these are activated and 'enjoyed' only in the interweaving of divine relationship. Or, to put it as succinctly as we can, there is no divine nature independent of its actualization in Father, Son and Spirit; so that it cannot be right to think of the three divine hypostases as 'countable' examples of a kind of life that we could

4   As several interpreters have observed, the fact that Basil the Great and Gregory of Nyssa tend to assimilate the threefold being of God to three instances of a shared *ousia* in some of their work (as in Gregory's *ad Ablabium*, for example) did not help terminological or conceptual clarity in the period.

independently identify as divine. Thus, as Beeley says, there is a difference between (i) talking about an eternal hypostasis, which is the divine nature in one unique activation of its eternal life, entering into the state of being the organizing or unifying reality of a human individuality, and (ii) talking about a single saviour in whom two kinds of abstractly identifiable life are equally operative.

Like most or many formulae of settlement, Chalcedon defines an agenda rather than a solution to the problems that have generated it. We should not exaggerate the 'dualism' of Chalcedon; the repeated insistence on 'one and the same' subject is important; there is a clear acknowledgement that the Word is eternally begotten and that it is this Word that is then humanly born of Mary; and there is a very deliberate echoing of Cyrilline language at key points. Even the novel phrase, 'acknowledged in two natures', can be squared with a Cyrilline recognition that the Incarnation does not make divinity and humanity conceptually indistinguishable from each other in the incarnate identity. But the agenda for the theology of the centuries immediately following Chalcedon was unmistakeably the clarification of the vocabulary and assumptions of the definition, so as to underline the asymmetry of the relation between the single hypostasis and the divinity and the single hypostasis and the humanity, and to avoid anything which might suggest that either hypostasis or essence could exist in a purely abstract way. The often useful flexibility of the term 'hypostasis' itself had to be disciplined somewhat – though, rather paradoxically, the effect of this process of clarification was to establish that the word could be and regularly was used in distinct, even superficially contradictory ways. In fact we are already well on the way in these discussion to the recognition by medievals like Aquinas that the single *esse* of the incarnate Word could intelligibly be discussed from two significantly different points of view; and the working through of the asymmetry between Christ's sharing of the divine essence and his sharing of human nature brought more clearly to light some of the ways in which the classical Christological model both reflected and illuminated fundamental convictions about the asymmetrical relation of creative and created act.[5]

---

5   See above, pp. 33, 35–37. And on the continuities between Byzantine and medieval Western discussions see Antoine Lévy, *Le Créé et l'incréé. Maxime le Confesseur et*

To summarize, there was a recognition that, if we start by trying to see the question from the point of view of clarifying the grammar of divinity, it is right to say that the sole hypostasis in the identity of Jesus of Nazareth is the eternal Word. No other ultimate principle of identity and coherence can be imagined, no other source of active presence and power. And for this to be true, the Word must be what it is quite independently of any external condition, any state of affairs within the world: what we are talking about is the second hypostatic reality actively exercising or realizing the divine life, 'consubstantial' with the Father, distinct within the divine life simply in virtue of the relation of having-been-generated by the Father so as to reflect and return to the Father what has been bestowed on it in its eternal generation. No state of affairs in the world makes this true; it is a specification of how the Christian God is to be identified. At the same time: if we start by trying to state how the problem is posed for us within the world's history – the problem of what must be said in order to make proper sense of the historical phenomenon that is Jesus of Nazareth – we shall be starting with the actual unique phenomenon that is Jesus, identified by a number of finite predicates: there are states of affairs in the world that make things true of this subject that is Jesus. And so the theologian has to say that when we talk about the one hypostasis of the incarnate Word, we may mean either the eternal and simple reality which is the eternal Word or the 'composite' reality which is 'Jesus of Nazareth as animated and actualized by the Word'. This is precisely the point that is ultimately addressed by St Thomas's discussion of whether we should speak of one or two *esses* in Jesus, the discussion examined in the first chapter of this book. It is a point that has to be clarified, in the light of the ambiguity of Chalcedon's language, where the 'one hypostasis' is evidently – and confusingly – both the unchanging eternal Word and the specific single phenomenon of Jesus as Word incarnate, 'in' or 'into' whom the natures converge to be realized. We have to find a way of saying that the animated, 'Word-embodying' human substance that is Jesus is a composite reality in which created agency is real and distinct, while *not*

Thomas d'Aquin, Paris: Vrin, 2006. This brilliant and formidable monograph is one of the most fruitful recent studies of the analogy between the union of human nature and the eternal Word and the relation between Creator and creature in general; for some lapidary formulations on this subject, see, for example, p. 368.

claiming that this human substance contributes anything to what the Word eternally is by definition. Such a claim would undermine the entire structure of the fundamental distinction, the non-dual separation, of infinite and finite on which Christological doctrine rests.

Christopher Beeley in the book mentioned earlier generally assumes that theologians who use strongly 'dualist' language about divinity and humanity in Christ are primarily anxious not to expose the divinity to suffering, and that this is a theologically dubious priority.[6] He says of Athanasius, for example, that he combines a purely triumphal divine activity in Christ with a purely passive humanity (with the emphasis heavily on the passible weakness of Jesus' material existence, since he has no discernible theology of a genuinely human mental or spiritual life in Jesus); 'It is also a scheme in which God lacks the desire and the ability to include human brokenness into the divine being without being threatened with decomposition himself.'[7] It is certainly true of Athanasius that his account of the duality in Christ of divinity and humanity gives little explicit place to what we would call a human subjectivity, so that the contrast is between the action of the Word and the sheer contingency and vulnerability of the 'flesh'; but that he effectively leaves no room for such a subjectivity, or is deliberately aligning himself with those who denied the presence of a created mind or spirit in Jesus, is less clear (and some of those who most admired him in the later fourth century certainly did not read him in this sense[8]). And it is debatable whether any early Christian writer would have seen the problem as one of God being threatened by 'including' human brokenness in divine life: the issue is not whether God risks disintegration but that – since it is agreed on all sides that the divine nature *cannot* suffer disintegration – we should simply not be talking about *God* if we were talking about

---

6   Beeley, op. cit., pp. 133–5, 206–7 and elsewhere.

7   Ibid., p. 196; cf. pp. 267–8.

8   As Beeley in effect grants: Gregory Nazianzen, for example, is someone Beeley sees as decidedly 'monistic' in his Christology, untroubled by issues around divine impassibility, in contrast to Gregory of Nyssa (op. cit., pp. 184–94), yet he is undoubtedly indebted to and respectful of Athanasius. Beeley's reading of Gregory, I think, underrates his fidelity to the general consensus about divine impassibility, which he definitely maintains; like others, he is equally prepared to underline the possibility of saying 'God suffered' in a homiletic or polemical context.

something vulnerable to dissolution, 'corruption', as the language of the patristic period would put it. To say that God cannot be conceived as the subject of disintegrative experience is not to ascribe some sort of failure or deficiency to God, but to assert God's freedom from failure and deficiency of *any* kind. That God desires to rescue human beings from the 'corruption' they undergo in this world is the premise of all early Christian doctrines of salvation; but it is certainly *not* assumed that this ought to mean that the divine incorporates corruption into itself; the divine hypostasis of the Word takes on, or takes to itself, the reality of *human* fragility and dissolution in order to transform humanity from within. And, as Gregory Nazianzen stresses, this entails the taking on of all the consequences of sin and death in humanity's experience.[9] The transformation arises from the fact of divine initiative, and that initiative is possible simply because the divine is free from constraint and passivity. Athanasius may be vague and unsatisfactory about *what* exactly suffers when the Word incarnate suffers (whether the body only or the whole created psycho-physical ensemble); but his statement in the Letter to Epictetus that the Word both suffered and did not suffer[10] is simply a statement of what any theologian of that era, however anti-dualist, however committed to the notion of the significance of Christ's suffering, would have had to make. It is echoed closely in the vocabulary of Cyril of Alexandria.[11]

But in the light of the discussion in the last chapter, we can say a little more. A theology of Head and Body, of Christ as living in and as the faithful community, tells us that the Word is embodied and communicated not

9   The classic text is the Fourth Theological Oration (*Oratio* 30, PG 36; see especially sections 5 and 6, 109A–112B).

10   Athanasius, *ad Epictetum* 6, PG26 1060C (*paschōn kai mē paschōn*: the body suffers, while the divine Word remains *apathēs*).

11   Cyril is associated with the phrase *apathōs epathen*, 'he suffered in an impassible way', though there is no instance in the surviving Greek texts where he actually uses precisely this form of words. For various approximations, see for example his Second Letter to Nestorius 5 (pp. 6–7 of Wickham, *Cyril of Alexandria: Selected Letters*), the Third Letter to Nestorius 6 (Wickham, pp. 201/21) and the Second Letter to Succensus 4 (Wickham, pp. 90–1). On this, see Beeley, op. cit., pp. 268–9, and Brian E. Daley, 'Antioch and Alexandria: God's Presence in History', in Francesca Aran Murphy, ed., *The Oxford Handbook of Christology*, pp. 121–38, especially pp. 133–4.

only in the individual Jesus of Nazareth but, derivatively, in the utterances of disintegrating and fallible human subjects in the Church. It is not that we must 'make' the Word suffer in its divinity in order for the Word to be credible to suffering humans: the suffering that the Word takes to itself in the Incarnation is the absolutely specific human pain of Jesus and, consequently, the specific human pain of all those for whom the Word in Jesus speaks. It is not an unimaginable 'divine' suffering but yours and mine in their historic particularity. And it is not that the divine Son by some supreme act of empathetic identification 'feels' our pain as if it were his own, but rather that the divine agency inhabits completely the pain that is ours, and gives it voice precisely as *human* pain and as *our* pain. There is no imaginative gulf to be crossed between a human subject and a divine one; this would reinscribe yet again the idea that there are two subjects which need to be connected in the way that two finite agents or substances might need to be connected.

2. Terminological Developments: Leontius of Byzantium and Leontius of Jerusalem

These are the questions that are being worked through in Byzantine theology of the sixth and seventh centuries, especially in the work of the two major theologians both confusingly called Leontius – Leontius of Byzantium and the possibly rather later Leontius of Jerusalem.[12] Leontius of Byzantium, in debate with anti-Chalcedonians of the 'Alexandrian' variety, i.e. those often called 'monophysites', goes a long way towards an unambiguous affirmation that the humanity of Christ in the Incarnation is fully individuated – a nature with defining finite characteristics. As Richard Cross puts it, Leontius manages a 'principled affirmation both of the individuality of

---

12 For an argument in favour of a later date (in the early to mid-seventh century) for Leontius of Jerusalem, see D. Krausmüller, 'Leontius of Jerusalem, a Theologian of the Seventh Century', *Journal of Theological Studies* 52.2 (n.s.) (2001), pp. 637–57. Patrick T. R. Gray, who has edited some of the texts (*Leontius of Jerusalem: Against the Monophysites, Testimonies of the Saints and Aporiae*, Oxford: Oxford University Press, 2006), defends the traditional earlier date. This conclusion is still slightly more probable.

Christ's humanity and its non-subsistence',[13] on the basis of arguing that every 'nature', every kind of subsistence, has to be individuated by particular features, otherwise it is indistinguishable from other instantiations of that kind. Leontius assumes that we cannot imagine 'particular natures', in the sense of actualizations of some *kind* of being that are not individuated by anything other than natural characteristics. 'Individual' natures, in contrast, are particular substances in which nature is given local and actual subsistence by individuating features. If that is the case, the interesting question for the theologian is what actualizes or activates a nature as an identifiable subsistent; and Leontius is clear that a nature can be made actual by an agency that is not exclusively its own. A particular kind of life, a nature, may as a matter of fact be real in the way it is real in virtue of another agent causing it to be characterized by the features that mark it out.[14] Thus in the case of Christ incarnate, there is of course a set of particular things that are true of Jesus of Nazareth, in virtue of which we can pick him out as an individual member of the human race. But that these things are true of him, that he lives thus and not otherwise, is in virtue of his union with the eternal Word. Cross quotes from Brian Daley to the effect that the converse must hold in some sense – that what 'picks out' the eternal Word within the Trinitarian life is the relation with, or the capacity for relation with, the humanity[15] – but this must be true only in the sense that our account of the three divine Persons in the narrative of salvation, or more generally in relation with the created order, can legitimately treat the Word's union with humanity as distinguishing the Word from the Father and the Spirit; any more than that, any suggestion that the Word's incarnate life is an intrinsic differentiating feature for the Word *in eternity*, is debatable for the reasons already sketched in this and the last chapter, and not something that any Byzantine theologian could claim.

The salient point is that the argument about a nature being 'actualized' by another counters the argument that, if Christ's humanity is fully

13 Richard Cross, 'Individual Natures in the Christology of Leontius of Byzantium', *Journal of Early Christian Studies* 10.2, 2002, pp. 245–65, quotation from p. 258.
14 E.g., Leontius, *contra Nest. Eut.* PG 86, 1277D–1290B; and see Beeley, op. cit., pp. 287–8.
15 Cross, art. cit., p. 264.

individuated, we must think of it as a hypostasis and so be obliged to accept the 'Antiochene' argument for a full-blown duality between the incarnate Word and the human Jesus. This is a significant conceptual refinement. It allows us to leave behind once and for all the confusing language implying that a 'nature' is itself a *thing*, and so to clarify that whatever has to be said about the union of divine and human in Jesus cannot be understood as the putting together of two pre-existing subjects or subsistents. The human nature of Jesus is, of course, distinguishable from other instances of the human because it is 'hypostatized' in a certain distinct way, in virtue of these particular characteristics; and ultimately, its distinctiveness from other human subsistents depends on the fundamental fact of its unique relation to the Word. Christopher Beeley once again expresses misgivings about the way in which this can give house-room to an abstract model of *hupostasis* as a single 'referent' for sets of divine or human attributes;[16] on such a model, we end up with a seriously weakened Trinitarian theology, in which the divine Persons are individual instances of divine life, rather than deriving their distinctness from their relation with one another in the inseparable eternal reality that is active divine being. It will not do to reduce divine nature to the bare 'sameness' of the three Persons, a sort of common substrate. The point is an important one. But Beeley's criticism raises the same problems we have already seen in the context of discussing Aquinas on *esse*, and we need to look carefully at what is and is not being claimed by Leontius and his successors. It is not so much that Leontius is looking for one authoritative definition of what a hypostasis 'is' so much as he is drawing attention to what work is done by using such a word; and that work has to do with providing for us a vehicle for speaking of how a kind of life or action is particularized in the actual world – as opposed to the language we need in order to speak of what makes us identify distinct agents as sharing a single kind of life. If a nature is indeed not a sort of *thing*, it cannot be the case that any actual subsistent agent is a compound of 'nature' and individuating features; you cannot add one to the other. You can only say that, when speaking of this active subsistent, you will need both a register that has to do with actual events and relations, and a register that allows you to identify continuity between distinct agents.

16 Beeley, op. cit., p. 290.

Beeley argues[17] that Leontius in fact uses two definitions of 'hypostasis', both theologically problematic. On the first account, the word designates simply the individual thing, the specific agent or subsistent, as opposed to the form or genus it embodies; on the second, the word refers specifically to what is not 'nature' in an existing subject, i.e. to the distinguishing features alone, *exclusive* of the nature. But this is surely too forensic a reading. To say, as Leontius does,[18] following Cappadocian precedent, that *hupostasis* does not refer to the common nature, the *katholikon pragma*, is not to say that it *excludes* that nature, as if there could be some separable thing that was the natural substrate distinct from the additional specifics; and it is precisely this view that Leontius rules out by insisting that there are no such things as natures subsisting in themselves. Indeed, the section of Leontius's argument from which Beeley quotes also specifically says that, while 'nature is not hypostasis' (i.e. to specify a nature is not the same thing as specifying a *particular* referent), 'hypostasis is nature', i.e. has nature as its referent, in the sense that that *hupostasis* contains or includes both what is singular (that is the identifying particulars of a substance) and the *logos* of the substantial form (*eidos*), even though this latter is the primary referent of language about *physis*. That hypostasis is a word referring to something with individuating characteristics (*idiōmata*) rather than what is common (*koinon*), as Leontius says, *cannot* therefore mean that hypostasis designates individuating features independently of nature.[19]

We do not therefore need to look with too much suspicion at Leontius's scheme. Granted that he echoes the Chalcedonian awkwardness we have already noted (assimilating the relation of divine nature and divine hypostasis to that between human nature and divine hypostasis), granted too the ambiguities around the Cappadocian legacy of simply distinguishing nature and hypostasis as 'common' and 'particular', Leontius clears the way for affirming that the human nature of the incarnate Christ possesses integrity as, formally speaking, a finite subject constituted as an activated, hypostatized kind of life concretely identified by a set of finite markers. That this set of finite markers is ultimately dependent on the agency of

17 Ibid., pp. 288–91.
18 *contra Nest. Eut.* PG 86.1280A.
19 Ibid.

the infinite and eternal hypostasis of the Word does not formally contradict what is needed for a finite nature to be a distinguishable individual. Like so many patristic writers, Leontius compares this with the way in which soul and body unite.[20] Body and soul are actualized together; their natures are radically different, and each may be specified or identified in terms that are independent of the other. It is possible to specify just what we mean by 'soul' without necessarily referring to 'body', and vice versa. However, if we want to identify *this* soul or *this* body, we have to speak of them as united: these two kinds of thing are actual and visible only in mutual relation, so that we cannot in *fact* divorce one from the other if we are speaking about the world of event or actuality. And this is an admittedly limited but still defensible analogy to what we affirm about human nature in relation to the eternal Word. That we can spell out what human nature is independently of the Word is taken for granted; and we can also, obviously, say that we can spell out what it would take for human nature to be individuated as an agent in the world without reference to the Word or indeed to any particular narrative (we should be specifying the sort of conditions that would constitute actual human identity – embodiedness, temporality and so on). The crucial point is that we could not ultimately spell out what was fundamentally distinct about *this* humanity, the humanity of Jesus of Nazareth, in the world without reference to its unity with the Word. The analogy is indeed awkward, as Leontius seems to acknowledge, but he is trying to establish that the possibility of independently specifying the conditions for individuation or identification as between finite agents is not the same as assuming that every such independently specified agent is *ontologically* an independent substance. We know what counts as a soul or a body, we know what would identify a soul or a body as such, and what would identify a soul or body as this or that particular soul or body; but in fact there are no *actual* souls or bodies 'as such', only the (hypostatic) unity of the two in actual persons. And the individuating features that constitute a soul as this or that soul are bound up with its union with a particular body. So it is not the case that an active instance of human nature has to be considered an independent finite hypostasis simply in virtue of its finite individuality. Nor is it the

20 *contra Nest. Eut.* PG 86.1280D–1285B.

case that an individual of another, uncreated, nature somehow supplants a created principle of individuality in this instance of humanity. The unique hypostatic (that is 'actually subsisting') reality that is God the Word, in full communion with Father and Spirit, fully identical with the entirety of divine life as far as its qualities go, actively constitutes this human substance as an active and identifiable presence in the world.

Without this constitutive agency, the human substance would lack the actual subsistence it has; it would, to use the term favoured by Leontius of Jerusalem, be 'anhypostatic' – which really just means 'unreal'. This second Leontius, probably (if not certainly) active in much the same period, and for a long time confused with his namesake of Byzantium,[21] takes the argument and the vocabulary of what we have so far discussed a couple of small but important steps further. To be a hypostasis is to be one indivisible agent, one *atomos*, normally as a fusion in *sustasis* or coexistence of a number of identifying features (*idiōmata*) or natural modes of existence; a hypostasis realizes several general potentialities, substantial and accidental, by uniting them in a specific act of being, to use a later formulation.[22] So if Jesus is 'a particular human being' (*tis anthrōpos*),[23] why is he not a hypostasis? This is presented as an argument advanced by Nestorian opponents of Chalcedon, and Leontius grants that the humanity of Jesus must be understood as a human *ousia* with individuating features. But the crucial point is what is expressed by Leontius in his use of verbal forms like *sunupostanai* and *enupostanai* to describe what is happening in the relation of divinity and humanity in Christ: the individuated human substance is taken into, 'inserted in', the eternal life of the Word,[24] so that it is actually or concretely subsistent only in and with the Word. It cannot thus be a hypostasis in its own right: it is not *idioupostatos*, but that does not mean that it is *anupostatos*, unreal, not a subsisting thing, only that it would be such if it were not united to the Word's hypostasis.[25] To be independently 'hypostatic', says Leontius, is to be 'diastatic' and 'apostatic' – that is, to be distinct and 'distantiated' from

---

21 See above, p. 92.
22 *adv. Nest.* 1, PG 86.1529C.
23 Ibid., 2.43, PG 86.1597B.
24 Ibid., 5.28, PG 86.1748D.
25 Ibid., 2.10, PG 86.1556A.

other agents.[26] But if the humanity of Jesus is inseparably held in a relation to the eternal Word, a relation of unbroken dependence, it cannot be distant, independent of relation. The unifying reality is the unbroken and unchanged unity of the Word, which unites with a set of diverse potentialities for finite human life that thus become inseparable from the Word's act in the world.

Leontius of Byzantium's scheme had concentrated chiefly on one aspect of this picture, the way in which the union of divinity and humanity 'produces' the united actuality that is the incarnate Christ, in whom divinity and humanity are both actualized. Leontius of Jerusalem has rather more to say about the balancing recognition that there is a single eternal hypostasis as the fixed basis of all this, whose activating work is the primary reality. It is the point about the *asymmetry* of the Christological mystery which we have noted earlier. The one hypostasis is not simply what is produced by the union but what makes the union possible. We have already noted the importance of understanding that using the term 'hypostasis' to designate 'what there is one of' in the incarnate Christ does indeed have a measure of ambiguity: it can be used both of the Word of God as such and of the complex finite phenomenon in its entirety that is Jesus of Nazareth, the saviour of the world. But at the same time the whole of this discussion also points to the basic importance of grasping that the unity is grounded in the first sense of the term, as designating the one divine Word. *Only because* there is a single divine hypostasis involved as the ground and condition of what makes this human nature what it actually is, is there a single, genuinely finite, phenomenon in the world that is the incarnate Son. The affirmation of an integral finite identity for the actualized human nature of Jesus is not a piece of residual Nestorianism. The human nature is *hypostatized* but not in itself a hypostasis (*idioupostatos* in Leontius's vocabulary). The act of the Word in making its own this complete finite phenomenon secures rather than compromises both the integral finite reality of an individuated human nature, and the unequivocally divine reality of that agency which gives it finite reality. Once again, we are brought back to the fundamental insight developing in and through

26 See the very good and clear discussion of this theme in Demetrios Bathrellos, *The Byzantine Christ: Person, Nature and Will in the Christology of Saint Maximus the Confessor*, Oxford: Oxford University Press, 2004, p. 45.

these Christological refinements – that it is by affirming the unchanging divinity of the Word without qualification that we are able to understand the integrity and freedom of the finite, and so to understand that this is the key to the entire relation between Creator and creature. And in this framework it is still true to say that 'one of the Trinity suffered in the flesh', a formula that Leontius of Jerusalem endorses wholeheartedly:[27] there is no break in action between the Word and the subject that is Jesus, and so we can say that no other subject than the Word is referred to in any account of what Jesus suffers. At the same time, it would be wrong to say that the Word suffers 'in his divine nature'; not – as I have been trying to argue – simply because of squeamishness about the appropriateness of speaking of God suffering but because something would then be admitted into the definition of what it means to be God that would be dependent on how things stood in the world, and this would be a fundamental confusion of categories. Equally, the idea that Jesus instantiates a composite *nature*, a kind of life that is both divine and human, is a category error,[28] implying that the two 'contributing' natures are mutually dependent in constituting a third; that what it is to be divine and what it is to be human condition one another as elements in a single logical landscape. And this would mean that the divine nature was under a sort of necessity of combining with the human in order to produce the composite, that the divine would not be the divine unless it were interdependent with the human. This would yet again entail that something was true about the definition of God that depended on finite facts, and would take us back to earlier confusions implying that a nature was itself an agent. The work of the two Leontii, both complex and tantalizing, at least offers a clear way out of that kind of confusion.

3. Maximus the Confessor: Christology and the Reconciled Cosmos

All of this argument forms the background to the work of the most important theologian of the seventh century, possibly the most important of all Byzantine theologians, Maximus the Confessor. It is Maximus who gives

---

27 The seventh book of the *adv. Nest.* (PG 86, 1757C–1768B) is devoted to a defence of this formula.

28 Bathrellos, op. cit., p. 100.

something like a definitive shape to the general theological approach of the Leontii, and puts their clarifications to positive use within a wide-ranging spiritual and metaphysical scheme.[29] Like the Leontii, especially Leontius of Byzantium, he takes for granted the Cappadocian convention of distinguishing *hupostasis* and *ousia* as referring respectively to the particular and the general; and his letters 13 and 15 and the *opuscula theologica et polemica* show him following through the Leontian argument about how nature has to be hypostatized, though not necessarily in a hypostasis exclusive to it.[30] But he brings to the discussion a number of significant new elements. Perhaps the most significant is to do with his vocabulary for what is single and what is dual in Christ; and here he offers an alternative terminology to the familiar language of *physis* or *ousia* and *hupostasis*. As we have seen, earlier writers like Leontius of Byzantium had spoken of nature in terms of the *logos* of *eidos*, the intelligible structure of a natural form. Maximus regularly uses the phrase *logos tēs phuseos*[31] to denote the characteristic pattern of action that makes a nature what it is. 'Nature' is not an agent, but it is what

29 The literature on Maximus's Christology is vast and growing steadily. In addition to the works directly quoted here, see François-Marie Léthel, *Théologie de l'agonie du Christ: La liberté humaine du Fils de Dieu et son importance sotériologique mises en lumière par Saint Maxime le Confesseur*, Paris: Beauchesne, 1979; Pierre Piret, *Le Christ et la Trinité selon Maxime le Confesseur*, Paris: Beauchesne, 1983 (and the summary of this work in Chapter 3 of Aidan Nichols, *Byzantine Gospel: Maximus the Confessor in Modern Scholarship*, Edinburgh: T&T Clark, 1993); Paul Blowers, *Maximus the Confessor and the Transfiguration of the World*, Oxford: Oxford University Press, 2016; and the essays by Atanasije Jevtic, Nikolaos Loudovikos and Sebastian Mateiescu in the special issue on Maximus of *Analogia: The Pemptousia Journal for Theological Studies* 2.1 (2017). Chapter 4 of Andrew Louth's superb introduction, *Maximus the Confessor*, London and New York: Routledge, 1996, is of great use, and this volume also includes translations of several important texts.

30 Letters 13 and 15 in PG91, 509B–533A, 544C–576D; see especially 525D on the definition of 'composite hypostasis' (and cf. 490C in Letter 12); for the use of Leontine vocabulary about hypostatization, see, for example, *opuscula* PG91 149C, 204AB, 205AC, 261A–264B.

31 See Lars Thunberg, *Man and the Cosmos: The Vision of St Maximus the Confessor*, Crestwood, NY: St Vladimir's Seminary Press, 1985, pp. 37–8; Lévy, *Le créé et l'incréé*, pp. 47–8, 143 n. 4, 311–17, and, on the previous history and evolution of the concept, Appendix 4, pp. 505–12.

gives to a particular agent the internal consistency in behaviour that allows us to identify the agent as this or that kind of being; it is, we could say, a set of basic constraints within which a subject of this particular kind works. But a substance, subject or agent is also identified in terms of its own particular and unrepeatable 'performance' within the world, the ensemble of things that come to be true of this and only this agent; for a rational substance, this includes, significantly, the succession of choices it makes, the acts it decides upon. This is what Maximus refers to as the *tropos* of a substance, literally the mode or way in which it is actual as an individual. As Antoine Lévy has well put it,[32] the distinction between *logos* and *tropos* is roughly that between the invariable and the variable in the life of a substance. It is a distinction that allows Maximus to explain, for example, why sin does not alter the definition of human nature, and so how nature itself can be raised to a new level of agency without its basic structure being changed. The *logos* of human nature remains the same through the drama of fall and redemption; what changes is the way in which it acts, and this can be altered by the relations in which the embodiments of that nature stand.

There is still a great deal of scholarly discussion about how the detail of this structure works, since Maximus never devotes a lengthy exposition to it. But its theological implications can be summarized in something like these terms.[33] In the Trinitarian life, the eternal Word is distinguished from the Father and the Spirit in virtue of, or as a result of (though this language is a bit problematic as it could be taken to suggest some sort of sequence in the divine life), the mode in which he derives from the Father and relates to the Father. The Word is *energeia ousiōdōs hupestōsa*,[34] 'a substantially existing activity'. The single *logos* of divine life is lived here as a life of dependence on the Father – lived as 'Son': the unique *tropos* of the Word is 'filiation', and the activity of living 'filially' is what makes the Word or Son exist as identifiably distinct within the Trinity. This is (to recall Antoine Lévy's phrasing) the identifying 'variable' in the divine life which allows us to speak of the distinct hypostasis that is the eternal Son. And it is this divine *tropos* which ultimately identifies the 'invariable' of human nature in the unique manner

32 Lévy, op. cit., pp. 311–12.
33 Ibid., p. 327.
34 Maximus, *ambigua* 26, PG91, 1268A.

that is the life of Jesus. The set of definitional constraints that make Jesus count as a human being is unchanged: the *logos* of humanity remains. But it is actuated and exercised in a mode that is perfectly continuous with the Word's way of being God. The enhypostatized humanity that is Jesus exhibits what Levy calls 'an identity of "comportment" between Christ in his divine nature and in his human nature, an identity characterized by filial relation to the heavenly Father'.[35] Christ's human nature receives the gift of 'subsisting/being hypostatized' in a divine way (*huphestanai theikōs*), so that it is not moved by anything unnatural to it:[36] the actuality of the eternal Word is his eternal and stable actualization of divine life in this particular relational mode. This 'act of subsisting' then realizes the *logos* of human nature in the relational mode, the finite and historical embodiment of unbroken filiation, that is Jesus.

There is an immediate terminological problem, though. If we are speaking of a single act of subsisting, this sounds like the affirmation of a single *energeia*. Every nature has its own characteristic mode of behaviour and there can be no *phusis* or *ousia* that does not have its distinctive way of acting: the very idea of a *logos* of nature implies an active presence in reality which can be identified as this rather than that sort of life according to its inner structure. Natures move towards particular ends and so their behaviour is given intelligible form according to the pattern of this movement.[37] As Lévy very helpfully explains,[38] the concept of *logos tēs phuseōs*, which in late Alexandrian Platonism denoted an ideal state from which actual finite existence had fallen away, was redefined by Maximus to mean a sort of inner regulatory principle shaping the activity of finite substance in the direction of its full and final actualization. Each finite reality contains in its ground or centre a pattern of movement that is making for a state of affairs in which the reality in question is most fully itself. 'Returning to the *logoi* does not define for the creature a movement towards an origin from which it has fallen away, but a movement towards a goal which it has not immediately

---

35   Lévy, op. cit., p. 330, n. 1.

36   *ambigua* 36, PG 91, 1289D; cf. the language of *ambigua* 4 (1044C) about the incarnate Word doing 'fleshly things divinely' (*sarkika theikōs*).

37   See, for example, *ambigua* 5, PG 91, 1045C–1060C, especially 1049 ff.

38   Lévy, op. cit., pp. 508–10.

arrived at.'[39] *Logos* has a clearly dynamic sense, defining the way in which an historical or temporal nature consistently grows into its optimal and complete identity, an identity in which its natural mode of existing is realized as fully as it can be in this or that particular subsistent reality within the world. The *energeia* belonging to a nature is, in short, the unifying form of its history.

But surely this means that a single *energeia* must imply a single *phusis*? Maximus inherits from both Cyril of Alexandria and Pseudo-Dionysius (whom he regards, of course, as an author of more or less apostolic authority) language about a single 'theandric' *energeia* in Jesus, and feels obliged to defend this. But his defence[40] in fact provides a really important clarification of a recurrent problem in the tradition. We need to distinguish between activation as the moving principle of an event – the 'moving force' in a situation – and what results from this, the action that is the happening of the event. Thus in Christ we recognize a single moving principle, the divine hypostasis, who brings about activity that is divine and activity that is human: the activity that is human is the integral human individuality of Jesus, which in no sense ceases to be human because of the source which activates it; similarly, the eternal act by which God is God remains unchanged by the fact that the agent of this act also activates human nature. The one hypostatic agent holds the two forms of action inseparably together, so that there is no way of understanding the human event that is Jesus without reference to its union with the divine, and so it is not impossible to speak of a single active phenomenon that is both divine and human, 'theandric' – even if, strictly speaking, we have to identify the *energeiai* as radically distinct from one another. But this makes it plain that a nature, although it cannot be conceived without ascribing to it a mode of acting, is not *as such* an agent; it is active because it is necessarily hypostatized, realized as the *logos of* this or that particular agent. This decisively rectifies the imbalance of Leo's language about *formae* acting: no nature is inactive (since it must be *enupostatos*, concretely realized), but no nature is *an agent*. It is always strictly the 'invariable' in an actual agent, specifying what kind of

39 Ibid., p. 510.
40 PG91, 84D–89A, 100B–110B.

agent it is, what its *logos*, its intelligible structure, is – and so also specifying what it is meant to be in God's ultimate purpose.

This takes us on to a second substantial contribution made by Maximus, connecting the vocabulary of Christology still more closely to an understanding of God's relation to creation. As is well known, Maximus explores in depth the relation between the eternal Logos and the *logoi* of finite substances, between the eternal life of God as active and creative intelligence and the diverse structures of intelligible life that make up the finite universe, the sum total of finite natures. The *logos* of any particular nature is its participation in the life of the eternal Word; every finite kind reflects one way in which the eternal Logos's life can be imitated or rather expressed in finite intelligible form. But this means that the more a created nature moves towards its optimal actuality, the closer it is to the Creator;[41] and the harmonious diversity of the finite order when it is acting as it should is in its entirety a reflection of the unity of the eternal Logos in whom exist inseparably all the multiple modes in which eternal being and intelligibility can be mirrored. Thus for humanity to be fully human is not only for it to be aligned with its own natural *logos* but also for it to exist in optimal relation with *the* Logos. This is of course true of all finite creatures; but what makes humanity unique in creation is that it is created with the capacity to mediate the Logos's own unifying agency within creation.[42] Humanity's vocation is not simply to be optimally human in the sense of exemplifying its natural qualities as perfectly as possible, but to be actively engaged in the harmonizing of the created order as part of a 'liturgical' service offered to God. We could put this more loosely by saying that humanity's calling is to be freely active in a certain way, to be more than 'just' natural. And where this vocation has been refused and overlaid by human sin, what has to be restored is the capacity of finite human agency to choose and act as it should. Thus when the hypostasis of the Logos takes on human identity, it will render human

---

41 See Melchisedec Törönen, *Union and Distinction in the Theology of Maximus the Confessor*, Oxford: Oxford University Press, 2007, p. 130.

42 See, for example, Thunberg, op. cit., Chapter 4, and his earlier and ground-breaking longer work, *Microcosm and Mediator: The Theological Anthropology of Maximus the Confessor*, Lund: Gleerup, 1965; also Aidan Nichols, op. cit., Chapters 5 and 6.

nature capable of a new level of 'hypostatic' agency in respect of the whole entire created order.

Filling this out a little further, we can see how Maximus is connecting two themes that might initially seem distinct. What happens in the Incarnation is that a human identity, an 'enhypostatized' nature, comes into being that fully realizes in finite terms what is true of the eternal Word's relation to the Father; that is to say, this human nature is identified ultimately and decisively by the fact that it actualizes divine filiation. Its mode or manner of subsisting is to be 'filial' as the Word is 'filial', to be absolutely, uninterruptedly, consciously and thankfully dependent on the self-gift of the Father in such a way that the fullness of that giving life is lived in the one who receives it. But in the light of what is said about the cosmological relation overall, the sharing of *logoi* in the Logos, this means in turn that what happens in the Incarnation is a revelation that the *logos tēs phuseōs*, which is the structure of human nature, is oriented towards realizing in the finite world the character or quality of the infinite reality which is the Word's loving dependence on the Father. To be fully human is to be an adopted child of God, to receive the *charis tes huiothesias*[43] and so (in Maximus's theology) to share the operation of the divine nature yet without ceasing to be created. The human *logos* is unchanged, but its full dimensions are shown to be realized only in the *tropos* of filial relation. Or, to put it slightly differently, what distinguishes Christ from other human beings is not that his human nature is in any sense different from ours, but that it is lived out differently. In the pithy phrase of Felix Heinzer, in his monograph on Maximus's Christology, there is in Christ a human 'what' and a divine 'how' (*Menschliches 'Was'* – *Gottliches 'Wie'*);[44] his humanity has 'a quality of existence that is at once natural and supernatural',[45] natural in that it satisfies every condition for being recognizably human, supernatural because its natural potential is actualized in a mode that transcends routine human behaviour because it is united with the eternal Logos's 'mode' of existing. And so what is eternal

---

43   From his treatise on the Lord's Prayer, *expositio orationis dominicae* PG90, 884D.

44   Felix Heinzer, *Gottes Sohn als Mensch: Die Struktur des Menschseins Christi bei Maximus Confessor*, Freiburg: Universitätsverlag Freiburg Schweiz, 1980, pp. 125ff., discussing Maximus's opusc.4.

45   Ibid., p. 130.

and simultaneous in the divine life – the origin of the Son from the Father and the Son's relation with the Father – is rendered in narrative or dramatic terms in the earthly life of the Word incarnate. The eternal self-emptying of love that is exchanged between Father and Son becomes the active obedience, even to the point of death (Phil. 2.8) of Jesus.[46] And our alignment with his humanity by incorporation into his sacramental Body makes possible our own *kenosis* and *ekstasis*, our self-emptying and self-transcending in love.[47] The finite and historical kenosis of the Son both realizes in history the eternal kenosis of the Word and opens the way for our finite and historical kenosis towards the Father.

What is perhaps most interesting in terms of the history of Christology is that this scheme says a good deal more than what many historians of theology recognize in patristic accounts of redemption. It is often claimed – eloquently by Daphne Hampson, for example[48] – that the patristic model depends on a wholly unreconstructed Platonism: Christ assumes 'human nature' as a general reality which exists independently of specific individuals, and restores it in its universality. And if we cease to believe in Platonic forms in the way that this kind of formulation implies, we have little reason to take seriously the Christology of the patristic and Byzantine church. But we have already seen that, while the theologians we have been examining in this chapter were undoubtedly 'realists' in their belief that universal natures were real, they did not believe that abstract universal human nature could ever be a subject in itself. Redemptive transformation is indeed the transformation of 'nature', considered as the defining set of human qualities. But – despite the looser language of some fourth-century writers – it is not the bare 'injection' of divine qualities into human nature that achieves this. The eternal Logos's way of exercising/living the divine nature is what now animates this particular human substance; and in animating as it does this human substance (that is, in 'enhypostatizing' humanity, realizing human possibility in a particular way), it creates a new set of relations between humanity and divine life precisely in and through the unique humanity that is Christ's. The relations thus created become the vehicle for a new level of

---

46   Ibid., pp. 140–1.
47   See, for example, *quaestiones ad Thalassium* 64, PG90, 93A–728D.
48   Daphne Hampson, *Theology and Feminism*, Oxford: Blackwell, 1990, pp. 53–8.

transformative engagement with the cosmos at large: in (personal) union with the incarnate Logos, human agents are enabled to act as they are meant to in regard to their entire human and non-human environment. For the Logos to be united to the *logos tēs phuseōs* of humanity is for a human substance to be activated by the divine agency exercising its divine *physis* in the distinct mode of 'filiation' so that the human *logos tēs phuseōs* is comprehensively defined and identified as 'filial'. The humanity of Jesus is drawn out beyond its static properties into an 'ecstatic' relation with the Father, a radically self-emptied and other-directed love.

It is true (as Törönen says[49]) that some of Maximus's interpreters have elaborated this into a metaphysic opposing fixed nature to 'self-transcending' person, and this is not what Maximus has in mind: he undoubtedly sees nature itself as endowed with an appropriate degree of freedom, rather than as the realm of necessity and impersonality. But it is also true that Maximus treats *ekstasis* as the proper culmination of humanity's growth towards God: it is the condition in which the knowing finite subject goes beyond its given limits, including the 'natural' limits of self-preservation: it is generated by *erōs*, a term the Confessor uses without embarrassment as designating the magnetic drawing of finite beings towards the infinite. For Christ to live in the believer is for the believer to be caught up into the self-abandoning love both of the Son for the Father and of God for creation. In both creation and incarnation, God has elected to live within the created order without ceasing to be what God eternally is. What God brings about in the finite is a movement of 'desire', *erōs*[50] – that is, a moving beyond what the intellect can master and a growth in love. But this growth in love manifests itself also as an overcoming of 'the divisions now prevailing in nature because of man's self-love':[51] the community of finite agents becomes more and more solidly

---

49 Op. cit., p. 112.

50 On *erōs* in Maximus, see Paul Blowers, op. cit., and Nevena Dimitrova, 'Desire and the Practical Part of the Soul According to Maximus the Confessor', *Analogia* (above, n. 29), pp. 35–46.

51 The phrase comes from the fifth of the 'Centuries' of 'Various Texts on Theology, the Divine Economy and Virtue and Vice' extracted from Maximus's works and preserved in the *Philokalia*; see *The Philokalia: The Complete Text Compiled by St Nikodimos of the Holy Mountain and St Makarios of Corinth*, Vol. 2, trans. G. E. H. Palmer, Philip Sherrard and Kallistos Ware, London, Faber & Faber, 1981, p. 10.

established in 'justice' as human beings recognize more fully in one another their common nature as rational. Paradoxically, universal rationality here means the universal realization of 'ecstasy', acting in other-directed love for all in their diverse conditions, so that believers '[belong] not to themselves but to those whom they love'.

Connecting this to the central theme of this book, what is significant in Maximus's theology is the clarity with which he affirms that the final fulfilment of human vocation *as* human, even *as* finite, is the realization in humanity of a divine mode or style of existing. Nothing ceases to be human when divine filiation is lived or enacted in a human individual: when that filiation is embodied unsurpassably and uninterruptedly, as in the humanity of Jesus, the image of God in which humanity was first created is fully activated, and human beings in communion with the Word incarnate are made able to live in kenotic love and mutual gift, reflecting the life that belongs to the Trinitarian Persons in eternity. And just as the Trinitarian God lives eternally in a relation to the created order that is free from conflict and competition, so the finite self united with the infinite reality of the Word is able to live in reconciled communion with other human persons and to overcome the various life-denying divisions that characterize the fallen finite world. As in Augustine's theology, the affirmation that God the Word is freely and unrestrainedly active in the human identity of Jesus opens up an understanding of how that human identity ceases to be merely individual in the ordinary human sense but must be seen as the founding and enabling agency in the lives of believers incorporated sacramentally into his relation with the Father. For Maximus no less than for Augustine, Christology is inseparable from a theology of the Church and a phenomenology of holiness. Maximus's doctrinal pattern – human nature realized in a particular mode by the presence in the finite world of divinity lived as filiation – is inseparably connected with the pattern of a restored creation in which humanity actualizes its long-lost potential for establishing just relationship and reconciliation among the diverse forms of earthly existence. It is here that Maximus makes his most significant advance over the earlier Byzantine thinkers we have discussed, in that he is equally concerned with settling a technical vocabulary appropriate for Christology and with the shape and sense of the baptized life, and more specifically the life of contemplation. Our association with Christ through the work of the Spirit in the Church and sacraments and contemplation does away with the kind of self-preoccupation that impedes both love and prayer. We are 'activated' by a divine action that is eternally moving out towards the other – the love of the Word as eternal Son of the Father, the love of the Trinity for creation. So to speak in this connection of a 'logic of creation' is to speak of the immeasurable diversity and interwoven complexity of a finite order destined to be drawn into harmony and mutual life-sharing through the reconciliation of humanity to God; that reconciliation is achieved in the self-emptying act of incarnation which draws us into self-emptying and self-transcending faith and prayer, whose natural by-product is universal justice.

In sheerly conceptual terms, Maximus also follows and further clarifies the development that emerges from the arguments of the two Leontii about the two distinct levels at which we speak of unity in Christ, unity of hypostasis. Christ is one primarily because there is one eternal agent, the divine Word, at the source of every act performed by Jesus of Nazareth; there are not two co-ordinate agencies at work in him. This means that his human nature is given its particular intelligible unity by the Word, so that the actual phenomenon of the incarnate life, the life of Jesus, is held together by the Word. This phenomenon can be referred to as a *hypostasis synthetos*, a compound or composite hypostasis.[52] From the perspective of the historical world, there is 'one Lord Jesus Christ', in whom divine and human nature are brought inseparably, 'synthetically', together. But from the point of view of eternity (insofar as we can presume to use such language), there is one eternal divine hypostasis to which nothing can be added and from which nothing can be taken away. The unity of Christ is thus both the outcome of the uniting of divine and human in the Incarnation and the timeless reality of the Word's subsistence. If the two Leontii show a tendency to stress one or the other of these perspectives, Maximus can be said to do equal justice to both; and the legacy of this balance is to be of considerable significance for the next stage of evolution in Byzantine theology.

52   As in, for example, Maximus's *ep.* 12, PG91 490C and 13, 525Dff.

4. A Byzantine Synthesis: John of Damascus

The conceptual developments we have been tracing were put to sharply practical use in the controversy over the veneration of icons which so bitterly divided the Byzantine world in the eighth and ninth centuries. What is of interest for our discussion here is the way in which John of Damascus, the foremost apologist for the veneration of sacred images, drew on earlier Christological debate in order to show that opposition to icon worship rested on a misunderstanding of fundamental Christological principles.[53] The argument he was contesting was that any attempt to depict Christ was implicitly heretical: given that the divine nature was incapable of representation in any image and that the humanity of Christ was a humanity inseparably united with and transformed by the divine nature, we could only make an image of Christ by representing a humanity severed from its union with the divine – which would be an impossibility. John grounds his response to this dilemma in a detailed discussion of terminology in his *dialectica*, a work which, although it is really for the most part a compendium of earlier textbooks, has been described as the most important philosophical text of the early Byzantine period, showing knowledge of both Aristotle and the major Aristotelian commentators of late antiquity, especially Porphyry, while devoting considerable attention – in the wake of the Leontii and Maximus – to defining the non-Aristotelian vocabulary of hypostasis and *enhypostasia*. He carefully examines the word *enupostatos*, concluding that it may be used in any of three ways.[54] It may apply simply to a nature as it is 'contemplated' (*theoreitai*) in a hypostasis, or to distinct natures joined together in a single hypostasis, or to a single nature taken by a hypostasis of another nature and existing only in it and for it. The first meaning is the most general; the second applies to humanity (body and soul combining in the hypostasis of a human individual, so that the individual is the hypostasis of both body and soul, which have no actuality independently of this united subsistence); the third applies to the incarnation of the Word. The

---

53   For an overall guide to John, see Andrew Louth, *St John Damascene: Tradition and Originality in Byzantine Theology*, Oxford: Oxford University Press, 2005, especially Chapters 4 and 6. Cornelia Rozemond's 1959 monograph, *La christologie de s. Jean Damascène*, Ettal: Buch-Kunstverlag, remains a very valuable study.

54   PG 94, 616–17.

significant point is that hypostasis becomes very clearly the medium in which, and in which alone, nature can be seen as active, contemplated in its various differentiations, both essential and accidental. He has already established that form and accident and differentia have no subsistence except in a hypostasis,[55] and nature or substance exists *en energeia*, 'in actuality', only as hypostatized.[56] It is not possible to make one nature out of two natures or one hypostasis out of two hypostases:[57] a nature simply *is* the set of defining characteristics that make something this kind of thing rather than another, a hypostasis simply *is* the actuality of some kind or kinds of natural action. The job of both sorts of word is to identify – either to identify a kind or to identify an individual; hence two genuine 'nature-sets' or two genuine individual identifications could not logically merge with each other. In theological terms, there cannot be a composite nature in Christ which supersedes the difference between the divine and the human, and there cannot be a single hypostasis that is the product of two already existing hypostases. The one hypostasis actualizes the two natures, though John is clear that the eternal actualization of divine life by the Word is the prior and determinative reality.

John's logical clarifications distil with great economy the themes we have examined in earlier writers. And the practical significance of this for the controversy about whether Christ could be represented in images is plain enough: the divine nature is indeed incapable of being represented – like any nature, it is not a *thing*. It exists only as actualized by the divine *tropoi huparxeōs* (John adopts Maximus's terminology for the Trinitarian Persons). The problem is not that divinity is inconceivable and unimaginable: it is, of course; but the issue is in a way more prosaic. There is no 'thing' to represent; we can no more represent the human *nature* of Christ than we can his divine nature. All we can represent is his hypostasis, which is indeed, as the critics of icon worship insisted, inseparably one. But if it is inseparably one, and if it is genuinely a hypostatization of human nature, it is no less representable than any ordinary human hypostasis. It does not

<hr>

55 Ibid., 611B; cf. 589 on the *anupostatos* – i.e. 'unreal' or 'non-actual' – character of accidents as such.

56 Ibid. 613A.

57 Ibid. 669.

cease to be its finite self, subject to ordinary finite passibility;[58] yet this finite passibility is the way in which the divine Person has willed to be seen and known. It is 'the visible aspect of God', *theou to horōmenon*.[59] And in the light of this, it is a bizarre piece of theological misconception to refuse to treat it as visible in the ordinary sense, as capable of being visually depicted. To believe otherwise would be to swallow up the humanity in the divinity. Orthodox belief envisages the moment of Jesus' conception in the womb of Mary as a moment when an animated and reasoning body comes into existence that is immediately and continuously the animated body of the divine Word,[60] unequivocally human and individualized as human by the unique and unitary subsistence of the Word. This humanity is properly venerated as the flesh of God, the finite human phenomenon in and as which God acts out what it is to be God in the *tropos* of filiation. Depicting Christ in an icon and venerating that image is a witness both to the unrestricted divine action in Christ and to the sovereign grace that transfigures finite humanity without destroying it.

John follows Maximus in arguing that the integrity of the two natures implies the presence of two 'wills' – that is, two natural 'instincts' as we might put it, two distinct kinds of mental and psychological motion, so that we can make sense of Jesus' natural shrinking from death in his prayer in the Garden of Gethsemane and his words to his divine Father, 'Not my will but yours be done.' And he makes explicit what is largely implicit in Maximus: 'will' in this sense is as abstract a notion as 'nature' itself. It has no existence except as actualized in a hypostasis. Thus what we have to think of is the one divine agent realizing a specific set of human possibilities in a fully human way, subject to human 'instinct'; but that instinct being itself the instrument of divine action as much as any other aspect of the human identity. Christ's natural vulnerability as human thus becomes a communication of the life of God the Word, and John's account distantly echoes in this respect some of Augustine's arguments about the way in which

58 John of Damascus, *de fide orthodoxa* 3.20–1, PG94 1081A–1085C.

59 John of Damascus, *de sacris imaginibus* 1, PG94 1245A.

60 *De fide orthodoxa* 3.2, PG94 985C–988A; it is notable that John has no difficulty in describing the concrete identity of the incarnate Word as a composite *nature* (*physis ... synthetos*) in this passage.

the Word in Jesus takes up and takes on himself all the varieties of human utterance, even the apparently questioning and rebellious, yet holds them in an unconditional obedience. In the words of an authoritative modern discussion of John of Damascus's Christology, Christ 'according to his divinity wills salvation. According to his humanity he chooses to be obedient to the Father (which is at the same time an act of obedience to the divine will in himself).'[61] To anyone objecting that the language of 'two wills' is confusingly abstract, John might have replied that this is the point: there is no such thing as a will any more than there is such a thing as a nature. What we are discussing is always the way in which abstract capacities or qualities become visible and actual. As his discussion of logical terminology suggests, the ultimate focus for talking about substantial reality must be at the level of hypostasis, where (to use his language in the *dialectica*) we have arrived at the point where *eidos*, 'species', 'specifying or particularizing form', reaches its most irreducibly particular level, and is not a generic form for anything else.[62] Hence to say that hypostasis is *atomos* is simply to recognize that we are at the ontological level where the subject of our discourse is strictly the historical reality of *particular* subsistent entities acting and interacting. These entities are not *types* of agency, not abstractions from a set of multiple phenomena, but indivisible subjects. At one end of the scale, the 'most generic genus' is that which is not the *species* of anything else – which is why God does not belong in a genus. At the other end, the most 'specific' species is that which is the *genus* of nothing else. God is not a case or instance of anything; and the individual hypostasis is not an abstraction from any set of phenomenal qualities.[63] Hypostasis is simply this unique, unrepeatable actuality, 'nature in act', as we have already noted.[64] And as such, of course, it is not itself an element in a composite, as if a concrete being were composed of substance to which some extra thing ('individuality') had been added. We have already seen in the first chapter how Aquinas's elaboration of the language of *esse* is meant to wean us away from any such model. The path to that conceptual resolution is firmly laid in John of Damascus's

---

61 Rozemond, op. cit., p. 36.
62 PG 94 568B.
63 Ibid.
64 Above, pp. 92–4.

analysis. His ontology is framed by the two extremes of the unconditional and eternal being that is God, the unclassifiable infinity of God's Trinitarian life, and the equally unclassifiable particularity of the single finite agent in its singularity; and the Incarnation is the place where these two points are brought together, the finite at its extreme of finitude, the limitedness of historically unique specificity, the infinite as that which necessarily escapes any classification along with anything else. The divine act of being, beyond all categorization and analysis, unites with and actualizes the 'most specific', the most particular, act of being that is a finite individuality. And in so doing – for John of Damascus as much as for Maximus – the divine allows the finite to become the means by which unlimited communion, transforming participation in the divine, is opened up to other finite agents. This happens primarily and definitively in the glorified humanity of Jesus, no longer simply a single closed-off object in a world of objects, and then derivatively in the life and practice of the community created by the Spirit of Jesus.

So John's reply to the anti-icon party adds a further dimension to the evolution of a coherent picture of Christ and the created order by defending the idea that, if Christ's humanity remains human while conveying divine meaning, finite and material representation of his humanity may likewise convey divine meaning and – even more precisely – be a carrier of divine *energeia*. The agency that is in Christ incarnate, in unique and unsurpassable fullness, is an agency that may be shared by realities that are connected to Christ in one way or another – by the holy lives of believers and by the holy vehicles of shared thought and imagination which make up the acts of the Body of Christ in its liturgy, its self-defining common work of worship. As has often been observed, the Western Christian response to this aspect of Byzantine theology was from the first rather puzzled, if not hostile, suspicious of a kind of over-realizing of the participation of the finite image in the infinite and in turn over-reacting towards an instrumental approach to the liturgical image, and sometimes to the liturgical action itself. That is another story;[65] but all that John is really doing is following through the logic of his fundamental Christological schema. If in Christ divine agency takes nothing away from the human and if his hypostatic unity takes

---

65 Parts of it are well told in Judith Herrin, *The Formation of Christendom*, Oxford: Blackwell, 1987, Chapter 10, especially pp. 437–9.

nothing away from the divine, that which is itself activated by his hypostatic presence, in the life of the Body of Christ and by the action of his Spirit, can also be seen as the bearer of divine act and meaning without compromising either the divine or the human. The created reality – and in this context very specifically the *material* reality – is not to be seen as 'excluding' the divine in virtue of its finitude or physicality. So far from the cultus of the icon compromising the transcendence of God, it reaffirms that transcendence by insisting that finite substance does not and cannot constitute a place where God is not. The Christological foundation of this insistence lies in the recognition that no nature or essence is an object as such; and that therefore the presence of the divine nature in the world can only be seen or understood as the actualization of finite reality. The uniqueness of Christ is in the fact that this uniquely individualized or hypostatized human nature is simultaneously and inseparably the making-present in the world of the eternal active subsistence that is the divine Word. The comprehensive assumption by the Word of a complete human identity declares decisively that such an identity is not something that stands alongside divine life as a separate item in a single set of identifiable objects.

As we have just noted, John and his precursors do not imagine that the unique and active subsisting reality is a compound of essence or nature and something else called 'individuality'. In this sense, the word 'hypostasis' in itself no more designates an object than 'nature' does – a point we have seen that Leontius of Byzantium insists upon in saying that hypostasis *is* nature, in the sense that the word hypostasis does not designate some thing that is separate from nature but picks out a nature as existing in *this* way or within *these* defining relationships. There is therefore no problem in speaking, as John of Damascus, like Maximus, unapologetically does, of the eternally simple hypostasis of the Word appearing in history as *sunthetos*, composite.[66] It is not that anything changes in the way in which the Word realizes or actualizes Godhead in eternity; what happens in the Incarnation is that the Word's way of being God (the Word's hypostatic being) – comes to be the ultimate identifying principle (the hypostatic being) of this particular finite phenomenon, Jesus of Nazareth. Or, to put it more carefully, so as to rule out any suggestion that this is a process in the life of the Word,

66   *de fide orthodoxa* 3.7, PG94 1007C–1010B.

it comes to be the case that at a point in finite history a finite identity begins its life whose hypostatic identity is that of the Word. To underline the point made earlier, the oneness of the hypostasis is being affirmed in two distinct ways: as the unchanging singleness of the Word's divine identity and as the unbroken continuity between the Word and the human agency and identity of Jesus. In the latter context, we can intelligibly speak of a 'composite' unity; but we should beware of understanding this as though the unity of Christ's hypostasis were the product of two pre-existing substances now somehow blended together.

Between them, Maximus and John of Damascus decisively clear the ground for the synthesis that Aquinas offers centuries later. The creation of a comparable vocabulary in Latin took time, as we have seen, and it was only with the Western Aristotelian revolution of the thirteenth century that both resource and energy were available to secure adequate precision. Aquinas's own increasing sympathy with and knowledge of a specifically Cyrilline approach to Christology mean that his ultimate positions are closer to John of Damascus's perspectives than any of his Western predecessors. The complexities of speaking about hypostasis in two significantly different ways foreshadow Aquinas's wrestling with whether it is possible to maintain the single *esse* of Christ while allowing that for certain purposes we might need to speak of a 'secondary' act of being – a way of speaking which he finally seems to leave behind as too confusing, so that he ends up, like John of Damascus, settling for the slightly risky but unavoidable model of a 'composite' unity. But the thread that connects the Byzantine with the Western medieval discussion is above all the recognition, at various levels of explicitness, that the language of ontology in general, and thus of Christology to the extent that it seeks to clarify the relation of finite and infinite being, is drastically misunderstood if it is seen as descriptive of objects, 'natures' or 'essences' or 'pure individualities' or whatever. What we are talking about is the diverse terms we need to isolate for intelligent discussion of the diverse ways in which we apprehend agency: as a 'kind' or pattern of life, as the record of a particular agent, as limited and (as with divine action) unlimited, as embodied or as abstract form. The problem with all the vocabulary of metaphysics, and perhaps especially the immensely complex idioms of late classical metaphysics, is that the proliferation of technical terms can readily be misunderstood as a catalogue of distinct subjects. Leontius of

Byzantium insisting that a hypostasis is not a separate *thing* from *physis*, Maximus assimilating hypostasis to *tropos*, John of Damascus describing hypostasis as nature *en energeia*, the whole exploration of what it means to examine nature only as *enupostatos*, all these themes point in the same direction: we have to recognize that a good deal of our confusion in the task of finding appropriate language for the Incarnation lies in the way we reify our terms. The replies offered by these theologians to those they regard as heretics are frequently, in effect, an exhortation to abandon such reified understandings and to look more broadly at the work these terms are actually being asked to do.

5. The Story So Far

It may be helpful at this point to draw together some of the main points so far outlined in this first part of our study, before going on to the related but very different debates of the later medieval and post-Reformation periods. The purpose of these chapters has been twofold: first, to show how what seem to be highly abstract terminological debates, in the patristic and medieval periods, are generated by problems that are rooted in the narrative of the New Testament – not by the importation of alien considerations, the agenda of 'Greek philosophy' or whatever; second, to argue that these problems ultimately have to do with the central issue of the relation of Creator to creation, infinite to finite, and that the search for adequate conceptual structures to speak of this is linked with some fundamental questions about how the gospel is to be articulated. Thus we identified the distinctive problem posed by the language of the New Testament as something more than just the oddity of describing Jesus of Nazareth in terms drawn from apocalyptic and visionary depictions of heavenly priests and angelic mediators. What is more lastingly unsettling is the refusal to turn the narrative of Jesus into one in which heavenly agency and revelation *displace* a story of highly particular and embodied transactions within the human world. As we noted, Paul can pass from straightforward, if ritualized, description of Jesus sharing a meal to speaking of Jesus as having a 'body' that is the kinship group of his disciples. As the Christian movement grows and matures, the degree of interest in or valuation of this story of human transaction increases rather than otherwise, producing the texts we know as the Gospels – certainly not, as we have constantly been reminded, simple biographies as we might think of biography today, yet moulded into what would have been a recognizably biographical shape in the Roman world. They present a picture in which the entire human identity of Jesus is seen as significant, even (eventually) including his birth and childhood. Even the Fourth Gospel with its intense, sustained discourses, where the embodied particularity can at some moments seem most remote, makes astonishingly liberal use of what we would call realistic dialogue and bluntly ascribes ordinary human weariness and grief to Jesus.

The significant point is that we are already looking at a style of speaking about Jesus in which the identifying detail of the human life is understood as inseparable from the communication of the divine which it carries. And this helps to explain the fact that the actual *teaching* of Jesus does not dominate the narrative (as it does in, for example, the later gospel texts associated with esoteric groups, the 'Gnostic' gospels of Philip, Judas or Bartholomew); the transforming effect of Jesus' presence is in the entire process by which he gathers a community that comes to see itself as bound together by kinship with him as if 'in' an ancestor's body. Teaching is not ignored, but it is not what makes the difference. And the process of gathering a community is understood as reaching its climax in Jesus' execution and its aftermath, as if the terminally violent breaking of the community's bonds in the crucifixion had to be shown as overcome by the unbreakable union between Jesus' human identity and the divine act. That (embodied) identity returns on the other side of death to re-establish the new kindred, the extended 'Body' of the Church. No account of the foundational story of Christianity can avoid having to come to terms with this central drama of breakage and restoration, violent death and restored shared life. To the extent that this depends upon the continuing finite identity of Jesus within the human world, we already have within the New Testament the fruitful tension that generates the whole of the Christological tradition we have been tracing: the challenge of affirming the unbroken presence of divine freedom in the human identity of Jesus without fracturing or compromising that identity in its finite specificity.

The debates of the patristic era can be read as a steady clarification of the terms of this formulation. The tension can be reduced – for example – if we agree that what is acting in Jesus is not precisely the divine freedom as such but a derivative mediatorial agency. It can be reduced by weakening the integrity of the human nature, either by the suggestion that it is only apparently a stable material phenomenon, or by removing some element from it that might compete for psychological space with the divine agency, or by imagining a complete human identity which had to be in some sense suspended in order for the divine to work. The century and a half leading up to the Council of Chalcedon saw all these options defended, considered and criticized in turn; and the Council itself represented less the triumph of a theory, let alone a vocabulary, than the reassertion of the basic elements of the problem. It declares in effect that there is no resolution possible by compromising either the completeness of divine freedom or the specificity of finite humanity. Once the unequivocal divinity of the divine Word had been established at Nicaea, the paradoxical consequence had to be accepted that it was equally inadmissible to question or compromise the full humanity of Jesus of Nazareth: embodied suffering and finite mental identity had to be located in a straightforwardly human subject as they now could in no sense be attributed to the divine Word, as if the Word (as Arius had argued) were more 'open' than the Father to change or embodied pain.

The unfinished business of Chalcedon was unmistakeably to do with terminology, and the often exhaustingly technical discussions of the two following centuries attempted, with a measure of success, to develop a consistent vocabulary. The word *hupostasis* stands at the centre of this process – not a simple import from 'Greek philosophy', but a notion developed and refined within the particular constraints of this set of debates. It is the word that designates *realized* action, the specific phenomenon or ensemble of phenomena in which a set of 'natural' or generic possibilities becomes concrete. It is a flexible word, and because of that can be ambiguous. To speak of the single hypostasis of Christ may be *either* to point to the unique actuality of divine life as Word and Son that determines the overall coherence and continuity of Jesus' identity *or* to designate the single finite phenomenon in which divine agency and human individuality are inseparably at work, the *sunthetos* reality that is the incarnate Christ. In other words, hypostasis-language points to the level of reality where unique specificity is in question. Within the finite world, this is necessarily a temporal and embodied specificity; the word is not meant to designate a component in a whole (nature *plus* individuation) but the whole as actively real – that which in Maximus is identified with the *tropos* of existing, the 'variable' as against the 'invariable'. By the time we reach the high scholastic era, Aquinas's use of *esse* attempts to undergird the recognition that 'hypostasis' does not designate an element in composition by highlighting the word's connotation of actuality or actualization, though the complexities of the different levels of reference for the term in eternity and in time do not disappear. But it allows him to state with unprecedented clarity the fundamental point that the relation of the human identity of Jesus to the divine agency of the Word is in no sense that of one determinate subject to another; it is a relation in which one reality is informed and defined by another which is real at a completely different ontological level. Hence the recurrent point in these chapters so far: that there is no sense in which we can suppose any 'competition' between humanity and divinity in Christ. The rigorous stripping away from the divine of any vulnerability to finite conditioning is designed to avoid the reduction of the divine to one partner in the mutually exclusive confrontations of finitely determined agents. The logic of finite and infinite overall has to be repeatedly clarified for the sake of affirming both divinity and humanity in their proper integrity.

It is precisely this 'zero-sum' perspective of mutual exclusion which is disturbed and reshaped by the fact of the Incarnation. The finite reality of Jesus embodies infinite divine relatedness, and so its own humanly and historically generated relations are more than instances of routine finite relations: they have the effect of extending and deepening human relations with God, so that the 'filiation' that characterizes Jesus is in some measure lived out in believers; and, connected with this, they establish between believers an organic interdependence that radically changes our involvement with and responsibility for others, inside and outside the visible community of faith. Because the divine hypostasis is what it is – divine, and thus without any ground for withholding love, filial and thus eternally related to the Father – its action draws finite agency into itself in such a way that finite agency moves outwards from its fallen state of mutual rivalry and hostility. As Maximus expresses it, the divine 'ekstasis' and self-emptying create in us a new capacity for communion. This is not a denial of the integrity of finite reality, since in Maximus's cosmology each created substance is a participant in and a reflection of the eternal Word; all *logoi* subsist in the Logos. And (recalling Antoine Lévy's important discussion of this) this establishes at the ground of finite reality a 'tending' towards the infinite, not back towards a lost equilibrium but forwards in *eros* towards a deeper consummation: the passage of time becomes the vehicle of grace, in that what is achieved and realized in the temporal order is genuinely more and deeper than the initial relation of Creator to creature. The union of finite and infinite in Christ is thus the pivot of a metaphysic in which there are genuinely new levels of integration or reconciliation to be realized in the temporal world. To quote from the conclusion of a recent and magisterial study of Maximus' theory of time, the process of change and motion in the world is 'the manifestation of a relationship'[67] in which we as humans not only return to our 'natural' integration with the rest of reality but acquire a life *huper phusin*, beyond our given capacities, in our relatedness to the incarnate Word.

So Christology troubles the supposedly impermeable borders between one self-contained individual and another, telling us that our connections with other human beings run deeper than we imagined (or are comfortable with). As we shall see in a later chapter,[68] this can generate a sharp-edged political and social critique, as it does in the work of Bonhoeffer, as well as fresh metaphysical insights. Understanding something of how classical Christology works and how its terminology evolves is bound in with understanding how and why Christian theological commitments reshape our map of the human world as comprehensively as they do. John of Damascus's defence of icons also reminds us that Chalcedonian and post-Chalcedonian theology provides the foundation for an understanding of material reality as capable of bearing meaning – that is, of being a vehicle for loving and intelligent relation, between God and creation and between one created subject and another. When the created subject is in communion with the relational life that is God, it is free to communicate dimensions of that relational life in ways that go beyond words and ideas: the communicative energy of the things of this world, once brought within the scope of Christ-centred relation, is expanded and transfigured. The sacramental practice of the Christian community is the place where we see this worked out most fully; but what is made plain there casts light on the entire world

---

67 Sotiris Mitralexis, *Ever-Moving Repose: A Contemporary Reading of Maximus the Confessor's Theory of Time*, Eugene, OR: Cascade Books, 2017, p. 216.

68 Below, Chapter 2.2.

of our systems of meaning and the way in which human culture makes signs out of the raw material of the world. As various theologians have argued, the semantically full reality of sacramental practice, itself deriving from the semantically 'saturated' materiality that is the historical body of Jesus, allows us to see our material environment as pregnant with significance which we may or may not immediately grasp. In this light, we can say that Christology conceived along these lines decisively rules out the reduction of the physical world to a mechanistic system whose meanings are established only in relation to human utility.

The synthesis constructed by Aquinas, whose main lines are so clearly marked out by Maximus and John of Damascus in particular, can reasonably be thought of as an achievement of both Western and Eastern Christian thought, particularly given Aquinas's late enthusiasm for Cyril and his careful restating of many of John of Damascus's themes. The story we shall be looking at in the second half of this book is less obviously a *common* Christian project. Late medieval and Reformation discussions tend to move away from the close integration of directly Christological, ecclesiological and spiritual themes that characterize Augustine or Maximus, and there is a curious amnesia about many aspects of the earlier terminological refinements that were designed to avoid major misunderstandings. But it is nonetheless intriguing to see the same issues returning, and the search for new ways of 'holding' the tensions in some sort of coherent theological language. It is also important to see how fresh philosophical impulses have an impact on Christology, from the nominalism of the later Middle Ages to Hegel and beyond, not to mention Wittgenstein.[69] If the general approach of this book is right, Christology, while it is never the instrument of any metaphysical scheme, inevitably poses metaphysical questions, in the sense that it requires us to think about the grammar of our talk about finite being and what might tentatively be said about its relation to infinite being. A scheme in which nothing could be said about substances beyond an account of the interaction of 'billiard-ball' particulars would leave little room for understanding relation with the infinite except by characterizing the infinite as a larger version of the finite (competitive ontology once again). But equally, an ontology in which particular substance was regarded

69   See below, pp. 255–272.

as entirely epiphenomenal, a sheerly contingent coming-together of forces or processes, would fail to do justice to the central role in theology of the relatedness of actual historical subjects in whom the processes of the universe achieve a unique specification in unrepeatable events. The intricacies of the terminological discussions of Leontius of Byzantium or John of Damascus as they try to nail down what exactly the language of 'hypostatization' means are not an idle or abstract indulgence. As we have noted with John of Damascus, the idea that reality is, so to speak, extended between the utterly trans-generic (God as beyond definition) and the utterly specific (the hypostatic moment in which possibilities are uniquely actualized) is a genuine claim about the nature of reality as such; not the repetition of an available ontology but the reworking of concepts and terms in the philosophical tradition to produce a fresh perspective.

The later Middle Ages sees the rejection of a great deal of this painstakingly assembled ontological model, and a consequent weakening of any idea that the union of humanity and divinity in Christ (or in any finite subject) can be more than extrinsic. And the Reformation debates about sacramental theology in connection with Christology are in essence debates about the proper way to conceive God's relation to finite and contingent reality, but deprived of some of the most resourceful traditional material for thinking this through. When we come to look at the controversies over incarnation and *kenōsis*, divine self-emptying, in nineteenth-century Lutheran dogmatics, and the twentieth- and twenty-first-century arguments over whether the incarnate identity of Christ is eternally determinative for the divine life itself, what we are seeing is an attempt to do justice to the main affirmations of classical Christology independently of a coherent metaphysical overview. This allows for some important restatements of divine freedom and a rhetorically forceful presentation of the impossibility of what we might call doing Christology by numbers – i.e. by defining and enumerating the ontological elements that have to be welded together in order to 'produce' the divine-human reality that is Jesus Christ. Insofar as the classical scheme could lend itself (as we have noted) to a reifying of the language used, the reaction is understandable and even necessary: Dietrich Bonhoeffer's impassioned protests about asking the question 'How?' rather than 'Who?' concerning Christ have a good deal of justification, and allow him in many ways to reconstruct a great deal of the classical synthesis by unconventional means. But it is in the somewhat unlikely shape of a twentieth-century conversation staged between the Thomist tradition and aspects of Hegel that we finally return to a full-blooded attempt at understanding Christology as the key to the logic of createdness and finitude in theology.

We shall explore the detail of all this in the remainder of this study; for now, the central point to bear in mind is simply that the elaborations of Byzantine and scholastic writers in the field of Christology represent not an irresponsible pursuit of conceptual abstraction for its own sake, but a serious and sustained effort to understand, and to find a coherent vocabulary for, the way in which the recognition of divine agency in the entirety of Jesus' human existence affects what can be said about the nature of the reality we inhabit as limited and temporal subjects and about the nature of that which sustains this reality without being in any sense part of it. As soon as it is granted that we cannot dissolve the problem by restricting the presence of divine action to parts of Jesus' life or by qualifying the transcendence and liberty of the divine agent who is at work, this larger issue is unavoidable. I have not discussed in depth exactly *why* Christians came to see it as necessary to assert the divine presence in the whole of Jesus' historical life rather than only in privileged episodes. It surely has something to do with the recognition that the difference he is believed to have made involves a particular kind of sustained relation to himself as a person rather than simply receiving revealed teaching or giving allegiance and obedience to a worker of wonders. But what is beyond dispute is that this concern about the life of Jesus as an integral whole, whose theological interest is not restricted to one period, episode or activity alone, is present as far back as the texts take us; and if this is the case, the challenge of making sense of the finite/infinite relation is there at the root of Christian reflection, and remains so today. The theologians of the early and medieval periods are not addressing abstruse and redundant questions, and the recovery of the reasoning which connects their explorations with the focal ontological problem is still a task that needs pursuing.

PART TWO

2.1

LOSS AND RECOVERY: CALVIN AND THE RE-FORMATION OF CHRISTOLOGY

1. Dismantling Aquinas: The Later Medieval Discussion

So far in this book, we have looked at the process whereby a highly complex and sophisticated scheme of Christological vocabulary was brought into focus and given, in Aquinas, as much terminological precision as possible within the terms of his metaphysic – and sometimes in a way that stretched those terms creatively. The notion, painstakingly if not always lucidly advanced, of a 'composite' act of being (*esse*), integral and undivided in its eternal 'principle' as the act by which the eternal Word is what the eternal Word is, yet wholly continuous with, informing of, an identifiable human identity, allows theology to grasp the possibility of a relation between finite and infinite action that is in no way mutually exclusive, thus opening up a wide range of theological topics to clarification and undermining any idea of a God whose will is hostile to the world he has made, or whose glory is served by the diminution of the finite in its integrity. Yet the history of doctrinal formulation is rarely if ever a smooth story of advance towards consensual resolution. The Thomist synthesis, built on the long process of argument sketched in the preceding chapters, was subject to serious challenge in the two centuries after Aquinas's death, and by the time of the Reformation had been to a substantial extent overlaid by new arguments and criticisms from a philosophical perspective increasingly at odds with that of Aquinas. This new look is regularly associated with Franciscan scholars, Duns Scotus and William of Ockham above all. But it is important to remember that this was not simply a quarrel between the theologians of the major mendicant orders. The Franciscan Bonaventure works in an intellectual framework not radically different to that of Aquinas and a good deal different from that of the later Franciscans.[1] As has repeatedly been observed, what happens in the half-century or so after Aquinas's death is the gradual emergence of a new approach to the language of 'being' itself, culminating in a philosophy for which the idea of any phenomenon 'participating' in an act or energy not contained in its own concrete particularity was alien.[2] This 'nominalist' philosophy produced sophisticated and innovative discussions of doctrinal themes; but, as we shall see, it could generate some very eccentric results, and generally represented a move away from the tight connections in earlier theology between such discussions and the ethical and spiritual life of the Christian community. It is not surprising that the Reformers looked for theological inspiration to sources other than late medieval scholastic writers, even when the way in which these writers had laid out some conceptual problems continued tacitly to shape the arguments of the Reformers, not least Luther, as we shall see later. But this chapter will be suggesting that Calvin at least ended up defending positions remarkably close to those of the earlier synthesis – and that the way in which he did so helped to lay

---

1   Like Maximus, he has a highly developed doctrine of Christ as the one who contains the intelligible forms, the *rationes seminales*, of all created beings, spelled out in his *collationes in Hexaemeron* (especially I.1.10); and he famously designates the eternal and incarnate Word as *ars Patris* (e.g., ibid. V.13, and in his Commentary on the Sentences I.d1.1ad 4). Zachary Hayes, *The Hidden Center: Spirituality and Speculative Christology in St Bonaventure*, New York: Paulist Press, 1981, especially Chapter 3, remains a good introduction.

2   The erosion of a participatory metaphysic in the later Middle Ages and the role in this of Scotus in particular has been the subject of much discussion in recent decades; see the discussion in Adrian Pabst, *Metaphysics: The Creation of Hierarchy*, Grand Rapids, MI: Eerdmans, 2012, especially Chapter 6.

the foundations for some creative reworking of its themes in more recent theology.

One way into understanding the dissolution of the synthesis in the generation after Aquinas is by way of examining at slightly more length a point touched on in the first chapter. It is one that at first sight seems to be (even by the standards of scholastic analysis) a somewhat recondite subject, one that will appear more than usually remote from contemporary vocabulary and interest. But in fact it proves to be something of a key to a number of broader questions. Aquinas, as we noted above, discusses[3] what it means to say that Christ's incarnate actions are 'meritorious', and, if so, what is the nature and the effect of their merit. It is language that can hardly fail to suggest to post-Reformation theologians, even Catholic theologians formed in a late twentieth- and twenty-first-century milieu, an embarrassingly mechanical approach to the life of grace conventionally expressed in a set of very questionable devotional idioms. But the topic has a substantial pedigree in medieval theology; Peter Lombard had discussed it in his *Sentences*,[4] and Aquinas had already commented on Lombard's discussion,[5] arguing that the actions of the incarnate Christ are of *infinite* worth (and thus capable of atoning for an infinitely serious offence against God, to echo the language of St Anselm), and that what he receives from God in his human life is boundless: he 'merits' all the dignity that could possibly be given to a human being. However, as Aquinas spells out in his own treatment of the subject in the *Summa*,[6] this does not mean that we can say that Christ as a *person* 'merits' divinity (his person is identical with the divine Word, so he cannot in any sense 'gain' divine status), or even that he merits grace or blessedness for his humanity, since he has all spiritual gifts in virtue of his own eternal personal relation to the Father with which the entirety of his humanity is united.[7] So what Christ acquires for himself through *meritum* must be

3   ST III.19.3 and 4.
4   *Liber Sententiarum* III.18, PL 191, 792–3. Lombard concludes that Christ merits no *spiritual* benefit for himself, only for the members of his Body, but can be said to merit 'the glory of impassibility and immortality' for his actual material body.
5   Comm Sent. III.19.
6   ST III.19.3.
7   Aquinas is clear that Christ as human possesses the fullness of 'habitual' grace – that is, the indwelling love poured out by the Holy Spirit which makes finite beings holy – in

simply whatever constitutes the glorification and perfection that accrues to human nature as it matures in the life of grace – the transfiguration or glorification of bodily existence, for example. The key text for Aquinas, as for Peter Lombard's earlier discussion of merit in Christ, is Paul's language in Philippians 2, where we are told, after the recital of Christ's total human obedience, that *'therefore'* Christ is exalted by the Father, which implies that something is given to Christ's humanity as a result of the quality of his actions. Now, since Christ's humanity is that of the Head of the Body of believers – since nothing impedes or limits his relation with and solidarity with those who are incorporated into his life through the Spirit – whatever he merits, whatever his human life makes possible in terms of relation to God, is by definition shared with that Body. Because his humanity is activated by the eternal Word, he does not need any kind of purification of his humanity so as to restore relation with the Father; but we do. So if he lives a life that would in abstract terms be counted meritorious, a life that *ought* to deserve or attract grace and divine liberty and blessedness, a human life which is fully and uninterruptedly oriented towards the Father, perfectly adapted for communion with the Father, this makes no *difference* to Christ himself, but all the difference to us who are associated with his humanity in the Mystical Body. Christ does not *need* what he (abstractly) merits, and so it is all ours; the only difference his merit makes to him is the glorification of his mortal condition as the culmination of the life of the Word which is embodied in him and which is realized, actuated, step by step in the course of his earthly life and death.

To understand what is going on here, we need to step back a bit to clarify the notion of merit itself. As Colman O'Neill shows, in his excellent note

---

his humanity. Because the incarnate Christ has a finite soul, this finite reality must be holy by participating in the love given by God; but because the incarnate Christ is perfectly united to the Word, the fullness of this habitual grace overflows for the good of others; there is no limit to the receptivity of a soul united to the divine hypostasis, or rather no 'requisite' amount of grace needed for sanctification, and so it is gratuitously abundant, 'redundant' in the old sense of exceeding need. Legge, *Trinitarian Christology*, Chapter 5, has a good discussion of the historic debates on this subject and suggests an approach which stresses the continuous role of the Holy Spirit in sanctifying Christ's humanity, rather than supposing that the humanity is made holy simply by the hypostatic union in itself.

on these (and other) passages in the *Summa*,[8] what happens in a 'merito-rious' act is that God *creates in us the conditions that will enable us to receive further gifts*. It is comparable to different stages in the growth of a plant – an 'active ordering of the creature towards its goal'.[9] God restores our freedom so that we are fitted for virtuous actions, and those virtuous actions make us fit for fuller communion with God (we cannot in our ordinary sinful state bear such communion; we must be transformed so that we have an 'aptitude' for seeing God and being in God's presence). It is a gross mistake (though a common one among both supporters and critics of this language) to think of this in terms of human actions somehow independently earning the reward of the vision of God. As we have observed, Christ as a person does not need to develop an aptitude for communion with the Father, so does not merit this 'for himself'. The divine glory and the contemplative vision he possesses as eternal Word are not things he has in any sense *gained*. But he is also personally the centre and living principle of the believing com-munity; his humanity is the ground of that 'kinship' with the human race that reaches its fullness in the life of the Church. His humanity is connected with that of the baptized believer in the Church; it acts upon the believer to change the believer's condition. So the abundant God-worthiness of Jesus' humanity is shared with us. In the grace of the baptized life, we, in our renewed human dignity and freedom, are made more open to receive God's gifts through our own personal actions enabled by Christ. As O'Neill puts it, the justified human person 'shares in [Christ's] worthiness before the Father, so that the justification of the sinner is Christ's reward, *in the new member of his person*, for his merit'.[10]

Although the point is not made fully explicit in the *Summa*, Aquinas – as we noted above – had already committed himself in his *Sentences* Commentary to the proposition that Christ's merit was infinite: merit belongs to the person, and Christ's person, with which the human soul of Christ is inseparably united, is of infinite worth; therefore the worth of his acts of love is infinite, even when those acts are performed in the finite

8 St Thomas Aquinas, *Summa Theologiae*, Vol. 50 (IIIa.16–26), ed. and trans. Colman E. O'Neill, OP, London: Eyre & Spottiswoode/New York: McGraw-Hill, 1965.

9 Ibid., p. 240.

10 Ibid., p. 242; my italics.

sphere.[11] To understand the debate that develops in the period immediately after Aquinas, it is important to recognize that he thinks of merit primarily in terms of the capacity or aptness of a person to receive the loving action of God so as to become what they are meant to be. Thus the infinite hypostasis of the incarnate Word may from one point of view be said to possess 'infinite merit' in that there is no limit to his capacity to receive from the Father. His finite actions as a human subject steadily and uninterruptedly keep his human soul open to the habitual grace a human soul needs to live well, and so his human 'constitution' is rewarded with the effects of divine action as it brings human nature to perfection. But the infinite worth of his activity draws into itself the infinite gift of the Father; and since he is Head of the Body, that immeasurable self-bestowal of divine life overflows into those who share, by sacramental grace, in his glorified humanity.

However, Aquinas's account is not the only way of looking at this issue, and Duns Scotus proposes and argues a significantly different approach.[12] Much of his argument begins from a careful analysis of what 'merit' essentially means: for Scotus, it is linked with the concept of *acceptatio* – not just 'acceptance' in the general sense, but in the very specific sense of 'reckoning something as adequate'.[13] Merit is precisely what makes a particular reward *just* or fair; such and such an act is reckoned to be justly

---

11 The power or force (*virtus*) of his actions derives from their union with the Word; they have the effect they have because the humanity is one with the Word, and are therefore efficacious without limit in making satisfaction for the sins of the whole world (Sent.III d.19 1a.1 qc.1 in corp.).

12 It is conventional to identify the main Christological difference between Thomists and Scotists as their divergent views on whether the Incarnation would have happened if Adam had not fallen. This is not really very helpful, especially not when allied to the claim that Scotists/Franciscans are more 'positive' about the created order than Thomists; Scotus, in his way as robust a predestinarian as Calvin, would have been surprised by this. As will become clear, the differences are more far-reaching and even this one can only be fully grasped in the context of their wider metaphysical divergence.

13 Scotus, *Reportatio* 1-A. B 2.59 (Allan B. Wolter, OFM, and Oleg Bychkov, eds, *Duns Scotus: The Examined Report of the Paris Lecture: Reportatio 1-A*, Vol. 1, St Bonaventure, NY: Franciscan Institute Publications, 2004, p. 477) for the definition of the word in this connection as the way in which one good is ordered towards the acquisition of a greater good, as in merit and recompense, where the good of the meritorious act is accepted as adequate for the conferral of the greater good.

and proportionately rewarded in such and such a way. But if we say that Jesus wins infinite merit, we effectively dissolve the whole concept of merit, since there must be some proportion between merit and reward, and infinite merit cannot be quantified and measured in any way that would make a reward fair.[14] But the problems do not stop there. The person of the Word as such cannot merit anything; the Word needs nothing and is never changed and certainly never 'rewarded'. So much is common ground with Aquinas and others. But Scotus argues that if we use language about the infinite worth of Christ's person then either we are ascribing the economy of merit and reward to the eternal Word, which all would agree is absurd, or we are assimilating the human soul and will of Jesus to the will of the eternal Word, which is heretical. It cannot be the case that the Holy Trinity loves the good will or good acts of the humanity of Jesus in exactly the same way and in exactly the same measure as it loves the eternal good will of the Word. The Trinity loves its own infinite goodness in virtue of its own eternal actuality; it cannot love any created phenomenon such as the human perfection of Jesus in the same way (as Scotus puts it,[15] the created cannot have the same *diligibilitas*, 'lovability', as the infinite). So the human soul and will of Jesus perform finite acts and those acts must be of finite worth. We can say loosely that they win an 'infinite' reward' in terms of obtaining grace and glory for those human beings who are predestined to salvation; they win a relation with the infinite goodness of God. But the meritorious action of Christ remains 'formally' finite; if we say that Christ's actions merit *pro infinitis*, 'for an unrestricted number', that is simply because God's eternal will and decision are what makes any finite action meritorious in any way, and God has determined that these acts will be 'acceptable' as sufficient to gain redemption for all (even if they are not *efficacious* for any except the predestined) because of the infinity of the person of the Word, whose acts they are. But they remain formally finite and thus finitely meritorious.[16]

---

14 Scotus, *Lectura in librum tertium Sententiarum* 19. un. A 2.13 (p. 29 in Vol. XXI of *B.Ioannis Duns Scoti ... Opera Omnia*, ed. Barnabas Hechich, OFM, et al., Vatican City, 2004): 'God does not accept anything unless it has a *quantum* of acceptability.'

15 Ibid., III.19 un. A 2a.13 (pp. 29–30).

16 Ibid., B 1.23 (pp. 33–4).

The difference between this and Aquinas's account is essentially that Scotus concentrates on the worth of the *acts* in question rather than the worthiness of the *agent*; as we have seen, Scotus holds that the ground of Christ's meritoriousness is God's prior will to *treat* his acts as meritorious. We can already see the beginnings of the kind of language used by William of Ockham in the fourteenth century, where the gulf has opened rather wider. Ockham wants to argue that God's power to bestow grace is always conditioned (as a result of his own divine choice, of course, in the ordering of the contingent universe) by the character of the subject receiving it, so that infinite grace cannot be given to a finite agent. Thus the incarnate Christ receives grace 'by measure', according to God's *potestas ordinata*, his power as it is displayed in relation to the specific conditions he has himself willed for the running of the universe.[17]

Where Aquinas gives priority to the character of the person doing the meriting, so to speak, Scotus's interest is in the specific actions, taken one by one, that are deemed by God to merit the reward of the human vision of himself – a discrete state of affairs within a finite human subject. The issues are prohibitively technical, but the central point of disagreement is whether the language of infinite merit can be used consistently. For Aquinas, infinite merit means that the acts of the Word incarnate, precisely because they are enacted by the Word, are unlimited in their capacity to make a difference to us and to open up the possibility of relating to God. As noted earlier, the capacity of the Word and therefore of Jesus to receive what God has to give is without limit, which is why it can overflow to all those associated with Jesus. This does not mean that the human *mode* of willing and acting is swallowed up in the divine, which is what Scotus suspects: the way in which Jesus thinks, decides and acts as a human individual is of course as a finite agent like all others, but the effect of those acts in disposing humanity afresh for communion with God is infinite, wholly unlike the effect of any finite act or transaction. From a Thomist point of view, Scotus's focus on the justice of particular rewards for particular meritorious actions might be seen as failing to see the wood for the trees.

17　William of Ockham, *Opera omnia* VI: *quaestiones in librum tertium Sententiarum* 1, ed. F. E. Kelley and G. I Etzkorn, New York: St Bonaventure, 1982, III.viii.ii, p. 262.

Scotus's argument is connected with some of his wider metaphysical positions, as several commentators have noted.[18] His fundamental unease with the strongly participatory cosmology of Aquinas and Aquinas's predecessors means that he is moving away from a model of reality in which *action* itself is a unifying intelligible structure that can be shared between different agents, and from the basic model of an infinite agency to which all finite and determinate action is related as wholly dependent. His metaphysics famously introduces a notion of *haecceitas*, sheer singleness, as that which differentiates one finite substance from another; and it also obscures the difference between finite and infinite being by its claim that in order to speak intelligibly about God we have to find some category under which God and creatures can both be subsumed as 'existing' – where Aquinas would have insisted that we could only give meaning to a word like 'existing' by referring it to the prior and infinite actuality of God as that which makes all being to be. Herein is the difference – as scholars of the subject usually put it – between Aquinas's view of being as *analogical*, a pattern of relatedness in which unqualified, wholly unrestricted free agency animates and conditions every variety of finite and particular agency by sharing its animating energy in differing degrees, and Scotus's *univocal* account, in which divine agency and finite agency, divine being and finite being, while still radically distinct and in most respects incomparable, may nonetheless be spoken of for certain purposes as variants of a single intelligible reality called being. In the light of these very fundamental features of Scotus's thought, his position on Christ's merits is readily intelligible. There is a sense for Scotus in which the sheer singularity of Christ's humanity has to be the 'terminus' of his acts in the world, and in that sense what he does is necessarily finite in merit and effect. Christ's existence as a human subject

18 Most recently, see Aaron Riches, *Ecce Homo: On the Divine Unity of Christ*, pp. 209–16: partly because of his insistence on the raw particularity, *haecceitas*, of individual substance, Scotus gives to the humanity of Jesus an 'ontological density' not directly constituted by its union with the one divine supposit (p. 210). Riches has very useful – and not unsympathetic – things to say also about the spiritual context of Scotus's work in connection with the Franciscan concern not to lose sight of the Word's embrace of real finitude, poverty, limit and so on (p. 211). It is worth noting, though, that Bonaventure agrees with Aquinas on the infinity of Christ's merit; his metaphysical starting point is still some way from that of Scotus.

is – to use what is admittedly a somewhat slanted description – a particular phenomenon distinct from the life of the eternal Word and thus not simply identical in action with that eternal Word. For Aquinas, the Word's infinite action is what is 'presupposed' in the actuality of this finite agency, as its foundational and formative principle, and it cannot therefore be thought of as an item alongside that finite agency; Scotus's position effectively denies that this model can work, insisting that the human individuality of Jesus must be seen as in some sense an agent with its own particularity, even given its unique dependence on its union with the Word. It is not – of course – that Scotus wants to dismantle the Chalcedonian settlement, and the accusation of 'Nestorianism' (teaching the existence of two full-fledged personal agencies in Christ) against him is unjust. But his metaphysic allows him to push as far as possible towards an affirmation of a human identity that is *in principle* separable from the life of the Word; and this implies that it is possible to ascribe to the acts of the finite individual that is the Word incarnate a distinct finite worth, sufficient to win for humanity the perfection God wills to give (no difference from Aquinas here), which is a condition enjoyed by finite subjects and so itself finite (a radical difference from Aquinas).

The effects of these shifts in the fine detail of Christological discourse are quite far-reaching. Paradoxically, although Scotus was among those who believed that the Incarnation would have happened even if Adam had not sinned (because the advent of divine presence in this form was a fitting culmination to the divinely purposed destiny of humanity), his Christology was a significant element in pushing theological argument to a point where the 'fitness' of human nature for receiving the incarnate Word was regarded as an irrelevance. As nominalism (the denial of any substantial reality other than individuals, so that terms of general reference were treated as no more than 'names', *nomina*) took an increasingly firm hold of the theology of the Franciscans in particular, it was harder to argue any kind of congruity or continuity between God and created agents. God's will and purpose were completely free and unconstrained by any created reality – and that must mean that God's decision to be incarnate could have nothing to do with any quality inherent in humanity. It was a pure act of will; consequently it could be said that in principle incarnation could happen in a donkey or a stone – a notorious formulation found in Ockham and often recycled in the fifteenth century and later (Calvin knows of it and deplores it).[19] Of course *as a matter of fact* the Incarnation takes place as it does in order to provide the means of grace and redemption; but we must not confuse what God in his inscrutable wisdom appoints as the means of our salvation with anything that is made possible by any kind of natural, predictable state of affairs within the world. A perfectly intelligible concern to safeguard divine freedom, and to avoid suggesting that God is in any way 'obliged' to become incarnate, led to a dramatic gulf being opened between finite and infinite in a way quite different from the way this distinction is understood by earlier writers, even by Scotus. The idea that the Incarnation takes place in order to allow humanity to be itself more fully could be said to be held in common by Aquinas and Scotus – Aquinas seeing it as the event that allows human agents to be incorporated into Christ's Mystical Body and so be able to receive grace which, because of sin, they could not receive before; Scotus more ambitiously seeing it as the crown of God's purpose for humanity. But the position advanced by Ockham makes the relation of the Incarnation to the natural end of humanity a more arbitrary one, and neither Scotus nor Ockham places the same stress as Aquinas or Augustine on the significance of Christ's Headship of the Mystical Body. The result is a somewhat thinned-out account of the relation between Christology and ecclesiology, and a doctrine of grace and merit more focused on the character of specific actions than on the continuous process of 'disposing' the created soul for union with the infinite.[20]

19 Ockham, *quaestiones* I.iii, ed. cit., pp. 33–4: humanity is not more fitted to receive the incarnate Word than a stone or a donkey because *indifferenter potest natura irrationalis sustentificari a persona divina sicut rationalis*, 'an irrational nature is just as capable of being sustained by a divine person as a rational one'; and see John Calvin, *Institutes of the Christian Religion*, Vol. 1, ed. John T. McNeill, trans. Ford Lewis Battles, London: SCM Press, 1960, II. 12.5, p. 470.

20 Late medieval thought was not monochrome in this respect: an adequate discussion of the period would have to take note of the brilliantly original cosmology and Christology of Nicholas of Cusa (1401–64), in which the themes of Maximus and other earlier writers are retrieved in a scheme that is a very long way indeed from the conceptual world of, say, Ockham. For Cusa, Christ is *universum concretum* and *maximum contractum* – the unifying energy and rationale of all things focused into a single finite reality. Human nature itself is already a microcosmic version of the rest of creation, destined to bring the creation to fulfilled significance and harmony; Christ fulfils

Martin Luther's radical reconstruction of Christology is a robust and uncompromising response to this.[21] He wholeheartedly denies the separability of humanity and divinity in the person of the incarnate, so that it becomes impossible to think in Scotist (let alone Ockhamist) terms of a human subject of action whose capacity is straightforwardly finite.[22] More particularly, as Scripture seems to tell us, the humanity of the Risen Christ, with its ability to pass through locked doors (John 20.19 and 24), is not confined by ordinary physical limitations, and this leads Luther to conclude that it is now fully united to the divine nature in such a way that it can be wherever God wants to be. 'Apart from this man there is no God', says Luther, provocatively[23] – a statement which, as we shall see in the next chapter, has a long and influential afterlife in Protestant theology; wherever God is, the human nature of Jesus will be found, 'naturally and personally', so that we can say that his humanity is now endowed with divine properties, including the capacity to be anywhere and everywhere. We are a good way from Scotist scruples about humanity receiving a finite reward for Jesus' merit; and Ockham's metaphysical objections to a divine gift

this human vocation and in so doing opens up creation to infinite grace. As the incarnation of the unifying eternal Logos, he is thus the foundation of all analogical talk about God in terms of creation. See especially Book 3 of Nicholas's *de docta ignorantia*, especially 2–4 and 7. Johannes Hoff, *The Analogical Turn: Rethinking Modernity with Nicholas of Cusa*, Grand Rapids, MI: Eerdmans, 2013, is a fine recent essay on Cusa; and the authoritative modern account of his Christology is R. Haubst, *Die Christologie des Nikolaus von Kues*, Freiburg: Herder, 1956.

21 There are not all that many recent general surveys of Luther's Christology. J. Siggins, *Martin Luther's Doctrine of Christ*, New Haven and London: Yale University Press, 1970, is one such; and more recently, see M. Arnold, 'Luther on Christ's Person and Work', in R. Kold, I. Dingel and L. Batka, eds, *The Oxford Handbook of Martin Luther's Theology*, Oxford: Oxford University Press, 2014. Luther's own (very lively) account of the Nestorian controversy is a good introduction; see *Luther's Works*, ed. Robert H. Fischer, Vol. 41, Philadelphia: Muhlenberg Press, 1966, pp. 93–109.

22 Thus in his summary of the pre-Chalcedonian controversies, he can write that it would have been possible and correct to say, 'There goes God down the street', during the days of Christ's incarnate life (LW 41, p. 101) and that it is theologically correct to say that 'the man Christ created the world and is almighty' (ibid., p. 103).

23 *Luther's Works*, Vol. 37, Philadelphia: Muhlenberg Press, 1961, pp. 218–19, from his 1528 *Confession Concerning Christ's Supper*.

that finite nature is incapable of receiving would have had little traction with a theologian as scornful of metaphysical fastidiousness as Luther. The glorified Christ, in Luther's theology, can exercise all three modes in which a substance may be present in the world – as taking up a determinate amount of space, as taking up a variable and unmeasurable amount of space, and as occupying all possible space. He can appear in his human nature anywhere; he can break the normal conventions of nature but still in bodily form (passing through locked doors, inhabiting the elements of the Eucharist); *and* he is omnipresent along with the divine Word.

It is a Christology at the opposite pole from that of the later scholastics like Ockham. Yet it is equally in tension with Aquinas's scheme, and with a great deal of earlier Christology. And, paradoxically, it can be said to share some of the problematic features of the theology against which it reacts. The analysis of the three different forms of presence is itself derived from Ockham, and, as Luther renders it, it risks reducing divine presence in the universe to a variant of physical presence, a matter of simple ubiquity: most substances are somewhere, some substances are in different places in different modes, one substance (God) is everywhere. 'Ubiquity', the belief that God's presence is not spatially limited, is here treated as if it were some sort of positive predicate, the ability to be in every place rather than in only one. But insofar as it can be called a distinctive doctrine in earlier theology, it is much more an aspect of the *denial* that spatiality is an appropriate category for speaking of God. There is a difference between unlimited spatial 'reach' and the denial of spatiality as a mode of divine presence, and it is this difference which Luther's approach obscures. T. F. Torrance famously argued[24] that this reflected a 'receptacle' model of space, at odds not only with modern scientific understanding but with the implication of patristic theology, which was concerned in this context not with the room taken up but with the relations established by agencies between themselves. The statement of the question in the way Luther inherits it from his late medieval predecessors once again tends towards seeing God's infinite life as an infinitely extended variety of finite life – thus creating the risk of seeing finite

24 As in *Space, Time and Incarnation*, London: Oxford University Press, 1969, Chapter 2; see also the posthumously published lectures, *Incarnation: The Person and Life of Christ*, ed. Robert T. Walker, Milton Keynes: Paternoster, 2008, pp. 216–21.

and infinite as within the same conceptual and even (in this case) literal space. The manner in which Luther's Christology handles divine attributes certainly poses serious conceptual problems, as the Lutheran scholastics of the next century were to demonstrate. The patristic notion of the 'communication of properties' between divine and human that is made possible by the Incarnation is in its origins a way of affirming that a single hypostatic agent is genuinely the subject of diverse and even contradictory predicates; because the Word is God and the humanity taken by the Word dies, we can truthfully say that 'God dies'. But this depends on admitting that the two natures through or in which different things are true of the Word remain unaltered by this relation. Without such a qualification, it becomes unclear what sort of solidarity Christ has both with the divine life and with actual finite human nature. Luther was not exactly a monophysite, as a Byzantine theological controversialist might have understood the word: he did not believe that divinity and humanity were merged in a new 'mixed' essence as a result of the Incarnation. But he does seem to have thought that both divinity and humanity *as natures* were in some sense altered through the union, in such a way that Christ's human nature is genuinely endowed with new *natural* properties.

Luther is notoriously hard to pin down on this matter, and his chief polemical concern is, of course, with the defence of a real (physical) presence in the Eucharist. But this concern undeniably led him into a Christological scheme that was just as much distanced from a theology of the Mystical Body as was Ockham's. Aquinas's account of how Christ merits salvation in effect says something like this: Christ's human life is such that it exhibits all the conditions for an unrestricted access to human beatitude in the shape of the vision of God the Father and participation in the life of the Trinity; but the Word who is the subject of this human life is always already in possession of these things. By the connection made by the Spirit between Christ's humanity and ours, possible because (as we have seen in earlier discussions) Christ's humanity is free from the limitations of relationship that sin imposes, we are made to be inseparable from him, and so able to receive what he 'merits' but does not need – that is to say, what God gives him as a human individual who is in no way impeded in his communion with the Father is given to us. And what is thus given is the entirety of the relational bond which is given eternally by the Father to the Word – the gift of being the Father's child, which never begins or ends for the Word as such but is realized moment by moment in the course of the Word's incarnate life, and made available to us because we share the same humanity as the incarnate one. If we introduce any uncertainty about the eternal gift that is the begetting of the Word, or about the identity of our humanity with Christ's, this structure gives way, and the relations between what is said about Christ and what is said about the Church become more obviously external or arbitrary. Luther's critics in the sixteenth century were concerned that his Christology (and his Eucharistic theology) compromised both the divine and the human in Christ in such a way that the infinite was reduced and the finite dissolved. In terms of the framework we have been utilizing in this book, the risk in Luther's approach is that we are offered a sort of resolution of the finite/ infinite tension as if the two terms simply needed to be glued together; the idea that a finite reality could be (without losing its integrity) the medium for infinite agency is seriously weakened, and the effect is (in a way counter to so much of what Luther wanted to affirm theologically) an undermining of the theological importance of finite and material reality as such. Luther had begun by rejecting what he – understandably – saw as a dangerously mechanistic picture of grace and holiness, but his remedy had produced fresh and complex issues, and had done little to clarify the challenge of thinking through how the integrity of the created order was affirmed by the Incarnation.

And it is against this background that John Calvin's Christology steers us back towards a Thomist and Cyrilline hinterland – even, it is tempting to say, a Maximian one, though in common with all his Western contemporaries, Calvin does not know Maximus's work. He is not – of course – deliberately seeking to revive Aquinas's Christology, which was also almost certainly unknown to him at first hand (he never quotes Aquinas directly). But the fascination of his discussion of this topic is that, in seeking to do justice to the full complexity of the patristic heritage (which he *is* undoubtedly seeking to do), he finds himself aligned with Thomas in a number of important ways. Where Luther, with admirable intentions, furthers the dissolution of the classical synthesis emerging in Aquinas, Calvin rather unexpectedly retrieves it, defends it, and adds some significant new insights.

2. The Catholic Calvin: A Theological Tradition Renewed

Calvin's idiom is deliberately non-scholastic, but he is aware of scholastic argumentation and willing on occasion to appeal to it. As David Willis demonstrated in his celebrated and still useful monograph on Calvin's Christology,[25] the reformer takes up enthusiastically Peter Lombard's distinction – originating in John of Damascus – between *totus* and *totum* in Christ: the whole Christ, the one person of the eternal Word (*totus*), is everywhere present and active, but the whole ensemble of natural properties which constitute him as incarnate (*totum*) is not. But the continuities extend a good deal further. Calvin begins his major systematic discussion of Christology, which is to be found in the second book of the *Institutes*,[26] with a clear statement (II.12.1) of the need for a mediating principle by which creatures endowed with intelligence and will may come to be fully united with God their Creator. Both angels and human beings need a 'head', 'through whose bond they might cleave firmly and undividedly to their God'. The form of that adherence is adoptive filiation (angels as well as human beings are called 'children of God', II.12.6), and so it is appropriate that the eternal Son is the agent in and through whom we arrive at this state. In this sense, we can talk of a Body of which Christ is the Head that is not simply the Body of Christ as we know it on earth. If Adam had never fallen from his first innocence, it would have been possible for human beings to participate in the Son's eternal life ('by his divine power ... by the secret power of his Spirit', II.12.7) as the angels do, as part of this cosmic 'Body'. In other words, Christ's status as 'Head of the Body', as the agency by which intelligent and free creatures are brought into the Trinitarian life and united to the Father, does not depend on the Incarnation. Calvin

---

25 *Calvin's Catholic Christology: The Function of the So-Called Extra Calvinisticum in Calvin's Theology*, Leiden: Brill, 1966, pp. 31–44. For a more recent treatment of the subject, focusing far more closely on Calvin's developing exegetical scheme, see Stephen Edmondson, *Calvin's Christology*, Cambridge: Cambridge University Press, 2004; pp. 210–15 on the *extra calvinisticum*. The discussion in the present chapter is restricted to Calvin's *Institutes* as the most systematic exposition of his Christology, but Edmondson is indispensable in showing its affiliations and consistent echoes in Calvin's exegesis.

26 All references to the McNeill and Battles translation (above, n. 19).

argues fiercely against the Lutheran Osiander on this point.[27] Osiander has defended a version of the Scotist view that the Incarnation is a foreordained implication of Adam's creation in the divine image, so that it would have occurred whether or not Adam sinned. But Calvin is clear that Scripture gives no ground for such a supposition; it is just as 'frivolous' as the notorious late medieval counterfactual which illustrated God's absolute liberty, the idea that it would be possible for God to be incarnate in an ass (II.12.5). Osiander wants to insist that human beings are made after the eternal image of a Christ who is already 'proleptically' incarnate, so to speak; Christ's status as our Lord and King would on this account be inseparable from his eternal modelling of our human condition. Calvin in response argues (II.12.7) that, since Adam is created in the divine image, he is a being whose 'head' is always already Christ as the second Person of the Trinity: it makes no sense to suppose that Christ's Headship in any sense depends upon some kind of natural solidarity with Adam. Christ, after all, is head of all creatures, and so his Headship cannot be in any sense a product of his sharing the nature of all of them as he shares human nature in the Incarnation. Christ's Headship over the angels certainly does not require or depend on his incarnation as a human being (as Calvin understands Osiander to be saying).

The reason for underlining here this concern with Christ's Headship over angels as well as humanity, and with the link between incarnation and the redemption of humanity from Adam's sin, is that both of these echo Aquinas in a couple of very significant respects. Aquinas, like Calvin, understands angels and human beings as equally created for the enjoyment of God's glory and equally members of a cosmic 'Body' which receives grace from the fullness of Christ's possession of the gifts that flow from the Father;[28] and he too repudiates any suggestion that the Incarnation is anything other than the mode by which Christ's Headship over humanity is reasserted or re-grounded in the wake of Adam's sin.[29] It would certainly have been *possible* for God to bring about the Incarnation whether or not Adam had

---

27 Osiander advanced the idea in a 1550 treatise on the incarnation; see McNeill and Battles, p. 467, n. 3. It did not help that the position was also defended by Servetus, one of Calvin's most bitter opponents.

28 ST III.viii.4.

29 Ibid. III.1.3.

sinned, but all we know from Scripture is that 'the Son of Man came to seek and to save the lost' (Luke 19.10). Aquinas is already dealing with some of the arguments Calvin rebuts in his comments on Osiander, and the convergence is striking. But perhaps one particular point is worth stressing here. One of the arguments Aquinas has to answer is the claim that the infinite power of God must of its nature have an infinite effect. No finite being in itself can be an 'infinite effect', so the only way in which an infinite effect can appear in creation is by the overcoming of an infinite gulf or distance between God and the creature. Such an effect would be the uniting of the *ultima creatura*, humanity, the final point or stage of the created order, with the *primum principium*, which is God, so that the Incarnation is a natural consequence of the very infinity of God in respect of creation. Thomas's reply is that the perfection of the created order lies in its natural orientation towards God as its goal and rationale; infinite power appears in the created universe *in the bare fact of the universe's being created*, not in some process of introducing the infinite into the finite. The finite is what it is by nature, and so the form of union with the infinite that is appropriate will be through person, not nature.[30] That is to say: the infinite cannot be introduced into the finite order with the purpose of making the finite order what it is, completing or complementing natural finitude: it cannot be a 'required' element among others in the definition of finite substance. Union between finite and infinite can only be a relation, not a natural fusion; hence the significance of the *person* here. Thus the Incarnation is not some kind of fulfilment of a natural capacity, nor is it the result of a logical necessity built in to the nature of infinitude. It is the bringing into being of a specific and unique relatedness between finite and infinite agency. It is, as we might want to put it, an historical moment within the narrative of human agency, not the outworking of a natural process. And Aquinas's arguments on this converge with Calvin's concern to make it clear that Adam could have been perfect in his humanity without any reference to an *incarnate* Christ – though emphatically not without reference to the mediation of the eternal Son of God. The substantive point, in relation to the theme of this book, is that both theologians recognize the risk of subverting the integrity of finite reality by speculating that it would need a certain kind of fusion with the infinite in order to be

30 III.1.3 ad 2.

itself. It is perfectly true that humanity can be human only in relation to Christ – as all finite reality is itself only in virtue of its relation to the one who is creation's 'head' and first principle. It is *not* true that humanity can be human (can realize the Creator's purpose for humanity) only if there is a guarantee of union between divine and human nature. Both the divine and the human are compromised if this is the case. We can quite properly say that creation becomes itself by way of a radical expansion of *what is possible in relation to the infinite* as the result of the union of finite and infinite in the one person of the Word. But this is different from the claim that the presence of the infinite as a crowning element in the created order is needful for creation to fulfil its purpose.

Thus Calvin's opening arguments in the Christological section of the *Institutes* work at the same issues that preoccupied the earlier writers we have examined. What differentiates his treatment from these earlier discussions is primarily his emphasis on how the Incarnation is required to satisfy divine justice, that is, to rectify in a very specific way the failure of humanity to be itself. The Word becomes human so as 'to impart to us what was his, and to make what was his by nature ours by grace' (II.12.2), a classically patristic formulation; but a more detailed exposition of this makes it clear that the Incarnation is the requisite means for this because our fallen nature must 'pay the price of sin'. God alone can overcome death; humanity alone can offer exemplary obedience to God and suffer for sin (II.12.3). The possibility of adoptive union with God that was blocked by Adam's sin is restored by an act of human obedience, an act that is initiated from the most powerless and humiliated human location imaginable. Because of his complete human obedience there is in Christ no obstacle to the outpouring of the Spirit; but because the person of the Word has no need of any augmentation of the gift of the Spirit and needs nothing for himself, all that is given to Jesus spills over into us as members of his Body (II.13.1). 'He received anointing, not only for himself that he might carry out the office of teaching, but for his whole body that the power of the Spirit might be present in the continuing preaching of the gospel' (II.15.2), and this holds true for all the gifts of the Spirit given to Christ's humanity. The Spirit is always given to the incarnate Christ *so that* all believers may 'from his fullness ... receive grace upon grace' (John 1.16) (II.15.5). Once again, there is a presumably unconscious echo of Aquinas, though with differences in nuance: for Thomas, Christ as Head merits salvation for himself and us, but does not need what he merits for himself and so becomes the conduit of unlimited grace to the members of his Body.[31] It is true that Calvin, when he turns to the question of merit later in his Christological treatise (II.17), dismisses the scholastic doctrine that Christ could merit anything at all for himself (i.e., as for Lombard and Aquinas, that he could merit the exaltation of his mortal body) as the product of 'stupid curiosity' (II.17.6). But what is significant is that both theologians see the importance of the Incarnation in its being the means whereby humanity recovers its lost dignity and its capacity for filial adoption into the divine life, and that this is understood in connection with Christ's freedom to transfer to us the gifts given him by the Father. Calvin stoutly defends against critics in his own day the propriety of using the language of 'merit' for the process of redemption: Christ '[by] his obedience ... truly acquired and merited grace for us with his Father' (II.17.3), and it is a moot point whether he really disagrees as much as he thinks he does with his scholastic precursors. As noted in the first part of this chapter, when Thomas speaks about the merit and the grace of Christ, he is speaking about the fact that Christ's incarnate actions are genuinely finite actions that dispose his human identity to receive all that the Father can give to a created being: Christ's created soul is closer than any other creature to the source of grace and so is uniquely receptive to that grace.[32] What Calvin really objects to is any suggestion that Christ acquires something *new* (II.17.6). But what Aquinas is claiming is simply that, formally speaking, it is the realized goodness that characterizes Christ's soul that makes possible the unrestricted inflow of divine grace. These are in fact simultaneous realities, not a process in which the eternal Person changes; there is never a moment when there is an obstacle in this finite identity to the action of infinite gift.

But Calvin also wants to make an exegetical point in this discussion. Scripture attributes to God in Christ a wholly selfless love, which can have nothing to do with any 'advantage' to the person of the Son: God gives up the Son to suffering solely out of love for the world. So, 'we conclude that he had no regard for himself: as he clearly affirms, "For their sake I sanctify

31 E.g., ST III.vii.9, viii.5, xlviii.1.
32 ST III.vii.9c.

myself'" (John 17.19) (II.17.6). 'Christ in a way forgot himself' (ibid.). This reflects a consistent theme of Calvin's Christological thought, in which strong emphasis is laid upon Christ's willingness to identify himself with 'a lowly and despised man' (II.13.2), and indeed with one who 'took the role of a guilty man and evildoer' (II.16.5). His fuller account of this in II.16 explores how Christ's entire renunciation of his own human security and well-being must extend to his reputation: he dies not only a human death but a contemptible, humiliating public death, an accursed death (II.16.5–6). He identifies himself with the damned in hell, allowing himself to experience the full sense of abandonment by God (II.16.11), so that he shares the worst of the human condition in spirit as well as body (II.16.12). Calvin is crystal-clear that Christ's cry of dereliction on the cross expresses nothing less than the condition and experience of the lost, experiencing God (in a chilling phrase) 'as if he [God] himself had plotted your ruin' (II.16.11). Jesus does not simply fear death as the destruction of the body, but fears this experience of 'God's curse', in 'unbelievable bitterness of heart' (II.16.12); only so can he be the redeemer of souls as well as bodies, by entering fully into the condition of humanity (ibid.). Calvin is equally clear that this recognition of the authentically human terror Jesus experiences in relation to the wrath of God or God's abandonment of him entails the definitive rejection of Monothelitism – i.e. it requires us to acknowledge the distinction of the 'will' that belongs to the human nature from the 'will' that belongs to the divine nature (ibid.). And, although he does not draw this out fully explicitly, it is the association of will and nature here that allows him to argue that Jesus felt, without any modification or consolation, the pains of the abandoned – and yet was in no way culpable: his *person* remains 'pure and free of all vice and stain' (ibid.), while his actual psycho-physical organism feels what such organisms feel in the face of extreme threat, internal and external. 'There is no reason why Christ's weakness should alarm us' (ibid.). The free embrace of the human condition in its most extreme wretchedness and pain is what underpins the narrative of this vulnerable life and humiliating death: the personal assumption of humanity is what makes possible the expression of the extreme emotions that Jesus voices in Gethsemane and on the cross. Calvin's emphasis on Christ's experience of literally hellish terror goes beyond what most patristic texts directly consider (though he can find some relevant quotations in Hilary and Ambrose), but there can be no doubt that his discussion of these questions is in the most direct continuity with the concerns of the Byzantine Christological tradition. The divine agency that is the eternal Word freely consents to speak in, as, and through the humanity of Jesus in all its aspects, and in so doing, to speak out of the depths of human dereliction – that is, the dereliction that belongs to the human condition in general, uniquely accentuated in the case of Jesus precisely because of his union with the Father, so that the *sense* of abandonment is uniquely intense and terrible. But the intensity of the suffering – the extreme case of a kind of suffering that belongs to the degraded state of human nature[33] – exists only because of the decision of the eternal Word to be our redeemer and to redeem through solidarity with us in our condemned state, to bear God's curse on our behalf. Calvin's distinctive emphasis in his doctrine of the atonement is what gives his version of the classical Christological model its unprecedentedly sombre colouring.

Yet the structure of the overall Christological argument is thoroughly familiar. We are saved because Christ exchanges what is his for what is ours, making 'what was his by nature ours by grace' (II.12.2); what is given in the Incarnation is – as for Aquinas – the maximal dignity that a human creature can receive, which is to become an adoptive child of God. And through Christ's identification with us, all that is given him by the Father in his incarnate life as human becomes ours (II.13.1). As noted already, Calvin, like Aquinas, sees the unlimited grace conveyed to the human individuality of Jesus overflowing to us, since Jesus does not claim or need any such grace for his own advancement in God's favour. His sonship cannot be augmented by grace; if the Spirit is given to him without measure – so Calvin interprets John 1.16 – then this is not for Christ's sake but for ours; hence, as we have already noted, Jesus' words in John 17.19, 'For their sakes I sanctify myself'(II.13.1, 17.6). In the background is Calvin's usual strictly Chalcedonian framework: the eternal person of the Word cannot receive grace or be sanctified, but the human nature that is assumed can be such a recipient. In line with the post-Chalcedonian clarification about what may be predicated of the composite hypostasis of the incarnate Word, we can say that Christ as incarnate receives grace, formally speaking; but since that

---

33 Although (see II.13.4) Scripture makes it plain that Christ is sanctified by the Spirit in his human nature in such a way that it is always to be described as 'pure'.

grace cannot alter his condition as a person in divine communion or even as a human individual living out God's purpose for humanity, it is all 'available' for the sanctification of the whole Body of those who are united with him not only by sharing a single nature but by the work of the Holy Spirit uniting believers with the *person* of the incarnate.

This set of assumptions about the 'composite hypostasis' model of Christ is spelled out further in II.14.1 and 2, where Calvin utilizes the popular patristic and medieval analogy with the body–soul compound that constitutes a human being, and, in the Latin text of the *Institutes*, specifically describes Christ as *persona composita* (II.14.1). 'The passages that comprehend both natures at once ... set forth his true substance most clearly of all', according to II.14.3, in that scriptural texts which describe the personal agency of Christ (especially texts from the Fourth Gospel) are texts about *what God does as human*: they are about neither divinity nor humanity in general, but about the unique embodied act that is the life of the saviour on earth. And since this is the effect of the eternal divine agency that is the Word, these 'mixed' statements offer the fullest account of who and what Christ is as the God who has chosen to be with and for us. But Calvin moves on in this same section (II.14.3) to one of his more idiosyncratic readings of Scripture (recapitulated later in II.15.5), arguing for a very distinctive application of the composite hypostasis thesis to the theme of Christ's kingship. God gives the incarnate Christ power or kingship up to and including the final judgement, when the elect become 'partakers of the heavenly glory' without mediation and Christ (as Paul says in 1 Cor. 15) hands over the kingship he has been given over human beings, the name above all names that he has won among us in the conditions of humiliation and death (Phil. 2). There remains only the *eternal* kingship that is proper to the divine nature; and redeemed human beings will relate to God in a way that no longer requires the mediation or Headship of Christ *as incarnate*. In the light of the earlier discussion about Christ's Headship of the angels, we should presumably conclude that this means that Christ now exercises that governance or direction of our filial communion with God that is eternally true for all intelligent creatures (cf. II.14.5: 'To neither angels nor men was God ever Father, except with regard to his only-begotten Son'), rather than the specific mediation associated with the Incarnation and the cross. But he also says that in this last state, 'God shall cease to be the Head of Christ', a very eccentric proposition at first sight. Giving this a charitable interpretation in the light of other passages, this must mean something like the idea that a certain kind of provisional or even 'tactical' subordination of Christ to the Father, which is inseparable from the historical dispensation of the Incarnation, is ultimately done away with.

But it remains a somewhat strained and puzzling argument. Its point is presumably to underline that what is said about Christ in Scripture has to be read carefully according to context, so that we do not make groundless deductions about the eternal Word on the basis of statements concerning the composite *persona* or *esse* – and this is pretty much what Calvin goes on to underline in the next section of his argument in the *Institutes*. Thinking about the 'constitution' of Christ as incarnate has to be, for Calvin, a matter of systematically keeping in focus what the Incarnation is *for*: it is to rectify the massive damage done to human nature by sin, and this rectification demands an unqualified commitment to the reality of Christ's humanity, and the consequential belief that this is a genuine object of divine grace. Without an integral human individuality, there would be no possibility of the Word bearing the consequence in human existence of human sinfulness, no possibility of his descent into the hell of abandonment where God appears as an enemy. Christ as human is as much a son to the eternal Father as is the Word in Heaven ('he possesses by nature what we receive as a gift', II.14.6); but that earthly sonship is uncovered, matured in its exercise, actualized in the midst of human sin and chaos, in such a way that it establishes that 'bond of brotherhood' (II.14.7) with the redeemed through which we come to share Christ's relation with the Father. Even before he could 'merit' anything as a human, he is in possession of his eternal sonship (Calvin quotes Augustine to this effect); but it is the fleshing out of this in the history of the incarnate life, above all in Jesus' atoning death, that makes this transformative for us. Christ's anointing as prophet, priest and king (II.15) shows how the gifts bestowed on him in this history become by the Spirit's agency the gifts given to Christ's Body (e.g., II.15.2); even the raising of Christ from the dead is a gift that secures connection with the members of the Body (II.15.3). His royal power is manifest in a resurrection that binds him for ever to his Church – even though, as we have seen, there is an end to his reign over and protection of the Church when he resigns his strictly mediatorial office – or, perhaps better, his mediatorial office as *redeemer*

(II.15.5), given that he retains his status as 'cosmological' mediator for all creation.

As Calvin has insisted already, the point of the Incarnation is that Christ should be able to act as a human being condemned to suffering for sin. The argument moves on, with Calvin dealing summarily (II.16.2) with those who are worried by the contradiction between the demand for punishment and God's prior and eternal love for creation. Of course Christ is incarnate because of the unswerving commitment of divine love (once again, Augustine is quoted in support of the argument that God does not love us because of the death of Christ but reconciles us in Christ because he loves us and has purposed to make us his children even before we are created); but we need to be made aware of the depth of the evil consequences of our sinfulness if we are truly to become aware of the depth of mercy. Language about God's wrath and curse is 'accommodated to our capacity' (II.16.2) – a notable corrective to the conventional textbook view of Calvin's ideas about divine wrath. But it is nonetheless true in the sense that we as we are in our sinful state cannot live in the presence of God: this sinful state must be shown to be utterly condemned and repudiated by God if we are to be in communion with him, and this is what Christ achieves by taking on the role of a condemned criminal. The Augustinian language that we have already discussed of Christ 'sustaining a *persona*' is developed in 16.5, which argues that Jesus needed to be condemned by process of law so that he could share with us the status of being a 'criminal'; despite his own personal innocence, he fully identifies with a humanity that is guilty. It is an aspect of his sacrifice in respect of his own feeling and natural will; Calvin echoes the classical consensus that the will that Jesus surrenders to the Father in Gethsemane is the 'natural' will of his human nature. And it is at this point that Calvin introduces his novel perspective on Christ as sharing the pains of the condemned, already summarized, and his appeal to the tradition of the two wills corresponding to the two natures.

The final stage of Calvin's exposition (II.2.17) deals explicitly with the question of merit, with which we began this discussion. He begins by defending the use of the word, despite its critics among the Reformed: he agrees (citing Augustine once again) that we cannot treat Christ's status as a reward for good behaviour, and that the cause of our redemption did not lie in a finite set of decisions but in God's predestining will. But as the work of redemption is actually carried through, it would be right to say that our liberation from sin is the effect – and the *just* effect – of the life and sacrificial death of Jesus. Justice is satisfied by Christ's death, and so we can say that redemption is a 'merited' result of it. It is, says Calvin (II.17.6), pointless to ask whether Christ merited for himself; he dismisses 'Lombard and the Schoolmen' in their discussion of this, though his further account in fact ranges him with Aquinas in its denial that anything could accrue as of merit to the eternal person of the Word. He is more blunt and radical, though, in insisting that Christ acquires *nothing* for himself: he 'forgets himself' (ibid.) and acts solely for our sake. If we are to use the vocabulary of merit, we can properly say that certain things are apt and just consequences of what happens in the life and death of Jesus: Paul's 'wherefore' in Philippians 2 simply states such a consequence, for our encouragement, rather than setting out a causal process originating in the finite action of the human Jesus (once again, the echo of Aquinas in this reading of Philippians is worth noting).

The Christological doctrine with which Calvin's name is most lastingly associated, that of the *extra calvinisticum*, is not in fact very much to the fore in any explicit way in the *Institutes* text, but it is not too difficult to see how and why it fits with the overall argument. The essential content of the doctrine is that there can be no simple substantive identity between divinity and embodied humanity; the unity that we affirm is a unity of action and of person. Lutheran critics of Calvin and more especially of Calvin's followers in the Eucharistic debates of the later sixteenth century presented the Calvinist Christology as positing a reality for the divine Word 'outside', *extra*, the humanity, such that a 'substantial' presence of Christ's humanity in the Eucharist could not be affirmed in the way Lutherans had always argued – on the basis that the glorification of Christ's humanity entailed the communication to that humanity of divine properties such as omnipresence, so that the incarnate actuality of Christ could be truly present in the sacramental elements. But the Calvinist point is that there is no sense in which the embodied humanity can *exhaust* the single divine agency of the Word; if we try to make Christ's human nature omnipresent, as if the action of the Word cannot be real without the local and material presence of his humanity, we are making a category mistake, whose implication would be that the divine action depended on the presence of the humanity. But Scripture makes it clear that the ascension of Christ to Heaven is the occasion for the manifestation of a kind of kingly rule and a kind of transforming power which would be impossible if he were restricted to what his humanity could effect in its necessarily local and finite reality. In II.16.14, Calvin deploys both the language of the Fourth Gospel and the arguments of Augustine to make the point: it is expedient for the apostles, and so for the Church, that Christ's 'humble abode of flesh' should depart from this world (John 16.7), enabling both the heavenly kingship of Christ and the full outpouring of the Spirit.

The *extra* functions not simply to distinguish the divinity from the humanity or to honour the principle that *finitum non capax infiniti*, 'the finite is not capable of the infinite';[34] it is a way of clarifying two focal issues for Christology. First, to put it rather crudely, it identifies what it is that the humanity has to *do* in the Incarnation: the Word becomes flesh so that human nature may be restored to its proper and 'natural' relation with the eternal Father through the eternal Son; and this restoration requires the Word to live through the full penalty of sin, in the dereliction of death and the terror of alienation from God. God the Word, out of free and unconstrained love, takes on himself the condition of a devastated humanity that has ruined its own nature; by voluntarily accepting this, as God and as a human agent, Christ overcomes the alienation between God and humanity, abolishes the distance between sinful humanity and divine life, refuses to accept the human decision to rebel against God, and so releases the love of God in the midst of fallen human existence. To say that divine justice is thereby satisfied is not – as is very clear in *Institutes* II.16.2–5 – to appeal to a mechanistic theory of substitution, but to affirm that the plain incompatibility between divine life and human sin or self-regard is taken away by what the Word Incarnate does. This is 'just' in that it does not require God to do less than justice to what he actually is or to pretend that we are not what we are. Without the divine act of eternal and unchanging love, this would make no sense; without the human reality of the terrible suffering of Christ in his absolute identification with our condition it would not touch us at the point of our deepest need. Christ's wholly selfless obedience has created in this world a form of humanity that is capable of the union with the Father

34 Willis, op. cit., is helpful on this point.

that was always God's purpose; by our association with him in the Spirit and in the life of the Body of Christ on earth, we too become capable of this. So it is essential, in Calvin's eyes, to maintain the first of these principles with total clarity, so that the hypostatic union is seen as what God does in order to redeem – not as any kind of quasi-natural process, not as the final term of any trajectory within created reality, and not as a fusion of natures. Through the Incarnation, humanity becomes *human* in the way God always intended – which is indeed to become united with the divine nature by adoptive filiation; it does not become divine in the sense of acquiring the properties that make the divine nature what it is.

The second focal issue is that for us to be truly incorporated into Christ requires that our relation to Christ should be both through his glorified humanity *and* through the agency of the Spirit. David Willis stresses[35] that Calvin's constant reference to the Spirit in his Christology is one of its distinctive features: 'it makes Pneumatology integral to Christology,'[36] insisting that the Word is never active without the Spirit and that the humanity of Jesus on earth is animated and activated by the Spirit's presence. Further, in his reflection (II.16.14) on the Johannine theme of the physical absence of Jesus as compensated by the presence of the Paraclete (John 16), Calvin is clear that the kingly authority of Christ after his ascension can become *universal* in its effect only through the work of the Spirit: his bodily identity as we have known it is bound up with the particularities of his time and place, and it is precisely this particular humanity that is taken into Heaven at the Ascension. Simply *as human*, the incarnate Word cannot be universally reigning, acting to transfigure and sanctify men and women everywhere: it is by the gift of the Spirit that he can fulfil his promise to be always with us, since the Spirit directly gives us the grace we need and forms the likeness of Christ in us as adopted sons and daughters. The Spirit is what *connects* us with the ascended humanity that has brought about our salvation and restored our human capacity to be God's children; the Spirit realizes in us what the Incarnation has made possible. Christ's active Headship of and life in the Church depends upon the Spirit's presence and mediation, giving

35 Ibid., pp. 82ff.
36 Ibid., p. 83.

believers the assurance they need in order to 'live blessedly but also to die happily' (ibid.). The ascended and glorified humanity is the source or, perhaps better, the 'occasion' for the outpouring of the Spirit; if the glorified humanity itself were the direct agent of Christ's present rule and grace and active presence, there would be no obvious rationale for the Spirit's work as making this rule and grace and presence effective in the world, making the connection between ourselves and the perfected incarnate life ascended in Heaven, and Calvin proceeds immediately in the *Institutes* (III.1) to enlarge on the role of the Spirit both in and through the incarnate life of Christ. As Julie Canlis puts it in her brilliant and innovative book on Calvin's spiritual teaching, 'With the sending of the Spirit at Pentecost, this man's history was made ours for participation ... It is the Spirit who brings us into a God-saturated life through his engrafting us into the human, ascended Christ who is in the presence of the Father.'[37]

Thus the *extra* becomes the cornerstone of a full-blooded Trinitarian theology, just as it has been shown to be the cornerstone of an adequate theology of the atonement. It spells out what Christ's humanity does and does not do: the human individuality of Jesus guarantees the healing of sin and the reversal of its consequences in the human world, and it releases the full agency of the Spirit as the divine agency conforming us to Christ. What it does *not* do is to reveal some principle internal to creation that secures its elevation to divine status or to act as some sort of universalized force in the world, separated from its identity-giving specificity in Jesus of Nazareth. Calvin's purpose in arguing for the ongoing finite reality of Jesus' humanity – as against the Lutheran belief that this humanity is directly endowed with divine attributes – is entirely in alignment with the overall way in which he retrieves themes from medieval and patristic Christology in affirming the fullness of creative and created action together in Christ without competition. The incarnate humanity can never be identical in its predicates with the divinity; it can only be the place in the finite world where relation with divine action is unimpeded. And so, when it ceases to be simply a phenomenon in our world (when it ascends into Heaven, whatever exactly we might mean by that), we do not need to suppose that it is

---

37 Julie Canlis, *Calvin's Ladder: A Spiritual Theology of Ascent and Ascension*, Grand Rapids, MI: Eerdmans, 2010, pp. 114–15.

then changed in its essential qualities. It is still, and eternally, a finite reality suffused with infinite agency; an *historical* reality with which we must now be united by that distinct divine agency that is the Spirit, so that what was and is true of Jesus' humanity may in appropriate measure be true of ours. What is fresh and distinctive in Calvin, as Canlis admirably brings out,[38] is the Trinitarian dynamic of the entire picture, with its unusually vivid emphasis on the Spirit's work in the incarnate life itself. And, to return to the point with which we began this discussion of Calvin, the centrality of the theme of Christ's Headship allows Calvin to develop a theology of Christ's radical self-dispossession which lays the foundation for a good many later developments: if Christ is indeed Head of angels and human beings, and thus – as an eternal Person – needs nothing to bring him into relation with the Father beyond the eternal energy of the Spirit, then what he 'achieves' in his incarnate life is wholly and unreservedly offered to us. 'He who gave away the fruit of his holiness to others testifies that he acquired nothing for himself' (*Institutes* II.17.6). We are seeing the first stirrings of a theology of divine self-emptying, *kenōsis*, that is emphatically about spiritual and ethical issues rather than awkward metaphysical adjustments; and in the next chapter we shall be tracing some of the ways in which this theme emerges in the development of kenotic theologies of incarnation, and how the twentieth-century discussion has, in effect, led back to some of the perspectives of Calvin (and to some extent of Aquinas, for the reasons outlined in the present chapter).

3. A New Diversity: The Varieties of Protestant Christology

So Calvin's Christology retrieves a good many of the themes of Byzantine and earlier medieval approaches, studiously avoiding what he and his followers see as a damaging over-reaction to late medieval developments on the part of Luther. Granted that Calvin emphasizes Christ's bearing of our punishment for sin in a way and to a degree unfamiliar in earlier theology, his Christology is, as the title of Willis's monograph on the subject claims, unmistakeably 'Catholic'. His Christ is a 'composite' reality to which eternal and temporal predicates can be truly ascribed, but whose

38 Ibid., Chapter 3.

identity is grounded in a single eternal act of being, a single divine *esse*, though he does not use this language. This single composite hypostasis involves the animation and individuation of a complete human individuality, for which no human experience is 'off-limits', including, crucially, the experience of dereliction and abandonment by God – a development in a rather different idiom of some of Augustine's insights about how the divine Word 'takes ownership' of the depth of human suffering and rebellion by 'taking the role', *personam agens*, of fallen humanity. From first to last, Calvin's discussion is pervaded by the conviction that it is only by beginning from the eternal Word's role as the 'Head' of rational creatures, the eternal form of life which makes possible the communion of created minds with the Creator, that we can make anything like adequate sense of the work of the incarnate Christ. To put it far too simply: where Luther seems to envisage an incarnate Christ whose glorified state 'expands' to fill the universe so that no human creature is now remote from his reality, Calvin begins from a universally present and active Logos, in perfect communion with the Father, whose relation with the human individuality of Jesus is the means by which humanity is freed to step into the place always already prepared for it in God's loving purpose.

As we shall see in more detail in the next chapter, the tension between the two approaches persists and becomes ever more complex in the history of Protestant theology up to the present time. With the fading away of 'Lutheran scholasticism' by the mid-nineteenth century, the Lutheran impatience with metaphysics generated two very different theological legacies. The tradition associated with Albrecht Ritschl and Adolf von Harnack stepped back entirely from any aspiration to doctrinal precision, regarding the language of classical dogma as representing a new Babylonian captivity, the enslavement of Christian discourse to a particular kind of philosophical idiom. But, with the revival of Luther studies in the early twentieth century, another and very different strand develops, associated with names such as Hans Iwand and Walther von Loewenich. For theologians like these, the essential theological insight of Luther in this context is to do with the direct involvement of God's eternal being with the cross of Jesus: traditional qualms about compromising divine impassibility simply reflect philosophical scruples which stand in the way of proclaiming the heart of the gospel. In more recent theology, this approach has found eloquent and sustained defence in the thought of Jürgen Moltmann[39] – though his confessional background is Reformed rather than Lutheran – and Eberhard Jüngel[40] in Germany, and Robert W. Jenson, the most sophisticated and original of contemporary Lutheran theologians in the English-speaking world. Jenson has been clear about his dissatisfaction with the Chalcedonian formula as it stands, arguing that it gives too much house-room to a dualism of agents, not just agencies, in Christ, and insisting that 'What Christology is – or ought to be – *about* is the Jesus who appears in the Gospels.'[41] For Jenson, 'the second identity of God [as "begotten"] is directly the human person of the Gospels, in that he is the one who stands to the Father in the relation of being eternally begotten by him'.[42] To affirm the pre-existence of the second Person of the Trinity is therefore not to speak of an eternal Word who can be conceptually separated from the humanity of Jesus 'as the existence of a divine entity that has simply not yet become the created personality of the Gospels',[43] but to recognize that God eternally chooses to be the God who is united with Jesus. This eternal divine self-determination is the presupposition and condition of the human life of Jesus, but not as a condition for something or someone *else*; the divine self-definition is precisely and inseparably the actual reality that is Jesus as Son of God. God's self-definition is to be *this* filial person in history.[44] In principle we might want to say that, had there been no creation, God would still have been in some sense triune, but we can say nothing at all positive about this counterfactual. The God we know is the God who has decided to be Word and Son in *this* unique historically specified way. Because God's eternity is not a parallel track to what happens in the finite order, we can even say that Christ's 'pre-existence' is the everlastingly real 'divine future' of what

39   Most fully in his classic work, *The Crucified God: The Cross as the Foundation and Criticism of Christian Theology*, London: SCM Press, 1974.

40   See, for example, *God as the Mystery of the World: On the Foundation of the Theology of the Crucified One in the Dispute Between Theism and Atheism*, trans. Darrell L. Guder, London: Bloomsbury/T&T Clark, 2014 (second edition), especially section V.

41   Robert Jenson, *Systematic Theology*, Vol. 1: *The Triune God* (second edition), Oxford: Oxford University Press, 2001, p. 134.

42   Ibid., p. 137.

43   Ibid., p. 139.

44   Ibid., pp. 140–1.

is born of Mary.[45] And in the light of all this, we need have no reservations about ascribing to the one divine Person who is Jesus the Son the sufferings of the cross: 'the sufferer of the Gospels is, without qualification or evasion, the second identity of God', raised, vindicated and glorified by the Father.[46]

We shall be returning in Chapter 2.2 to the issues raised by this direct identification of Jesus of Nazareth with the second Person of the Trinity, without remainder, so to speak. For now, the point is that Jenson's powerfully argued position reminds us that the sixteenth-century bifurcation of Protestant thought about the person of Christ is not a thing of the past; Calvin did not simply emerge victorious in the confessional battle, and, as Jenson's careful discussion shows, not every version of Lutheran Christology is an exercise in anti-metaphysical primitivism. But a discussion like Jenson's nonetheless underlines just the problems that Calvin sought to address. If there is something in the eternal divine life as such that is a necessary condition for the identification of the 'second divine identity' as Jesus of Nazareth, however abstractly this is allowed, we cannot say simply that there is an *exhaustive* identity between Jesus of Nazareth and the second divine Person such that the absence of one would mean the absence of the other. Exhaustive identity is what is in question when it is the case that two different names truly refer to the same individual – as when we recognize that there is no difference in the extension of reference as between Mary Ann Evans and George Eliot, or Archibald Leach and Cary Grant. Clearly, Jenson is not claiming anything like this sort of identity, as if between two putatively different individuals who turn out to be the same: it is rather that Jesus of Nazareth provides us with all that can be said if we want to identify the 'second divine identity' – which is clearly not, for Jenson, just another individual. The distinction, basic to what has been argued throughout the present study, between how we speak about finite and infinite reality is not being overturned. But the difficulty arises when Jenson writes – for example – that the 'subsisting relation' to the Father which is the eternal Logos, God in the eternal and irreducible mode of 'having been begotten', simply *is* the one who appears to us as Son of God in the scriptural narrative.[47] Either this means that the filial

45   Ibid., p. 143.
46   Ibid., p. 144.
47   Ibid., pp. 136–7.

identity of God, the divine life actually subsisting in the *tropos* of sonship, has no content independently of Jesus, or else it is a strong way of saying that we cannot ever speak of what divine filiation is or 'looks like' without reference to Jesus. Even if we follow Jenson's complex model of Jesus's realized human sonship as something we must 'project' forwards and backwards on to the horizon of God's life, we still have a question about whether the filial form of divinity is inextricably part of what it is to be God, rather than something *decided upon* by God; and on this issue, Jenson seems to be with the majority view in classical Christology, allowing for some sort of formal *extra*, even if absolutely nothing can be said of it (except, presumably, that it is whatever is the necessary condition for Jesus being Jesus, for Jesus being the particular human individual he was/is).

We shall be looking in the next chapter at recent debates on this in connection with the theology of Karl Barth. But our brief examination of Jenson's Christology rather reinforces the point that – whatever may be said about the possibility or otherwise of saying anything intelligible about the divine Word without reference to Jesus – Calvin's perspective may still be necessary if we want to say that the divine freedom to act for our salvation in the incarnate Christ is grounded in an eternal relatedness in God that is not in any way secondary to the definition of divine life. And this recognition of a *grounded* divine will for salvation, in that it rules out any notion of a purely arbitrary divine decision, connects with Calvin's concern to understand the work of salvation as flowing from what is *intrinsic* to the life of God, what is in no way 'reactive' to what happens in the history of creation. As we have seen, this is how the persistent issue of the non-competitive relation of finite to infinite appears in Calvin's thought. It is always clear to him that a divine life or action that is in any way conditioned by what happens in the world would thereby be constituted as part of a single system or story. Finite and infinite would become two aspects of one conceptual frame – or two levels in a univocal account of being (Duns Scotus once again). Jenson's eloquently Lutheran Christology stops short of this, but only just. To say that God determines to be Jesus of Nazareth from all eternity is very close indeed to saying that God decides to *be who God is* by taking part of creation into the divine self. Now, one might want to say something very like this as a strong statement of the indissoluble union of the Word with the flesh of Jesus – and indeed it would not be wrong to say that God does indeed determine to be who God actively is in relation to creation in and through the determination to be the God who is fully united in act with Jesus of Nazareth. This kind of language becomes deeply problematic, though, if it is heard as implying that God would not be triune, or, more specifically, would not be constituted by the relation of Father and Son, independently of the world's existence. And to rehearse again a familiar point, the importance of this is not to do with philosophical fastidiousness (although even Jenson sometimes seems to think it is), but with the fundamental significance in a theology of salvation of affirming the goodness and integrity of the finite as such. The paradoxical problem raised by Lutheran Christologies is that, in a thoroughly intelligible and indeed laudable concern to do justice to the radically transformative effect of the Incarnation and the incorporation of creaturely life into uncreated communion, finitude itself is compromised or implicitly undervalued, as if it cannot be transformed without ceasing to be what God has made it to be.

Calvin's argumentation is an attempt to find a way around this: to do full justice to the absolute liberty of infinite action, to the created capacity of human beings in their finite humanity to bear the divine image (i.e. to share the filial love and delight that belongs eternally to the Word[48]) and to the self-consistency of the divine will and purpose, the divine 'decree', by which God establishes the conditions under which he deals with creation in general and humanity in particular. As every reader of Calvin is aware, this last concern sometimes leads to what Calvin himself seems to have recognized as a problematic stress on the satisfaction of divine justice; but if we understand its relation to the other theological concerns that animate his Christology, we may at least see it as more than merely a repressive, mechanical or pre-Christian element (even if his followers, and he himself in some of his writings, cannot be wholly absolved from such charges). If finite reality is not to be swept away in its finitude, its actual and historical conditionedness, these points need to be kept in focus. Ultimately, they are

48 'The divine image in us, despite all, is an act of God, immune to our sacrilege'; this summary statement of Calvin's conviction comes from one of his most imaginative modern defenders, the novelist Marilynne Robinson; see her collection, *The Death of Adam: Essays on Modern Thought*, Boston and New York: Houghton Mifflin Company, 1998, p. 256.

to do with a concern that the Incarnation should not be seen either as an *arbitrary* exercise of divine power or as a predictable consequence of the way creation has been organized; it is a free act of love and thus an act consistent with God's eternal character.

In this context, we can better grasp the importance for Calvin of two themes which will (as already hinted) be of signal important for later Protestant theology. Christ's absolute solidarity with the extremes of human loss and suffering, his endurance of – literally – the pains of the damned, is an emphasis which, if not quite original to Calvin, is certainly given by him a quite unprecedented importance; and this stress on solidarity in human extremity takes on increasing significance as theology itself becomes more conscious of its need to hear and absorb the voices of those living and dying in extremity (this is why Moltmann's Christology, for all the conceptual issues it raises, still has the powerful evangelical appeal it does). Since Bonhoeffer's terse comment that 'only a suffering God can help', modern Christology has struggled repeatedly to find ways of expressing the unqualified nature of divine solidarity in suffering, and no amount of worrying about how exactly this is squared with doctrines of divine impassibility (worrying which is not to be ignored or despised) is likely to turn the clock back on this. Calvin's reasons for stressing Christ's participation in the deepest kind of human alienation from God are not exactly those of the modern theologian: he is interested in how the Descent into Hell establishes beyond question Christ's annihilation of what is most guaranteed to annihilate us – not death only but the death of the soul's hope, which is for Calvin the ultimate consequence of human sin. But, as his text makes clear, it is also important to him to underline that this is the clearest possible demonstration of Christ's goodness and thus of the saving will of God (II.16.12). Nothing is held back in the work of re-creating humanity from within: that 'within' has to include the furthest reaches of the *experience* of alienation, terror and culpability, even though those things are not in themselves ever ascribable to Christ. And this is linked with the second theme of enduring force in Calvin's treatment, his uncompromising assertion that Christ 'merits' nothing for himself and is entirely defined by his action and passion for the sake of the created other – humanity – which he transforms by the overflow of grace and glory from his fullness. Once again, we are reminded (II.17.6) that this is a revealing of the Father's love: he needs to give nothing further to the Son, and the Son needs nothing further from him than what is given and received in the eternal Trinitarian life; so what is given through the Son is wholly directed to our humanity. That God does not 'consult the advantage of his Son' in the work of incarnation and atonement is once more a sign of the rootedness of this work in the eternal character of the Trinitarian God. So the radical selflessness and other-directedness of Christ's identity is affirmed as a necessary corollary of what is said about the perfection of the Trinitarian life: the Son needs nothing and so is free to give everything. In the theologies that develop in the early modern and modern periods, Christ's self-emptying or self-dispossessing is increasingly a focal question (and the next chapter will be touching on some of the ways this is handled in the earlier modern period). What is significant is that Calvin's approach to this question shows no interest at all in the metaphysical issues around what would need to be involved in the Word of God 'renouncing' divine attributes as a condition of the Incarnation; for him, Christ's selflessness is bound up with the quality of his saving merit, that is to say, his relations with the human beings whose 'Head' he is. *Kenōsis* is a question of what the incarnate does for us, not about the mechanics of incarnation (a point drawn out in some modern Eastern Orthodox theology in a parallel way, as well as in Bonhoeffer's Christological reflections). In this connection, Calvin again displays his concern to provide what we might call a stable Trinitarian background for his Christology and his instinct for the importance in Christology of disentangling finite and infinite agency so as more adequately to affirm and understand their inseparable relatedness.

In all these ways, Calvin can be helpfully read as challenging much of the later medieval agenda in Christology and retrieving aspects of the tradition that had led up to Aquinas – but also as introducing significant modifications of that tradition which in due course open doors to the perspectives of Barth or Bonhoeffer. He is no less wary than Luther of the possible 'Nestorian' implications of Ockham's Christology, but his response to the conceptual challenge posed by it is very different. Where Luther explores the ways in which the absolute inseparability of humanity and divinity might be grounded in what we might call the interpenetration of the two natures in the phenomenon of Christ's human identity, Calvin's priority is to be as clear as humanly possible about the fact that divinity and humanity never stand side by side: 'interpenetration' is thus not a helpful idiom for thinking about what is involved. As he notes in what is almost a throwaway comment in 2.13.4 of the *Institutes*, 'we have no idea of any enclosing' in the Incarnation: there is no *spatial* relation whereby the humanity somehow contains and confines the divinity, no sense in which the Word cannot be both in Heaven and in Galilee; and so there are no problems about reconciling a finite and an infinite spatiality. The idea of infinite spatial extension is precisely not relevant to divine infinity, because the limitlessness of the divine act and presence is not an indefinitely enlarged variant of finite act and presence. The Word changelessly 'occupies' all Heaven and earth because the Word changelessly abides as that personal divine identity or agency in and through which creation is related to its maker. Thus it is in the *person* of the Word that the divine and the human find their *communication*, not by any modification of what 'nature' designates.[49] It is not that the conditions of finite spatiality or even finite materiality are dissolved by the Incarnation, but that divine action, present with unique integrity and directness in Jesus, radically alters the scale and scope of the relations in which any portion of finite reality stands to others and to God. In connection with those intractable issues in Eucharistic theology which divided Lutherans and Reformed Christians, what Calvin in effect argues is that the miracle of Eucharistic presence is not in the fact of God bestowing on the human nature of Jesus a unique set of extra natural properties, including the capacity to be spatially anywhere, but in the freedom of God to make both the finite elements of Jesus' humanity and the finite elements of bread and wine which Jesus adopts as signs of his identity effective vehicles of transforming relation with God and thus effective vehicles of the transformation of relations within the finite order. What is changed is the level and character of how finite substances are connected with each other and with the infinite.

It is in this context that Calvin can appear as a perhaps unexpected champion of the true glory of humanity in its full created purpose. The God of the *Institutes* has attracted plenty of opprobrium on account of the emphasis on his justice and his wrath, and there are undoubtedly elements of Calvin's picture (as of most theological schemes) which do indeed show an imperfectly Christianized model of the divine and a disturbingly atomized and

---

49   See T. F. Torrance, *Incarnation*, pp. 209–10, 221–6.

even mechanical model of 'justice'. But what makes Calvin at his best a genuinely theological thinker is his passionate intent to do (another kind of) justice to the sheer difference of God and creation. For him, this means God's commitment to be faithful to the integrity of the finitude of what he has made. Creation does not need specific supernatural completion in order to be itself (hence the rejection of Osiander and, by implication, Scotus on the motive for the Incarnation), and neither does it need to be endowed with properties not natural to itself as a condition of redemption. God 'does justice' to the createdness, the limitedness, of the creation he redeems, not overruling or replacing. And Jesus Christ, the supremely and perfectly human agent, as he is also the perfectly divine agent, enacts what is properly, justly, human; and because he needs no reward or augmentation of his personal eternal bliss in communion with the Father, it is similarly 'just' that what he merits is shared with those who share his life, not somehow accounted to him as an individual. It is this that puts him firmly with the mainstream of a theological tradition that utilizes Christology to clarify simultaneously the absolute difference and the unconditioned freedom of engagement that characterizes the relationship between finite and infinite.

In terms of the overall argument of this book, Calvin is a bridge between the apparent abstractions of the tradition we have been tracing, the tradition which finds its culmination in Aquinas, and the new idioms of a theology shaped by the challenges and nightmares of twentieth-century Europe – the theology of Barth and, still more, Bonhoeffer, as they work out what Christology means in a context where debates over the definitions of human nature have become matters of life and death. The centrality of the theme of Christ's 'Headship' in thinking about Christology is already visible in Paul and Augustine as well as Aquinas, and Aquinas's account of what the merit of Christ means gives a further stimulus to developing its implications. If we try to draw together briefly what this kind of reflection has brought into focus, it adds up to something like the following. Because of the union between the human individuality of Jesus and the infinite act of the Word in whom all finite things are related to the Father, that human individuality is radically unlike all other individualities, while remaining straightforwardly a phenomenon within the finite world. It is given its ultimate distinctness by its relation with the Word, and thus with the 'filial' realization of divine life (Jenson's complaint that Chalcedonian Christology increasingly focuses on the relation between Jesus and the Word not between the Son and the Father rather misses the point), with God as 'Son'. Because that relation with filial Godhead is not the result or product of any finite process, it is not the achievement of one individual: and thus, for those who are brought into union or communion with Jesus, who are brought to stand where he stands, this same relation to the Father is accessible as the gift given in and through association with Jesus – not an achievement, not even simply something 'reckoned' to the believer by divine fiat, but a specific possibility of life and experience bound up with the bare fact of the believer's relation to Jesus in the Spirit-filled community, the Body of Christ. Jesus Christ, as the one who thus both embodies and communicates fully reconciled relation with the Father, never acts so as to gain profit or growth for himself; all is already given him in the eternal self-communication of Father to Word. All his acts therefore are oriented towards the opening up of other finite lives to the gift he intrinsically possesses or lives from. Hence the self-dispossessing and healing, life-giving *service* which characterizes his earthly life, up to and including his death as a reconciling and absolving event, is the way in which he abolishes any boundary between his life and ours: he defends nothing of himself and holds back nothing of himself. He refuses, we might say, to be our rival at any imaginable level. And so the conclusion of Calvin's Christological chapter in the *Institutes* is a strong affirmation of Christ's embodiment of the divine will to give without condition, so that the gift of divine life in the Spirit will heal and finally cancel the effects of human rebellion against God. What Christ does in the incarnate life and above all in his atoning death is already the work of the Spirit in him, in that it lays the foundations for the coming to birth of the reconciled community in which the divine image is restored.

By thus linking the unity of hypostasis/*esse* in Christ, the status of the Word/Son in time and eternity as Head of the created order (that is, the point in which creation finds its principle of life-giving relatedness to the Father), and the actual character of the human life of Jesus as 'for others', Calvin begins to connect the high-level analysis of the grammar of essence and hypostasis more closely than earlier theologians with the narrative of the Gospels – and also, by implication, with the narratives of the lives of believers. In the next chapter, we shall be attempting to trace how Dietrich Bonhoeffer uses the model of Christ's existence as unreservedly 'for others' as the foundation for an ethical and spiritual interpretation of the Church's identity against the sombre background of post-humanistic, totalitarian and racially exclusive politics. Making the connection with Calvin, and with the tradition that Calvin is working to clarify and revivify, reminds us that all that we say about Christology will be vacuous if it does not finally issue – as it did for Bonhoeffer – in a reinforced sense of Christian possibility and Christian vocation, especially in the moral desert of modern ideology. And, to look forward to the concluding chapter of this study, following through these implications of Christological language should enable us more effectively to see classical Christology as the proper ground and focus of a whole theology of political and environmental engagement, since it establishes not only what we must say about the character of the triune Creator but also what we must say (and do) about being creatures. That we are 'deified' by our communion with Christ in the Spirit is, by a nice theological irony, the one sure way of avoiding the illusion that we are or can become gods. Calvin, with his clear insistence on both the deifying effect of the Incarnation and the total dependence of the redeemed on an act and initiative that is not theirs and not guaranteed by anything other than the loving will of the Trinity, would have understood and relished such irony.

2.2

CHRIST, CREATION AND COMMUNITY: CHRISTOLOGY IN THE SHADOW OF ANTICHRIST

1. Barth, Bonhoeffer and the Legacy of Protestant Orthodoxy

The Christology of Dietrich Bonhoeffer is still one of the less carefully studied aspects of his tantalizing theological legacy. His lectures on the subject were never edited by him or published in his lifetime, and the reconstructed texts are notoriously dense and difficult.[1] Yet the themes of the lectures are foreshadowed in earlier lectures and sermons, and are developed with extraordinary creativity both in the fragments of Bonhoeffer's *Ethics* and in the prison letters. The clear unifying theme is one that has its roots in the Reformation principle that the essential thing to say about Jesus Christ is that his person and work must be understood as radically

---

1 For the latest reconstruction, see the text in the English translation of Bonhoeffer's complete works (*Dietrich Bonhoeffer: Works*, Vol. 12: *Berlin: 1932–1933*, ed. Larry Rasmussen, trans. Isabel Best and David Higgins, with Douglas W. Stott, Minneapolis: Fortress Press, 2009); also in *The Bonhoeffer Reader*, ed. Clifford J. Green and Michael P. DeJonge, Minneapolis: Fortress Press, 2013. References here are to the latter.

and entirely 'for us'. There is nothing to say about God that is not ultimately grounded in this understanding; and Bonhoeffer's radical language in the prison letters about the 'non-religious' future of Christian faith has to be read as a gloss on this basic point. If God is wholly for us in Christ, God is never seeking to displace our createdness in order to win for Godself a space in the world; thus faith can never be a matter of securing a territory within the world, over against some alternative space of human action and aspiration. The challenge of the incarnate Christ is to see God's work as directed towards the wholesale pervading of created reality by the divine without any loss of its integrity. This is how Bonhoeffer deals with the recurrent theological problem of how divine and human exist together in Christ and in the entire work of redemption; it is his own distinctive version of the non-competitive vision of finite and infinite that runs through the tradition of classical Christological discourse, and it is worth reading it explicitly as a kind of commentary on this mainstream of doctrinal reflection rather than as a drastic departure or a modern eccentricity.

But Bonhoeffer comes at the end of a long story of Protestant argument about how the classical themes might be stated in a way that does justice to the priority which all the Reformation's major figures accorded to Christology. In the twentieth century Bonhoeffer's mentor and critical friend Karl Barth attempted to find a way between what had become rigid and ossified self-definitions of Lutheran and Reformed approaches to Christology, and his own recasting of the theological agenda needs to be looked at alongside Bonhoeffer's, so that it becomes easier to see how far Bonhoeffer's understanding is distinctive. I shall be arguing that it is indeed distinctive, and in some respects resolves some of the unfinished business, even the imbalance, of Barth's account; and that, although Bonhoeffer is regularly – and to some extent rightly – seen as holding to Lutheran emphases in reaction to Barth's (often heavily modified) Calvinism, the younger theologian is arguably more successful in preserving what Calvin himself would have most wished to safeguard.

To get to this point, we shall have to spend some time on the technicalities of historic Protestant Christology, before looking briefly at Barth's own schema and at some of the recent controversies over its interpretation which bring into sharp focus some of the ways in which the historic issue of the finite/infinite relation continues to generate conceptual confusion and creativity in pretty well equal measure. In the last chapter, we began to look at the divergences between Lutheran and Reformed Christologies and their roots in the different Christological priorities of the two greatest magisterial Reformers – the different ways in which they responded to the curious atrophy of Christological imagination in late medieval theology. Between the seventeenth century and the nineteenth, various attempts were made to systematize what was emerging from the Reformation debates about sacramental theology and the doctrine of the Church – these being the frontline questions of the Reformation's first generations. As we have already seen, the interweaving of questions about the Eucharist with the central issues of Christology was already significant in the sixteenth century. By the end of that century,[2] the Lutheran position had solidified into the doctrine that the humanity of Jesus Christ was possessed of the full dignity of divine nature, including omnipotence and omnipresence, but also that this full divine majesty was manifest 'when it pleased him'.[3] Christ as divine Word thus habitually holds back from showing forth his full divine glory during the time of his incarnation, but the effect of the hypostatic union on his humanity is such that this glory is always there, even if hidden (hence 'cryptics' as a designation for the proponents of one variety of Lutheran theology); and that underlying presence is what allows the humanity to share in the divine capacity to be anywhere and everywhere, and thus to be specifically in the Eucharistic elements. Without entering into the detail of this (notably the criticisms and modifications made by theologians associated with the Giessen school, who denied that Christ's incarnate and vulnerable humanity could be the organ of divine rule over the universe[4]), we can see that it assumes that there is a prima facie incompatibility between the essential divine attributes and the living of a recognizably human life, such that there must be some 'mechanism' that allows the appearances of humanity

2   Particularly in the work of Martin Chemnitz, 1522–86. For an overview, see Mark W. Elliott, 'Christology in the Seventeenth Century', pp. 297–314 in *The Oxford Handbook of Christology*, ed. Francesca Aran Murphy, Oxford: Oxford University Press, 2015, especially pp. 301–3.

3   The phrase is from the 1580 *Formula of Concord* 8.16/11 (*Creeds and Confessions of Faith in the Christian Tradition*, Vol. 2, *Reformation Era*, ed. Jaroslav Pelikan and Valerie Hotchkiss, New Haven and London: Yale University Press, 2003, p. 192.

4   See Elliott, op. cit., pp. 303–4.

to be saved – and, more importantly, the provisions of the Council of Chalcedon to be honoured and no 'confusion of natures' implied.

But by the nineteenth century, criticism of the classical Lutheran model had pushed theologians towards a stronger statement of incarnational self-restraint. Gottfried Thomasius of Erlangen[5] argued that the eternal Word must divest himself of certain divine attributes in order to be incarnate: properties like omnipotence and omnipresence are (according to earlier Lutheran orthodoxy) *consequences* of the intrinsic glory and majesty of God, specifying what must be true of God in relation to the finite world if his eternal and intrinsic attributes are what they are. These can therefore be in some sense 'suspended' in the context of the incarnate life without any change being ascribed to the divine nature in itself. In his later work, Thomasius spells this out further: if what God relinquishes in the Incarnation is those properties that are *relative* to the world's existence and so not essential to God's being, then God as incarnate remains holy, loving, merciful and just, and nothing changes in regard to these characteristics as a result of the Incarnation. All that defines God's relation to the created order – that is, all that constitutes God's *difference* from the created order simply in virtue of God's being Creator – is what is suspended. This in turn allows us to say that Jesus' self-awareness is distinct from that of the divine Word in eternity: divine omniscience cannot exist in a human psyche. But since omniscience is one of those attributes that derive their meaning from the relation of God to the world, its abandonment in the Incarnation can be maintained without compromising God's integrity as God. It is an ingenious structure, but its problems were painfully clear to many nineteenth-century critics, the most serious being that it in effect reinforces precisely the problem it is meant to solve. In Thomasius's scheme, the divine Word strips himself of certain divine characteristics in order to be able to 'function' as a finite consciousness; but the underlying model is of a single subjectivity undergoing a radical modification in order to be active in the flesh. That is to say, it is assumed that there must be a continuity of self-consciousness – we could almost say a continuity of 'psyche' – between the eternal Word and Jesus of Nazareth. And this creates obvious difficulties for any doctrine

---

5   See Bruce McCormack, 'Kenoticism in Modern Christology', pp. 444–57 in Murphy, op. cit., especially pp. 450–3.

of the duality of natures in Christ. The Incarnation is seen as posing something like a spatial or quantitative problem – how to squeeze an infinite
subjectivity into the tangible form of a human personality; and the very idea
of incarnation is then compromised, in that divinity and humanity are both
seen as involved in the event only by losing certain aspects of their essential and habitual reality. The Word that is incarnate is less than the eternal
Logos, its/his consciousness is adjusted and reduced so as to leave behind
the attributes that do not fit into the space provided by human nature; and
the assumed humanity is one in which this necessarily 'reduced' Logos effec-
tually replaces a human subjectivity. The persistent Christological problem
of seeing the two natures as competing for space is here at its most acute.

A fair amount of modern Protestant Christology is an attempt to deal
with this legacy, and we shall later be looking particularly at the ways in
which Bonhoeffer responds to its questions. The most serious difficulties
are to do with how the duality of the incarnate Christ is maintained. Put
like that, it sounds like a very abstract consideration, but in fact it is an issue
about the heart of classical Christology: the double solidarity of Christ with
God and with us, a solidarity which does not require any aspect of either
term to be brushed out of the picture. The Lutheran solution arises from
a proper concern about the impossibility of speaking of Christ independently of his incarnate form – the usual reproach entered against Calvin's
more scrupulous dualism. The difficulty posed by this Lutheran solution,
however, is that it elides two distinct issues: it may be impossible to speak of
Christ independently of his humanity, but this does not entail that there is
then nothing that could in principle be said of Christ that is not said of his
humanity. If these two things are not kept distinct, this can lead (as we have
already noted) to an erosion of any recognition of two natures – or wills
or 'energies' – that is, to the unpalatable conclusion that the Incarnation is
simply a matter of divine agency operating directly in the world by being
transformed into a 'worldly' agent, rather than by being embodied in the
finite agency of a human substance or subject (this explains why Thomasius
was accused of replacing the Incarnation with a 'theophany', a simple manifestation of divine presence[6]). It can also create another kind of problem,

6   The accusation was made by I. A. Dorner in a discussion of Thomasius's work in his
      1853 survey of the history of Christology; see McCormack, op. cit., p. 452.

to the extent that the unified subject of incarnation is conceived as simply identical with the eternal Word, the second Person of the Trinity: if the experiencing subject that is the incarnate Christ is ultimately *identical* with the eternal Word, does this imply that there is a dimension of the divine life that is in some sense *constituted* who or what it is by its relation to the created world? So here is another irony: a theological tradition which initially seeks to identify divine attributes unrelated to the reality of creation (holiness, justice and so on) as those aspects of divine life which are communicable to the humanity of Jesus ends up generating a theology in which relatedness to finite reality, though admittedly in a somewhat different sense, is pushed into the heart of divine eternity.

'If the concept "Word" and the concept "flesh" are both taken seriously but are considered as mutually conditioning each other, is the statement of John 1.14 an understandable statement at all?' The question is thus trenchantly put by Karl Barth,[7] and the problems associated with Barth's own engagement with these issues have come sharply into focus in recent discussions of his thought. Barth undoubtedly had at times a somewhat conflicted relationship with the traditional Reformed emphasis in Christology:[8] beginning as a strong supporter of the *extra Calvinisticum*, he steadily moved towards a more critical stance, though without ever simply repudiating it. The Calvinist approach, he observes,[9] can license speculation about a *logos asarkos*, a divine Word who can be known apart from Christ. At the same time, Barth never goes back on the conviction expressed much earlier in the *Church Dogmatics*[10] – that the divine Word *derives* nothing from the created order: he is what he is in virtue of his eternal generation and articulation from the Father. It is central to Barth's entire theological project that God freely, from all eternity, elects to be the Word Incarnate. God has made it to be so that there is no way around or behind this determination – which

---

7 *Church Dogmatics* I.2, *The Doctrine of the Word of God*, Edinburgh: T&T Clark, 1956, p. 167.

8 There is a good discussion in Darren O. Sumner, 'The Twofold Life of the Word of God: Karl Barth's Critical Reception of the *Extra Calvinisticum*', *International Journal of Systematic Theology* 15.1 (2013), pp. 42–57.

9 *Church Dogmatics* IV.1, *The Doctrine of Reconciliation*, p. 181.

10 *Church Dogmatics* I.2, pp. 136, 163–70.

is why he rejects the Calvinist account of double predestination as precisely the kind of speculation divorced from God's own self-determination as incarnate reconciler that the *extra* just might legitimate. There is no divine decree prior to or independent of the decision for incarnation; yet Barth is as clear as Aquinas that the Incarnation adds nothing to what can and must be said about the Word in eternity. The discussion in I.2 is untypically inconclusive. While recognizing that Reformed theology probably wins on points as far as the patristic foundations of Christology are concerned, Barth wonders aloud[11] whether the theology of the future will need to have both Lutherans and Calvinists arguing over the priority of what Barth himself prefers to call 'static' and 'dynamic' approaches – the Lutheran sense of the absolute and inseparable simultaneity of divine and human agency in Christ and the Reformed concern with the genuine novelty of the incarnational event as something that is 'brought to be' and which does not simply open up to contemplation some eternal fusion of Creator and creature.

Opinions differ as to whether the Barth of CD IV has moved from this position – and indeed whether the implications even of his earlier formulations may imply a more novel theological position than appears on the surface of 1.2. Bruce McCormack, in an important discussion of Barth's evaluation of the *extra Calvinisticum*,[12] has argued that Barth is not interested only in epistemological questions in this context; he is concerned with 'divine ontology'[13] with the question of whether or not there exists a divine identity prior to divine act and will. McCormack reads Barth as implying that the free self-determining act of God is what *constitutes* God's being in eternity: if Barth means what he says about how God in Christ crucified and abandoned 'gives himself over in this way to our contradiction of him and the judgement which falls upon it', then, if God does not cease to be God in this event, God must eternally be determined in his own divinity 'towards' this event; God must be not simply eternally capable-in-the-abstract of taking on the abandonment

11 Ibid., p. 171.
12 'Grace and Being: The Role of God's Gracious Election in Karl Barth's Theological Ontology', pp. 92–110 in *The Cambridge Companion to Karl Barth*, ed. John Webster, Cambridge: Cambridge University Press, 2000, especially pp. 95–101.
13 Ibid., p. 96.

and dereliction of the cross, he must be precisely the God who is who he is in virtue of that specific historical moment. There is no divine identity that can be separated out from this, no divinity 'complete in itself apart from and prior to all actions and relations of that [divine] Subject'.[14] This emphatically does not mean that Barth is suggesting that the events of Jesus' history make God what God is, as if God were being conditioned by events in the finite world: God is God because of his free determination to be for us in Jesus. 'History is significant for the being of God in eternity; but it is significant only because God freely chooses that should be so.'[15] And the further implication – perhaps more startling still – is that the Trinitarian life of God is likewise a matter of self-determination: 'Eternal generation and eternal procession are willed by God; they are not natural to him if "natural" is taken to mean a determination of being fixed in advance of all actions and relations.'[16] In other words, the ultimate statement we can make about God is not that God is Trinity but that God is the one who elects, whose being is freely defined as being 'for us'. What we may say about God rests at every level on the divine freedom; this, for McCormack, is the essence of Barth's theology, and its implication must be, so he argues, that this radical freedom to be for us is the definitive truth about the divine 'nature'.

McCormack makes a related point in another article, dealing with the variety of kenotic theologies from the Reformation onwards.[17] The traditional options for thinking about kenosis have been either a self-emptying on the part of the eternal, non-incarnate Word in order to take human nature or a self-emptying as a human subject which establishes Christ as an exemplar of selfless love. But on McCormack's reading of Barth a third possibility presents itself. The divine Word renounces any existence, and especially any exercise of power, that is not shaped and identified by the man Jesus: in place of the classical account in which the single divine hypostasis is active and the human individuated nature is receptive, we need a counter-narrative in which the divine hypostasis is freely

---

14 Ibid., p. 98.
15 Ibid., p. 100.
16 Ibid., p. 103.
17 'Kenoticism in Modern Christology' (above, n. 5), especially pp. 455–6.

and completely receptive to the humanity of Jesus. The Word, without relinquishing divine power and initiative, *elects* to use that power so as to receive the identity defined by Jesus. When Paul in Philippians writes of Christ's self-emptying, this is ultimately what he is talking about: the Word refuses to be 'God alone', self-defining, but abandons the claim to be as fully free as the Father and the Spirit in exercising divine liberty, because he accepts definition in the form of a slave. And this echoes the language used by another idiosyncratic Barth interpreter, Eberhard Jüngel, who writes, 'God's own eternal being is moved by the man Jesus ... The history of the eternal self-movement of God was intended to be a history affected by a human being in time.'[18]

As various critics[19] have pointed out, McCormack's reading takes us well beyond Barth's own statements of his intentions. The pattern of the *Dogmatics* assumes that there is no path for theology to go 'behind' the threefold life of the Trinity; and surely the appeal to a primordial indeterminate divine will is just such a strategy. Barth can write[20] of 'the ultimate reality of the three modes of being in the essence of God above and behind which there is nothing higher'; and this should make us wary of any reading of Barth – the later no less than the earlier Barth[21] – that suggests a divine will prior to the divine life of the Father, the Son and the Holy

18 Eberhard Jüngel, *Karl Barth: A Theological Legacy*, trans. Garrett E. Paul, Philadelphia: Westminster Press, 1986, p. 129; for a fuller discussion see section 19 of his *Gott als Geheimnis der Welt*, Tübingen: Mohr Siebeck, 1977 (second edition); English Translation: *God as the Mystery of the World*, Grand Rapids, MI: Eerdmans, 1983.

19 Out of a substantial and still-expanding literature, two early responses to McCormack's approach are particularly important: Paul Molnar, 'Can the Electing God be God without Us? Some Implications of Bruce McCormack's Understanding of the Doctrine of Election for the Doctrine of the Trinity', *Neue Zeitschrift für systematische Theologie und Religionsphilosophie*, 49.2 (2007), pp. 199–222; and George Hunsinger, 'Election and the Trinity: Twenty-Five Theses on the Theology of Karl Barth', *Modern Theology* 24.2 (2008), pp. 179–98, which includes a good round-up of what had so far been published around this issue in nn. 1 and 2, p. 196.

20 *Church Dogmatics* I.1, *The Doctrine of the Word of God*, Edinburgh: T&T Clark, 1975 (second edition), p. 382.

21 One point at issue is whether the later elaboration of the theme of divine election in Vol. IV of the *Dogmatics* should lead us to ignore or at least radically rethink our reading of statements such as that just quoted from the earlier volumes.

Spirit. The complaint against a theology that speaks of a divine nature prior to all relations or actions rests on a misconstruction of the very idea of divine action. For classical theology, Barth included, divine action is not something that 'follows' divine being in some contingent sense, awkwardly attached to a static and self-contained divine identity: the being of God is eternally and necessarily active in its self-relatedness, the fundamental *fact* in virtue of which any other agency is possible and actual. Primordial will detached from language about actual divine life opens up an empty 'abyss' of divine pre-being such as features in the kind of speculation associated with thinkers like Boehme and Schelling, and reworked in the twentieth century by Berdyaev and a small number of others.

This is in fact an intellectual tradition with which Barth's own thought is in a slightly more uncomfortable relation than some have granted: he is clearly opposed to any idea of divine indeterminacy or infinite potentiality, as we have seen; yet at least one modern Hegelian scholar can suggest in passing that it is precisely Schelling's notions of divine freedom that, indirectly at least, mould Barth's vocabulary.[22] That being said, the last thing Barth seems to want to leave room for is any *thinkable* or *speakable* divine identity apart from the always already determined will that is eternally realized in what God eternally *is*. There must be no gap here between being and act. And on top of this, the model of God as causeless will before all else, a will that eternally settles on and actualizes a finite potential (a potential within the created world) to which it binds itself, raises a number of serious logical as well as theological problems. It is one thing to say that the Trinitarian God eternally determines a relation with this specific finite subject in history, and that this relation is crucial to our created knowledge of the eternal divine nature and relations; it is another to say that God decides to be *nothing but* the God whose action in human history ultimately reaches its climax in Jesus of Nazareth. God cannot of course choose to be Jesus without choosing the entire complex of finite events which make Jesus possible within the finite world, and thus God's choice to be Jesus is

---

22 Dale Schlitt, 'German Idealism's Trinitarian Legacy: The Twentieth Century', pp. 69–90 in *The Impact of Idealism: The Legacy of Post-Kantian German Thought*, Vol. IV: *Religion*, ed. Nicholas Boyle, Liz Disley and Nicholas Adams, Cambridge: Cambridge University Press, 2013, p. 76.

a choice to define the divine identity in relation to this world.[23] But this in turn must logically mean that God first chooses to be the creator of this world, without which there is no finite reality called Jesus of Nazareth with which to be united. Can we intelligibly say that God thus 'elects' a Jesus-containing world on the presupposition that this specific element in that world determines an aspect of his self-constitution as Trinity? And that this in turn determines God's existence as Spirit? If the divine election is not in some sense dependent on divine being, the 'choice' to be Jesus and thus the 'choice' to be God-as-Son (in this scheme) cannot reveal anything about God's being as God; yet that revelation of God's being as God is for Barth the key to how and why the Trinitarian doctrine matters. The further argument about the kenosis of the Son once again drives a wedge between God as such and the Trinitarian life. If we say that the eternal Word is as he/it is in virtue of the quality of the *incarnate* life, and that the Word's self-emptying is simply the Word's acceptance of this, the question we are left with is whether the incarnate life, 'imprinting' itself on God's eternity, modifies or adds to that life. Are the filial quality of the incarnate life, its compassionate selflessness, its devotion to the Father's will shaped by temporal contingency and then 'received' in Heaven? Clearly there can be no simple 'then' about it: the Word timelessly relinquishes all that is not Jesus in its/his self-defining action. But can we then say nothing about the eternal Sonship of the Word or indeed the eternal act by which the Father is Father in begetting the Son? Because if we do want to affirm this, we are allowing that the divine life is in some vital way the absolute condition of the incarnate; if not, we are left with both a 'Father' and a 'Son' existing in eternity somehow logically prior to the determination created in the incarnate life of Jesus – and who therefore may be thought to have no *intrinsic* relation between them as begetter and begotten.

This is to do less than justice to a highly complex and currently very lively debate.[24] McCormack's contentions seem hard to reconcile both with

---

23 See the discussion of Robert Jenson's theological proposals in the preceding chapter, pp. 158–61.

24 George Hunsinger's *Reading Barth with Charity: A Hermeneutical Proposal*, Grand Rapids, MI: Baker Academic, 2015, is the fullest recent treatment; Philip Cary, 'Barth Wars: A Review of *Reading Barth with Charity*', *First Things*, April 2015, offers

any classical vocabulary of divine self-subsistence and with Barth's explicit theological intentions. But what must be allowed is that McCormack has identified some points of potential tension in a theological tradition which emphasizes as Calvin did the absolutely 'for-us' character of the life of Jesus. Barth – as his statement about John 1.14 makes plain – wants to insist that the statement that 'The Word became flesh' assumes a real difference that is reconciled or overtaken by God's free act. But if God's act is itself simply and exhaustively in being constituted as the election of Jesus, even if (with Barth and against McCormack's reading of him) God is already eternally Word and Son, do we not still have a problem about the relation of finite and infinite? The transcendence of God as God, the character of God's infinity as we might say, is preserved by both Barth and McCormack by an emphasis on the divine freedom: God freely elects to be Jesus. For Barth this is the free communication of a divine selfhood already and everlastingly real, while for McCormack it is the self-determination of the primordial and eternal divine will to be God with us and for us. But for both, it is as though the only way of securing the divine difference is by opposing finite *substance* to infinite *will*. This is evidently one way of resolving the conundrum of how finite and infinite coexist without rivalry or contradiction; but by – in effect – denying God a nature prior to the divine will, we are left unclear as to what it is that humanity is united *to* in the Incarnation. The classical schema imagines human nature endowed (through union with Christ) with the realization of its capacities for filial communion with God; humanity is liberated to enter the 'space' in the divine life that is appropriate for dependent beings, the place occupied by the eternal Son. In so coming to new life in Christ, the finite self both remains itself and is fully actualized by divine agency – that agency which is the outflowing in the Spirit of the exchange of life between Father and Word. What a finite subject cannot by definition be united with, or assimilated to, is causeless divine will, the will that freely elects finitude to define and manifest itself as being for the finite. So the 'revisionist' Barthian thesis we have been considering leaves out of the picture the assimilation of the creature to a real and eternal relation, the eternal Son's relation to the eternal Father – a theme pervasive

a spirited summary of the controversy with some provocative conclusions about the future of Protestant theology.

in the Christology of earlier ages. Paradoxically, the insistence on election, understood in the theology of Jüngel and McCormack as an affirmation of the eternal significance of humanity for God (God as 'affected' by a human life, in Jüngel's words), risks leaving humanity as simply the passive object of divine will rather than a subject in its own right, a subject which is being transformed by grace into a subject of divine love and relational freedom – into a filial liberty.

The mature Barth has undoubtedly and decisively moved away from any perspective that ignores or plays down the theme of the new 'subjecthood' of redeemed humanity. When Nigel Biggar sums up Barth's ethics as grounded in 'the filial invocation of God for the coming of the Kingdom',[25] he identifies a key point in the later Barth's theology. The gift of the Spirit in baptism is, for Barth, that which enables us to discover the history of Jesus as '[our] own salvation history': we 'come to ourselves' in this moment, becoming aware of where we stand in the eternal counsel of God as brothers and sisters of the elected Jesus; and in doing God's work we are 'normalized' as humans.[26] And it is the prayer 'Abba, Father' that expresses precisely the essence of our rediscovered normality, the humanity that corresponds to what God has eternally purposed and chosen in Christ. In other words, Barth, by his last years, had recognized at least implicitly the problems of certain ways of understanding the freedom of divine will and the election of Christ, and, in his reflections on 'Baptism with the Holy Spirit' in IV.4, he is able to identify the potential distortion of his own theology that would displace human agency as such and replace it with the Spirit's action. 'The omnicausality of God must not be construed as His sole causality';[27] and 'the very intention of the Holy Spirit is to bear witness to our spirit, not to a non-human non-spirit but to the human spirit that we are the children of God'.[28] In the light of these and comparable statements, we should not, I think, assume that Barth's earlier Christology carries some kind of

---

25 Nigel Biggar, 'Barth's Trinitarian Ethic', pp. 212–27 in the *Cambridge Companion to Karl Barth*, p. 224.

26 *Church Dogmatics* IV.4, *The Doctrine of Reconciliation*, Edinburgh: T&T Clark, 1969, pp. 27–8.

27 Ibid., p. 22.

28 Ibid., p. 28.

inexorable logic that pushes towards the priority of divine will in isolation. The sometimes almost exclusive focus on the language of election has its theological difficulties, but Barth works his way through to a theology of a humanity restored in Christ by incorporation into eternal filiation – though this is emphatically an eternal filiation wholly inconceivable, incapable of being talked about, independently of the elected history of Jesus as the basis not only of our election as human beings but of our transformation as agents.

How far these developments in his theology owe anything directly to Bonhoeffer is an interesting question, but hard to answer. Barth is critical of Bonhoeffer's *Ethics* and evidently perplexed and even distressed by aspects of the prison letters – though some have read his later Christology as marked by Bonhoefferian themes in certain respects, particularly in his responses to some of Bonhoeffer's ideas in *Creation and Fall*.[29] But the point of this long excursus into Barth and the Protestant theological debates that preceded (and followed) his work is to demonstrate some of what defines Bonhoeffer's own theological agenda. He is not primarily an exegete of historical debates, and some of what he has to say in the Christology lectures about the history of Christology is, on the most charitable reading, rather broad-brush. Yet what he argues in the lectures, as we shall see, is closely tied in with the underlying questions raised for Reformation theology and classical Protestant dogmatics by the debate over the character of the union of natures in Christ. The Lutheran concern that there should be no weakening of what could be called the commitment of God to be Jesus Christ, with nothing withheld, is bound in with the fundamental Lutheran theme of the complete trustworthiness of God: God leaves himself nothing, so to speak, that could give any grounds for thinking that God was not wholly for us. Compromise this and you compromise the most basic conviction of all the Reformers; you are back with the oppressive mythology of a transcendent being whose will for your salvation is somehow provisional, temporary, contingent.

---

29 For an excellent, sensitive and comprehensive treatment of their relation, see Matthew Puffer, 'Dietrich Bonhoeffer in the Theology of Karl Barth,' pp. 46–62 in *Karl Barth in Conversation*, ed. W. Travis McMaken and David W. Congdon, Eugene, OR: Pickstock, 2014.

Bonhoeffer begins with the same concerns and the same basic unwilling-ness to compromise – not because of a simply theoretical anxiety about Christological orthodoxy as read by Luther but because that orthodoxy is seen as the pastoral centre of Reformation thought. And the Calvinist concern that God does not cease to be God in dealing with creation points to the same fundamental convictions of Reformation theology. God's absolute freedom, the fact that God's act is conditioned by nothing but God's own nature or character, is the necessary presupposition of God's commitment to be Jesus Christ. Without this presupposition, the free grace of God in assuming human nature cannot be affirmed and we are left with the prospect of a God who is acted upon by the initiative of creatures (and is therefore on the same level as they are). For the Calvinist as much as for the Lutheran, the question is about how we secure the trustworthi-ness of God: for the Lutheran, the presenting issue is how we secure the completeness of God's presence in the decision God has made; for the Calvinist, the issue is securing God's freedom to make that decision quite independently of any created condition, and thus of any human deserving.

Bonhoeffer and Barth are equally seeking to hold the precarious balance between these two sets of concerns. Both are critical of aspects of the Protestant dogmatic heritage: we have noted that Barth is cautious about what the *extra Calvinisticum* might permit, and Bonhoeffer, as we shall shortly see, argues strongly against the mechanisms of kenosis devised by Lutheran Orthodoxy. Both are in search of a starting point and a method-ology for Christology that will avoid these false trails. For Barth, the focus on the election of Christ serves as a way through the minefield, according clear priority to a free divine determination, a divine commitment whose relation to the humanity of Jesus is not one of necessity or strict implica-tion but yet one that closes off any possibility of looking elsewhere for truth about God: this is how the eternally self-revealing God actually reveals God. For Bonhoeffer, what matters most is the repudiation of what he calls the 'how?' question. Confronted with Christ, we can only ever ask 'who?' Any theology that seeks to show how the Incarnation is in principle or in theory possible (like the theologies of seventeenth- and nineteenth-century Lutheranism) is an attempt to stand at an angle to the actual encounter and to speak of Christ as if he were a possibility rather than always and ines-capably an actuality. In reimagining a starting point for Christology, both are engaging with the history of their traditions and also revisiting some of the perennial issues in Christological discourse – above all, the challenge represented by the Chalcedonian balance of inseparability and non-confusion. Unlike some of their readers, neither of them wants to sacrifice either pole of the tension, recognizing implicitly and sometimes explicitly how imbalance on these questions unsettles the grammar of speaking about the relation of finite to infinite. Humanity does not 'contribute' anything to the Godhead, and as soon as anything is said that suggests this, something essential is lost from our language about divine freedom, the freedom to determine our salvation irrespective of our deserving. Divinity does not replace anything in the human constitution, and anything suggesting this makes the created order a mere instrument for divine action, 'external' to God's being as one agent is to another.

The Christology lectures of Bonhoeffer's short-lived academic tenure in Berlin attracted wide interest largely because they unapologetically demonstrated a theological method that owed a good deal to Barth, yet that was not simply 'Barthian' either in style or content, and it is clear that the reception of the lectures secured his academic reputation – still a little uncertain, give what was felt to be the eccentricity of his earlier theological work. But 'When Bonhoeffer reached the high point of his academic life in 1933 he brought it to an end', as Bethge puts it.[30] The lectures have been described as tantalizingly lacking in positive dogmatic proposals. But in fact they contain a substantive and original set of arguments, which, as Bethge and others have consistently maintained, connect directly with the major themes of the *Ethics* and the prison letters. They are more than a ground-clearing exercise; the very fact of identifying – as Bonhoeffer does – a fresh starting point carries doctrinal implications, to be spelled out in his later writing. In the next section we shall look in detail at his critique of some conventional approaches to Christology, and at the various ways in which he draws the discourse back to the fundamental question addressed most fully in the *Ethics*, the nature of Christ's being 'for us' in a sense even more comprehensive and radical than we find in the magisterial Reformers whose legacy he is attempting to revive and clarify.

---

30 Eberhard Bethge, *Dietrich Bonhoeffer: A Biography*, London: Collins, 1970, p. 165.

2. Bonhoeffer's Christology Lectures

The lectures which Bonhoeffer delivered in Berlin in 1933 were immensely popular; contemporary accounts describe the crowds who attended them, and the excitement with which they were received. The text we now possess is, frustratingly, a reconstruction from different sets of student notes: the effect is like trying to view a great painting through frosted glass, but something of the initial impact is still discernible, even in the sometimes evidently somewhat garbled version that has been painstakingly collated by various editors. Commentators have noted the importance Bonhoeffer clearly ascribed to these lectures and their formative role in his development both as theologian and as activist;[31] they represent his coming to terms with the complex Protestant heritage we have been considering – a stark rejection of some of its presuppositions and also a recognition of the seriousness of some of its questions. At least as much as Barth in his Romans Commentary, Bonhoeffer here deploys strongly Kierkegaardian argument and rhetoric so as to distance himself from a particular style of dogmatic speculation. The opening salvo of the lectures is directed against the notion that Christology can be an engagement with the *idea* of transcendent Logos: this will inevitably constitute that Logos as an object for human *logos*, locating it within the territory of things about which we can ask 'how is it possible?' or 'how does it work?' But if Christ is what we say he is, if Christ is the divine Logos, there is no way in which he can be an object of this sort. As Bonhoeffer memorably puts it, the question is no longer 'how?' but 'who?' Who is it that I confront when I look at Jesus? But also, and equally importantly, 'Who am I?' 'With the "who question", the person asking is queried about the limits of his or her own being.'[32] Encounter with Christ thus threatens human *logos* at the most fundamental level, denies it any standing as an activity that can map reality from its own standpoint. My own *logos* is revealed as limited, and so my very existence discovers its limit. But in that discovery it also discovers that it cannot successfully ask even the 'who?' question without turning it into

---

31 Charles Marsh, *Strange Glory: A Life of Dietrich Bonhoeffer*, New York: Knopf, 2014, p. 170.

32 *The Bonhoeffer Reader* (above, n. 1), p. 264.

a variety of 'how?' That is to say, a 'who?' question that seeks to select an identity for what is encountered from an existing repertoire of possibilities is simply reinstating human *logos* by the back door. We must ask but we cannot.[33] Or rather, the 'who?' question becomes askable only when it has already been answered, in the sense that the very fact of encounter with Christ, within the community of belief, establishes the questioning initiative of Christ, his right to ask us who we are – and so establishes who he is as divine Logos. We have always already been met and judged and called to account where Jesus is present,[34] so that there is no possibility of going behind this moment, prescinding from the engagement we are actually in, without rebelling against the divine Logos. Such rebellion is always at the edge of the finite mind as it absorbs all this: faced with the radical challenge to its own *logos*, humanity seeks the death of the divine Logos. 'When a human being confronts Jesus[,] the human being must either die or kill Jesus.'[35] The reality that is Jesus cannot be made to reflect us back to ourselves in our own terms, so that if we do not accept the mortality and death of our human *logos* we are going to be complicit in the death of the Word of God.

Somewhere in the background here is the Kierkegaard of the *Philosophical Fragments*. Bonhoeffer's language echoes Kierkegaard's account of the passion of human reason to encounter what it cannot include or control. We want to encounter what we *cannot think*;[36] and when we encounter it, we

---

33 Ibid., p. 265.

34 Ibid., p. 266.

35 Ibid., p. 268.

36 Søren Kierkegaard, *Philosophical Fragments, or a Fragment of Philosophy/Johannes Climacus, or De omnibus dubitandum est*, ed. and trans. Edna H. Hong and Howard V. Hong, Princeton: Princeton University Press, 1985, p. 37. A detailed examination of Bonhoeffer's relation to Kierkegaard still remains to be done: the generally excellent *Oxford Handbook of Kierkegaard*, ed. John Lippitt and George Pattison, Oxford: Oxford University Press, 2013, has only one reference to Bonhoeffer, associating him simply with the 'radical theology' of the late 1960s. This volume has a useful summary of Kierkegaard's Christological thinking on pp. 297–303 of the essay by Sylvia Walsh, 'Kierkegaard's Theology' (pp. 292–308). On other aspects of Kierkegaard's legacy in Christology, see the appendix to this book, 'Wittgenstein, Kierkegaard and Chalcedon'.

know it as 'the god', a 'god' whose existence we cannot demonstrate because the god's appearance simply *is* the reason's encounter with the irreducibly alien and unmasterable. To know anything of the god, we must therefore know that he/it is different from us, different in a radical and unique mode;[37] the difference is constituted by 'sin', says Kierkegaard, by our choice to live in untruth. 'Through the moment [of encounter with the god], the learner becomes untruth; the person who knew himself becomes confused about himself and instead of self-knowledge he acquires the consciousness of sin.'[38] And the moment of encounter is something created solely by the god, who can be a teacher only by the total renunciation of anything we would regard as the intelligible form of divinity; to appear as a god would in one sense satisfy the human learner but would not satisfy the god, who would have achieved his end without truly re-begetting the learner, annihilating in the moment the learner's categories or processes of understanding by the very fact of *descending* to be equal with the humblest.[39] Kierkegaard thus presents us with one of the most complex of modern theological arguments: what looks like a speculative deduction of the Incarnation as the culmination of the very idea of intellectual activity (seeking its own limit and silencing, meeting a god who can manifest his utter difference only by concealing what can be thought of as godhead) is in fact necessarily a retrospective account of what the 'moment' entails once that moment of learning in faith has happened. The parallel with Bonhoeffer is clear. As, for Kierkegaard, the passion of reason is to seek out its limit, so for Bonhoeffer human *logos* recognizes its true destiny only when confronted with what demands its death; and we are able to think or speak of this only when it has already interrupted our reasoning. What is more – and this will be a theme central to Bonhoeffer's further exposition – for the divine Logos to address us or engage us it must not be through an experience that simply embodies the kind of difference we instinctively associate with the divine. The divine revealed as overwhelming power or unconstrained agency *as we understand those things* will not recreate us, re-beget us; it will not require the death of our *logos*.

37 Ibid., p. 46.
38 Ibid., p. 51.
39 Ibid., pp. 30–2.

Bonhoeffer reinforces the point in his discussion of the sort of authority exhibited by Jesus. Jesus is not an authorized spokesman for some other; his authority is dependent on his embodying in every aspect of his existence what is being communicated:[40] he is entirely and without remainder an act of communication, an incarnate word. Bonhoeffer would – no less than Kierkegaard (see, for example, the *Book on Adler*[41] as well as the *Philosophical Fragments*) – insist on the difference between Jesus as teacher and Socrates as teacher: Jesus does not remind us of what we have forgotten but creates the conditions for knowing him. He *is* what he teaches. And he does so by establishing an authority that cannot be seen as derived from anything in the world external to him. Bonhoeffer shrewdly and correctly observes (once again with a clear echo of Kierkegaard) that the miracles of Jesus 'do not jeopardise his incognito' in a world that is full of miraculous claims and magical display:[42] 'When Jesus performed miracles, he was preserving his incognito in a world of magic' – a neatly provocative suggestion that the miracles are a *concealment* of true divinity rather than a manifestation of it in the context in which the Incarnation takes place, a context in which claims for the supernatural origins of unusual events are routine, a context in which anyone can claim to be doing 'miracles'. What is theologically significant in the human career of Jesus is not the exceptional or preternatural but all those things that make his humanity difficult, embarrassing or ambiguous. More than once in the lectures, Bonhoeffer insists that the humiliation or self-emptying of the divine Logos in Jesus Christ is not so much in the fact of the Incarnation itself as in the specific human humiliation of the cross, the rejection of Jesus as a sinner or a criminal: 'The doctrine of the stumbling-block has its place not in the doctrine of God's taking human form but rather in the doctrine of the God-human's humiliation.'[43] In other words, it is not that *humanity* as such conceals God – not even that *finitude* as such conceals God. It is the suffering and failure and ambiguity

---

40 Bonhoeffer, op. cit., pp. 269, 276.
41 Ed. and trans. Howard V. Hong and Edna H. Hong, Princeton: Princeton University Press, 2009; Kierkegaard distinguishes in this book between the genius and the apostle, arguing that the question posed by the apostle is simply, 'Will you obey?' (e.g., p. 34).
42 Bonhoeffer, op. cit., p. 311.
43 Ibid., pp. 273–4; cf. pp. 308–12.

of *this* particular human being that is the issue, the fact that God exists in and as this specific human identity. In developing this point, Bonhoeffer is not only glossing Kierkegaard's stress on the incognito of God in Jesus but distancing himself from those aspects of classical Lutheran dogmatics that we looked at earlier – indeed, if the analysis of Calvin's Christology in the preceding chapter is accurate, Bonhoeffer stands close to Calvin in concentrating on the cumulative historical self-emptying of *this* particular historical humanity rather than some sort of a self-emptying of divine attributes. His approach gives no purchase to the idea that, in order for the Incarnation to be possible – that is in order for God to assume human nature as such – some kind of metaphysical surgery has to be carried out. If the kenosis of incarnation is seen not as the taking on of human nature but as the living-out of a humiliated and vulnerable life, the scandal, the 'stumbling-block' is not humanity but *this* kind of humanity, a humanity that entails solidarity not simply with humanity in general but with the most powerless and apparently distant from God.[44]

Kenosis is every bit as central to Bonhoeffer's thought as to the Lutheran tradition he argues with, but it works in a radically different way. Kierkegaard had insisted that the 'form of a servant' taken by the god in the Incarnation was intrinsic to what was being communicated in the Incarnation: God in humble form *is* the teaching,[45] in the sense that our liberation from untruth and sin is effected only by the act of unconditional love and this love can be manifest only as a total renunciation of power or advantage, in which the god undertakes never to overwhelm and coerce the human learner.[46] The visible form of a suffering and failing humanity absolutely refuses to

---

44 Reggie L. Williams's important book, *Bonhoeffer's Black Jesus: Harlem Renaissance Theology and an Ethic of Resistance*, Waco: Baylor University Press, 2014, shows how Bonhoeffer's experience of sharing the worship of black churches in New York opened up for him an understanding of Jesus' solidarity with humiliated human beings in a way that his own classical theological formation had never done. Charles Marsh's biography (above, n. 30, pp. 116–18) has a brief but helpful account of the impact on Bonhoeffer of the preaching of Adam Clayton Powell Sr at Abyssinian Baptist Church in Harlem at a time when Powell's theology was increasingly turning to Christ's identification with the marginal and dispossessed.

45 Kierkegaard, *Philosophical Fragments*, pp. 55–6.

46 Ibid., pp. 31–4.

constrain a response. So too for Bonhoeffer: the freedom of the divine Logos is supremely active, supremely itself, in being embodied as the entirety of a human subject, uninterrupted in its humanness (in Kierkegaard's celebrated and provocative formulation, 'he has himself become captive, so to speak, in his resolution and is now obliged to continue (to go on talking loosely) whether he wants to or not'[47]). And in the particular vulnerability of this humanness – rejected and killed – the Word abandons any resort to proof or force and renounces any possibility of external confirmation to endorse its divine authority. Bonhoeffer connects this explicitly to what becomes an increasingly important element in his theology, a development deriving ultimately from Luther rather than Kierkegaard – though the Danish theologian has a certain amount to say about the god's sorrow in carrying the constant possibility of rejection, the 'destitution' this entails for the incarnate saviour and the difference between a clear manifestation of divinity that would satisfy the hungry human soul but fundamentally frustrate the will of the god.[48] Christ's essential identity lies in being *pro nobis* and *pro me*; Christ is who he is as the one who exists for my and our sake. If Christ for a moment sought to coerce my response, that would mean that he ceased to be 'for me' in this radical sense; he would be seeking to implement his will as a rival to mine, *and this is precisely what he has forgone in becoming human.*

So I cannot think about Christ except as involved with me; a conclusion that, so far from implying an individualistic theological perspective, puts my selfhood in question at its foundation. To think about Christ, to acknowledge who he is, is, in Kierkegaard's language, to recognize my own being as 'untruth', and, in Bonhoeffer's, to recognize that I must die in Christ's presence. My *logos* cannot live with Christ; as we have seen, the choice is between my death and Christ's. But this needs some clarification. It might sound as though this were another example of the theological zero-sum game that the whole history of Christology battles to overcome; as if there were simply a competition between me and Christ, human and divine, finite and infinite, in which there could be only one victor. But in fact this is more or less the opposite of what Bonhoeffer is saying. The *logos* of my self-affirmation, refusing to live in the presence of and for the sake of the

47   Ibid., p. 55.
48   Ibid., pp. 29, 32–3.

other, is a poisonous fiction, an unreality, and as such it cannot be affirmed or undergirded by God: it is simply not *there* to be affirmed, since it exists only in the fearful imagination of a human self threatened by the incursion of God's truth. In other words, what must die in the encounter with Christ is precisely *not* finitude or createdness but the delusion that we can live in denial of our finitude, our dependence on infinite agency. Thus Bonhoeffer can write:[49] 'Only on the basis of having been judged by this Logos can the old logos learn anew to comprehend the relative rights to which it is entitled. Only from the question of transcendence does the human logos receive the rights peculiar to it, its necessity and also its limits.' As Bonhoeffer notes, this is both a formal point about the possibility of telling the truth about finite reality – Christology as a foundation for epistemology itself, in that it establishes the integrity and substantiality of finite existence as such – and something more, in that the content, not merely the form, of this relation specifies the shape of the life of faith as radical directedness towards the other and the willingness to live under the question of the divine Logos in its mortal human incognito. Living in faith, so far from destroying the finite as finite, affirms finitude and promises the glorification of finitude by grace: 'God's self-glorification in the human is thus the glorification of the human.'[50] Once again, the point is that God's taking of human flesh is not the problem, as though an incompatibility had to be overcome by some adjustment in the terms of the relation. Incarnation is not and cannot be the destruction of its own vehicle. The *stumbling*-block is that the incarnate life is as it is, vulnerable and other-directed.

On this basis, Bonhoeffer sketches what is entailed in this for the life of the Church, developing the fundamental understanding of the Church as 'Christ existing as community' which he had developed already in his earlier theology. Life in the community is a 'being-there' on behalf of humankind, history and nature,[51] declaring in its existence and practice that Christ is the centre of all human reality. This raises two enormous issues on which the text we have is tantalizingly brief. First: the affirmation of Christ at the centre appears to make a claim about Christ as the focus, hidden or revealed,

49 Bonhoeffer, op. cit., p. 266.
50 Ibid., p. 308.
51 Ibid., p. 282.

of all human religiousness – a claim about the absoluteness and uniqueness of Christ. Bonhoeffer insists, however, that this cannot ever be a matter of theoretical demonstration: start comparing Christ with other religious systems and you are comparing what cannot be compared, reducing Christ to a system among systems. Paradoxically, the attempt to *justify* Christ's superiority is a surrender to a distorted 'liberal' agenda. All we can do is proclaim that human imaginings of the goal of history have now been judged by the humiliation and death of Christ on the cross: every programme of human narration and sense-making is brought to silence here, and everything now depends on the underlying agency of God breaking through. This can only be declared and embodied by the community; it is not an argument from outside about the relative merits of 'religions'. And this leads to the second issue. If Christ is the centre of history, Christ's Body is the centre of the common life of humanity and so of the *state*: human law and order are challenged, shaken to their roots, in the cross, but at the same time the lawful ordering of human life is affirmed. Thus the Church is the necessary condition of the legitimate state: it announces the radical judgement of the state as an achievement of human self-organizing, yet offers a ground for believing that law is of God, a means of fulfilling the vocation of human beings in creation. The argument here is compressed to the point of impenetrability, but two themes emerge which we shall see to be important in the later discussion of Bonhoeffer's *Ethics* manuscripts. There is a clear distinction between claiming 'centrality' for the Church and claiming some 'visible position within the realm of the state';[52] and there is an insistence, very much in tune with the whole argument of the lectures, that Christological discourse manifests the limits of all human attempts to make sense of the world in terms of its relation to human needs and narratives alone. Christology posits limits to human *logos*, in politics as elsewhere – not to de-realize or dissolve the solidity of the finite but precisely to ground its finite nature, its density and temporality and locatedness. And this connects with the equally tantalizing paragraphs[53] on what is involved in 'being there for nature': the sacramental life of the Church allows the elements of creation simply to speak for God, released from their bondage to human sense-making. Adopted by the

52 Ibid., p. 284.
53 Ibid., p. 285.

living and active Word, they 'say what they are'; their reality as signs of the
new creation announces the end of a creation in which human interpretation, human need, human curiosity and acquisitiveness, no longer have the
determining power over the material environment.

Bonhoeffer comes back repeatedly to the starting point of his
Christological scheme: the divine Logos is apprehended as the enemy of
human *logos* precisely to the extent that the latter seeks to define itself as a
solid thing over against divine life – and so seeks to define its entire social
and material environment as existing only in relation to its thoughts and
needs. It is in this light that Bonhoeffer goes on to survey the history of
Christological debate, as he does in the first two sections of the second
part of his lecture series.[54] True to his general approach, he stresses that the
definition of the Council of Chalcedon must not be treated as a positive
'theory' of Christ's constitution;[55] and he also says – in flat contradiction to
the orthodoxy of the theological scholarship in which he had grown up –
that 'nothing is further from being a product of Greek thinking than the
Chalcedonian formula.'[56] The problem with the language of *ousia* in the
formula is not in the way the concept is deployed but in the regular misunderstanding, then and now, of the word itself, as if it could designate an
object rather than an agent in relation. The account given of the various
heresies and controversies of the patristic period is schematic and rather cur-
sory; Bonhoeffer was not a patrologist, though there are some insightful
observations about patristic concepts here. And in a way fairly typical of
his milieu, he passes briskly from patristic to Reformation debates, with
the result that there are some confusions over terminology (notably in
the brief discussion of what *enhypostasia* means[57]). Bonhoeffer is wary of

54   Ibid., pp. 285–307.
55   Ibid., p. 298.
56   Ibid., p. 306.
57   Ibid., p. 291. The reconstructed text here is evidently based on very faulty note-taking,
     as it speaks as though orthodoxy required acknowledgement of the 'impossibility' of the
     incarnate Christ having only one hypostasis – the exact opposite of what was actually
     taught by the patristic theologians, as the rest of Bonhoeffer's discussion makes plain.
     But it is also clear that Bonhoeffer thought of the Byzantine doctrine of *enhypostasia* as
     implying that something is lacking in Jesus' humanity rather than that the individuality
     of this humanity is as it is because of its relation with the person of the Word.

attempts to 'go beyond' Chalcedon, since he sees these refinements less as grammatical fine-tuning than as covert strategies for returning to the 'how' question which Chalcedon, rightly understood, prohibits. Chalcedon, for Bonhoeffer, states that 'God is no longer other than the one who has become human': 'the concrete existence of the one nature is expressed by the concrete existence of the other nature'.[58] This is consciously a quite Lutheran formulation; Bonhoeffer suggests that Reformed Christology is problematic in that it implies an abstract separation of natures, two static terms whose integrity needs to be conserved: the Logos has to be kept apart from the humanity,[59] and thus there is no glorification or deification possible for that humanity. Bonhoeffer defends the Lutheran notion of the *genus maiestaticum*, the possibility of speaking about the humanity of the Incarnate Christ as entirely suffused with divine glory. Yet when this becomes yet another vehicle for 'how' questions, as in the classical Lutheran theories about the concealment (*krupsis*) or evacuation (*kenōsis*) of divine attributes, it defeats its own object: the fundamental point is that the entirety of Godhead is present in Jesus (a broader and very basic theological point, as Bonhoeffer recognizes: 'wherever God is, God is wholly there'[60]). If there are elements of the Godhead that must be 'left outside' the union, the very idea of two natures in one person has been undermined. We are stuck at the stage of trying to put together two abstract entities which can be fully characterized without reference to each other.

So Bonhoeffer ends up with a scheme that is neither straightforwardly Lutheran nor straightforwardly Reformed in its vocabulary. The Lutheran emphasis on refusing to seek ways to go behind the actuality of the God-human is clear and unambiguous in his writing; but equally Bonhoeffer echoes a characteristically Reformed concern to the extent that he refuses to see the integrity of the finite somehow disrupted or diminished by the infinite: the union of natures is a union that allows the finite to be supremely what it is.[61] No less than Barth, he is looking for a Christological language

---

58   Ibid., p. 299.
59   Ibid., p. 300.
60   Ibid., p. 303.
61   In this sense, Bonhoeffer in fact echoes the concerns of the Byzantine theologians he has criticized (above, n. 55). And, as we shall see at more length in the next chapter,

that steps around the more technical points of debate between the two Protestant traditions; but, in contrast to Barth, he places in the foreground of his exposition a particularly radical statement of what is implied by seeing Chalcedonian Christology as a way of dismantling a false account of the finite/infinite distinction. The very intensity of his language about how human *logos* either kills the divine Word or dies itself is, as we have seen, a consequence of this reading of the tradition. And out of this emerges the ecclesiology and the ethics that will take shape further in the fragments of Bonhoeffer's last years, above all in the steady development of the notion of being-for-others: the divine Logos confronts a persistent human project of being-for-self, which cannot coexist with it. The acceptance of divine judgement on this project (not the same as a judgement on humanity as such, as Bonhoeffer makes plain[62]) means that our humanity is reshaped in its true form, as defined by 'responsibility'. Bonhoeffer uses the word almost casually in discussing the event-character of revelation as involving 'a word between two persons';[63] it will become the key to much of what he works through in the *Ethics*.

The only way of speaking truthfully about Jesus Christ is from that mutually defining relationship in which human existence responds to the summons to self-abandonment, life for the other, which is the life that Christ embodies, in history as in preaching and sacrament. So Bonhoeffer's formulation, already quoted, that 'God is no longer other than the one who has become human' is an intelligible corollary of this conviction. But how exactly does Bonhoeffer mean us to take such a statement? Is it a version of the interpretation of Barth we discussed earlier which sees him as presupposing a foundational role for the Incarnation in defining the eternal being of God? Some of the phraseology in the text of the Christology lectures undeniably comes close: 'God in his timeless eternity is *not* God',[64] he says – though it is important to note that this is one wing of a rhetorical doublet in which he goes on to say that Jesus Christ in his temporal humanity is not Jesus Christ.

his way of expressing it has some significant parallels with the Christology of Barth's Roman Catholic interlocutor, Erich Przywara.

62 Ibid., p. 308.
63 Ibid., p. 276.
64 Ibid., p. 273.

And the balancing rhetoric is the clue to reading him accurately on this subject. *In our apprehension of and response to* the presence of the God-human, we cannot isolate either a divine nature that is not bound up with the historical concreteness of Jesus or a human nature that is not suffused with divine agency. The way God is present is as the humiliated and suffering Jesus. Divinity is not something added to the humanity; it is what is confessed and affirmed in the response to the humanity as Word – as summons and judgement and death-sentence and transfiguration. It is in fact a way of conceiving the divine presence in Jesus that is closely congruent with some Byzantine and medieval versions of Christology.

We are not here dealing with a speculative essay in reconfiguring God's aseity, or with a theory about God's eternal self-determination. What we know and can speak about is the God who has expressed divine life in the entirety of a human life, so that human nature comes to be expressed in terms of God's life. There is no other God we can speak about positively; but this also means that recognizing God in Jesus Christ is not – as a certain kind of classical Lutheran would have insisted – ascribing to Jesus Christ a set of divine attributes.[65] My surrender in faith to the ambiguous and humiliated figure presented in the Gospels and in the community's proclamation is the 'statement' of Christ's divinity that most matters. It is to take this human subject to be constituted by and as the act of the eternal and divine Word – very much as, in a totally different idiom, Aquinas implies. Bonhoeffer does not seek to resolve any issues about what might make it possible for God to be thus in Jesus; and so it is not really possible to determine whether he would want simply to block off the concerns of classical and Reformed theology to avoid compromising the meaning of the word 'God' itself. But he would probably have responded to such a question by saying that the grammar of that word could establish itself only by the nature of our response – that is, by the abandonment of self-centred thinking and action. *This* would be the way in which the utter difference of God from a self-enclosed world of finite individual substances would be most unambiguously stated; and it would be in the process of reflecting on the implications of this that we would also be able to see finite reality as both limited and sustained by the illimitable – a connected and intrinsically meaningful world of related subjects

65 Ibid., p. 307.

rather than an ensemble of atomistic and impermeable substances. What we cannot ascribe to Bonhoeffer is a straightforward denial of the language of God's freedom from conditioning by the facts of the finite world; what concerns him is rather the way in which this can and cannot helpfully be brought into speech, and the risks that accompany any metaphysical idiom that allows us to 'objectivize' the divine nature.

So, while Bonhoeffer would almost certainly have resisted any attempt to translate his analysis of what it is to acknowledge God in Jesus Christ into any kind of ontological vocabulary, this does not mean that he would necessarily be sympathetic to the kind of replacement of ontology by divine will that was discussed earlier in connection with interpretations of Barth. What it does mean, though, is that Bonhoeffer's Trinitarian theology remains at best inchoate. Reference to the Holy Spirit in his entire corpus is slight – not absent, as a glance at his hermeneutics will confirm, but not strongly developed in relation to the Christology. And one of the most tantalizing silences in the Christological schema is the lack of any exploration of what Jesus' being-for-the-other means in connection with his being-for God the Father. Connections are not difficult to make: if the key to divine life is what Byzantine theology would call the divine *tropos* of not being for oneself, a mode of eternally and comprehensively other-directed action, this seems to require a Trinitarian context. But Bonhoeffer characteristically focuses upon Christ's divinity as the authoritative communication of God's summons to truthfulness – rather than as something revelatory of the element of filiation that is eternally within the divine life. The significance of his exposition is in the way it connects the Chalcedonian legacy – and the legacy of Reformation debate – with an account of the Christian calling, and thus (as we shall see in more detail in the next lecture) with ethics. Bonhoeffer's consistent refusal of any model that implies treating finite and infinite as comparable forms of a single reality, or that threatens to reduce their relationship to one of difference in scale, points towards a basic theological clarity about the 'Godness' of God, and thus affirms the classical belief that God can have no territory or interest to defend over against the created order. In the context of a more fully developed dogmatic picture, this is part of the rationale for understanding the divine life as intrinsically selfless or self-displacing. For Bonhoeffer, the immediate consequence is the corporate and individual self-displacement that appears in the being-for-others that he so eloquently sketches in the Christology lectures (and which he explores much more fully in the *Ethics* manuscripts): what we begin from is the divine selflessness in its agency *pro nobis*, in good Reformation style. But there is a road not taken here. The Chalcedonian framework presupposes that the human life of the Word Incarnate embodies the prior reality of the eternal Word, not least in its directedness to the love and will of God the Father. The other-directedness of the incarnate life is wholly conditioned by the eternal reality in which the Word's agency and love are what they are because directed towards the eternal source, the Father – whose loving agency is what it is in the act of generating the eternal other who is the Word and the eternal 'overflow' of their relation who is the Spirit. This is a long way from Bonhoeffer's idiom, but it is arguably a necessary filling-out of his schema if this schema is to have behind it the fullest possible theological resourcing.[66]

The Christology lectures, however, should not be read with inappropriate expectations of dogmatic completeness. They are visibly shaped by a sense of mounting crisis in Church and state, and they end with a passionate reiteration of the need for the Church to recognize and accept its 'humiliated' condition as the way it can embrace the humiliated Christ. Humiliation is not a strategy, so that the Church can make yet another defensive weapon out of its own failure ('we are humiliated, so we are justified'): the Church *seeks* neither success nor failure in worldly terms, but simply articulates its repentance in whatever condition it finds itself.[67] Central to the entire argument here is Bonhoeffer's conviction that our theology of the Church goes astray when the Church becomes the focus of its own thinking, a fixed object to be organized, defended, promoted – as opposed to being the communal consequence of a faith that is 'pressured' into being by encounter with God in the form of the suffering Christ. Speaking or writing connectedly about this has in it a certain paradoxicality, of which Bonhoeffer is fully aware; the later work that flows from

---

66   Puffer's essay on Barth and Bonhoeffer (above, n. 28) has a very good discussion of how Barth's development of the theme of an *analogia relationis* between God and humanity picks up and modifies some of Bonhoeffer's earlier theology and locates it in a more explicitly Trinitarian context, especially in *Church Dogmatics* III.2 (e.g., pp. 203, 218).

67   Ibid., pp. 312–13.

his Christological reflection is a sustained attempt to keep this paradox in focus as he explores more fully and urgently what a Christocentric or Christomorphic life might be in the heart of the twentieth century's moral catastrophe.

3. Christology, Ethics and Politics: Discourses of Transformation

Bonhoeffer believed that his unfinished work on ethics was at the heart of his theological vocation; he wrote from prison in December 1943[68] that he felt sometimes that all he had left to do was to finish his *Ethics*. Clifford Green, introducing the English translation of the new critical edition of Bonhoeffer's texts, underlines[69] the fact that his focus in these manuscripts is twofold – laying foundations for a post-Hitler Germany, and making sense of the transgressive politics in which he had by this time become engaged, the politics of clandestine resistance and – perhaps, given the uncertainties around Bonhoeffer's knowledge of and involvement in this – the plot to kill the *Führer*. Equally, though, Green stresses[70] the Christological foundation of Bonhoeffer's entire argument – a foundation whose significance earlier discussion of the *Ethics* manuscripts had largely overlooked or looked at somewhat askance. The complexity of Bonhoeffer's argumentation has led some commentators to complain that he offers little help with specific decision-making and provides only a hermetically closed theological description of human relations. James T. Laney, in an essay of 1981, charges Bonhoeffer with confusing 'is' and 'ought': Bonhoeffer describes the theological meaning of the given patterns of interrelation between human agents, the relations that exists prior to any of our decisions about them, and then fails to explain why we should act in this or that particular way on the basis of these patterns; and by making extravagant theological claims for our interdependence, he obscures the need to work out how we are to

---

68 Bonhoeffer, *Letters and Papers from Prison: The Enlarged Edition*, ed. Eberhard Bethge, London: SCM Press, 1971, p. 163. I refer to this edition as the most familiar and accessible to English-speaking readers.

69 Bonhoeffer, *Ethics*, English translation ed. Clifford Green, trans. Reinhard Kraus, Charles C. West and Douglas W. Stott, Minneapolis: Fortress Press, 2005, p. 10.

70 Ibid., pp. 6–9.

persuade agents to adopt conscious voluntary moral policies on the basis of any such convictions.[71]

But this slightly misses Bonhoeffer's point. His concerns about what would need to be taken for granted in a post-fascist state, and about what might be entailed for such a state if its foundation rested upon an act of supreme 'lawlessness' (political revolution, even political assassination), push him towards two related but distinct areas for reflection. There is first the question of what the patterns of relation are that state power cannot override; what it is about human interdependence that cannot be subordinated to either political interest or individual aspiration, the forms of solidarity between us that pre-exist choice or reasoning. And then there is the question of what the *ultima ratio*, the extreme case, is that would – without suspending the *fact* of these solidarities – make it intelligible for human agents to go against the routine expectations in respect of them, to make a breach in the normal pattern of respect or obedience to the imperatives that they imply. These questions, however, cannot for Bonhoeffer be addressed in abstraction from the prior issue of how we are to characterize and understand the non-negotiable reality that we confront simply in virtue of being human agents. It is indisputably a reality of interwoven or interdependent finite lives; but much more importantly it is the reality that has been embraced by God and renewed, re-constituted, in Christ. '*In Jesus Christ the reality of God has entered into the reality of this world*':[72] the event of Jesus Christ is the place where the unconditional eternal reality of God's life coincides with the life of the finite world, not displacing it or 'conquering' it but penetrating and suffusing it in such a way that it is now the case that I may participate in God's reality in and through participating *in the world*, since God has committed Godself to that world in all its aspects.[73] The interrelatedness of finite reality is always already related to God; but that deepest of relations is not something undialectically 'given' in the world, as if all we needed to do in order to apprehend God or learn God's will was to look

---

71 James T. Laney, 'An Examination of Bonhoeffer's Ethical Contextualism', pp. 295–313 in *A Bonhoeffer Legacy: Essays in Understanding*, ed. A. J. Klassen, Grand Rapids, MI: Eerdmans, 1981, especially pp. 302–3.

72 Bonhoeffer, *Ethics*, p. 54 (italics in original).

73 Ibid., p. 55.

around us.[74] At the same time, it is impossible, in the light of Christ, to think in terms of two parallel realities, crystallized in two parallel jurisdictions or institutional orders, one sacred, one profane. The habitual reality we think we perceive is opened up to God's, and this creates tensions: we must 'die' in order to come to life in God's world. Yet this death and rebirth is not a transition from one territory to another. This is the error of so much Lutheran thinking, according to Bonhoeffer;[75] and we might recall his warning in the Christology lectures against a false understanding of the Church's 'centrality' in the world in terms of 'its visible position in the state'.[76] There is no 'static independence' in the relation between sacred and profane, only the unceasing dialectical struggle for the world to become tangibly and historically what it actually is.

'There is no part of the world, no matter how lost, no matter how godless, that has not been accepted by God in Jesus Christ and reconciled to God.'[77] But the implication of this is that all the 'patterns of interdependence' between human beings that we have mentioned already are, at one and the same time, established on a firm foundation *and* re-evaluated or reimagined: they must now be understood as oriented towards the reality of Christ. Bonhoeffer calls these patterns 'mandates', a doubtfully clear designation for them, but manifestly a way of avoiding the use of the fatally compromised language of 'orders of creation'[78] while underlining the fact that these are relations that carry immediate implications for how we should act. What he is in fact doing is recognizing that our humanity is *necessarily* involved in three sorts of relation. There are relations with the material environment (through work and – as he spells out at a later stage – 'culture' in its widest sense[79]), the relations that constitute the intimate partnerships of family life, and the relations through which we are involved in the life of broader political units (government). But on top of

---

74 Ibid., pp. 53–4.

75 Ibid., pp. 55–8.

76 Above, n. 50.

77 Bonhoeffer, op. cit., p. 67.

78 See Green's introduction to the *Ethics*, pp. 17–22, and also the 'Editors' Afterword to the German Edition' in the same volume, especially pp. 415–19 and 429–33.

79 Ibid., p. 388.

these natural solidarities, there is the further, historically specific, 'mandate' implied in the Church's social and embodied form. This last exists in order that the other solidarities do not become exclusive or divisive: the Church declares that all forms of basic human solidarity point to and are subsumed in the fulfilled solidarity of the Body of Christ,[80] and are thus themselves never in competition, since they all lead towards that supreme connectedness. If we want to understand – and to *inhabit*, prayerfully and intelligently – any of our patterns of connectedness as humans, we need to keep alive the critical question of how the exercise of any action based on such connectedness relates to or makes possible or manifests the ultimate form of solidarity – the explicit participation in the divine life that is the life of discipleship in the Body. The Church inevitably appears as a visible social unit – and thus it occupies real space in the world; it jostles up against other social forms. But its fundamental challenge is to occupy that space *solely* for the sake of the world's eschatological solidarity: 'The space of the church is not there in order to fight with the world for a piece of its territory, but precisely to testify to the world that it is still the world, namely the world that is loved and reconciled by God.'[81] So the Church is not simply a *realm* of reality, a subdivision, but a locus from which the world can be seen as a whole and responded to with a wholeness of service and compassion. The Church exists to say to the world that it need not be afraid of the Church, of a Church that seeks to displace it or control it: it is 'still the world', that is, still a system of interwoven relations ('mandates') into which God has entered in order to realize the true nature of the worldly. The irony in the Church's very being is that it is there to make a universal and comprehensive claim that has nothing to do with any aspirations to be a universal and comprehensive system of control; its 'territory' in the world exists only to be the guarantee of the integrity of the world's territory as a whole. Its particular interest, the corner it exists to defend, is the interest of no specific human group or party in exclusion or isolation.

All this holds together in the framework of Bonhoeffer's Christology. 'In Christ the form of humanity was created anew', says Bonhoeffer; but this is again not a displacement of some other and alien form of humanity but the

---

80 Ibid., pp. 73–4.
81 Ibid., p. 63.

uncovering of what the actual 'worldly' form of humanity means: 'Human beings become human because God became human.'[82] The pre-existing, unchosen forms of human solidarity already tell us that we are not autonomous and isolated agents, but are involved in other lives; and the form of Christ's humanity is the most radical imaginable embodiment of solidarity. It is *the solidarity of Creator and creation* – which in this case is not a matter of pre-existing 'natural' interdependence, like finite solidarities, but a free divine act of self-immersion into the networks of the created world. And this divine act seeks to extend itself as human agents are incorporated into Christ, and Christ's solidarity with the whole world is formed in them. Bonhoeffer entitles the relevant section of his manuscripts 'Ethics as Formation' and defines this formation as 'Jesus Christ taking form in Christ's Church'.[83] More specifically, this means human agents taking on the representative and responsible role that Christ exercises.

The argument needs some spelling out. God's unconstrained and unlimited involvement in the human world means that God accepts universal solidarity; God is not 'immune' from the compromised and struggling reality of our world. In the ordinary forms of human solidarity, each of us has to recognize that we are not answerable only for ourselves but for those whose lives are intertwined with ours in whatever degree. In work and culture, in family life and in social/political engagement, we have to accept that we cannot make decisions as if our interest were capable of being isolated from that of others. And in this sense we exercise some level of what Bonhoeffer calls *Stellvertretung* – translated in the most recent versions as 'vicarious representative action', a great improvement on the eccentric earlier translation of the word as 'deputyship', but still not quite catching all the resonance and concreteness of the German. *Stellvertretung* is acting in or from the place of another, 'standing in' for the other, being actively there on behalf of the other, negotiating for the other. As we have noted, Bonhoeffer (ambitiously) sees this as basic to the life of the 'mandates', basic to the interwoven character of our life as agents; his prime example is the father of the family (a revealing choice, reminding us of his instinctive social

82 Ibid., p. 96.
83 Ibid.

conservatism[84]), who is never able to ignore his involvement with the lives of others for whose well-being he is answerable. 'By working, providing, intervening, struggling and suffering for them ... he really stands in their place.'[85] At the same time, this responsibility is a responsibility for *liberating others into their responsibility*;[86] anything other than this would be a violation of the other's dignity. The overarching theological point in all this is that God, by embracing this world of representation, mediation on behalf of others so that they are equipped for the same task, shows us that routine human life under the 'mandates', within the routine forms of mutuality, can be a mediation of participation in divine life. So far from all this being a compromising and spiritually ambiguous area of life, to be overcome or set aside by the life of grace, that life of grace appears as the life of 'mandated' human sociality – work, family, political society – now revealed as potentially the vehicles of God's own life among us.

What this means in practice is that what I have called routine life is understood and judged according to its openness to the Christological reality out of which ultimately it arises. The mandates exist in order to provide human existence with a structure that will eventually appear as the structure of Christ's own life, Christ's being-for-the-other.[87] Thus, where the interdependence of human life shows the radical quality of Christ's responsibility and representation, where familial, political or cultural action realizes a more and more unqualified degree of being-for-the-other, it becomes a manifestation of Christ's underlying and ongoing agency. The Christological transformation of humanity is the transformation of all our constitutive relationships as humans so that they are now able to move more freely towards this maximal for-otherness. It should be clear that this is inextricably linked with Bonhoeffer's fundamental insistence that God – and thus relatedness to God – does not simply displace finite solidarities; equally it is clear that it would be wholly mistaken to read Bonhoeffer as

---

84 Barth, who was not a great admirer of Bonhoeffer's *Ethics*, commented critically on Bonhoeffer's 'North German Patriarchalism', in *Church Dogmatics* III.4, *The Doctrine of Creation*, Edinburgh: T&T Clark, 1961, p. 22.

85 Ibid., p. 258.

86 Ibid., p. 269.

87 Ibid., p. 390.

reducing relation with God to such finite solidarities, or identifying God with the ensemble of worldly realities. And to see life under the mandates in this light is also to see how Bonhoeffer can arrive at his notion of the *ultima ratio* – the extreme or exceptional argument that might have to be made in extreme or exceptional situations – that could prompt a transgression of the routine order of 'mandated' relation. What if the routine pattern of relations has come to be so corrupted that it now actively blocks or subverts the possibility of redirection towards Christ? What if – in the most obvious instance in Bonhoeffer's context – the order of political solidarity claims to override all other solidarities, so that the mutual reinforcement and convergence of the mandates, their being for and with each other,[88] breaks down? This, Bonhoeffer argues,[89] leaves us stranded beyond the normal scope of reasoned moral argument, so that our responsibility, instead of being (as it normally is) bound to the daily maintenance of ordered relation, is a matter of direct confrontation with life-or-death choice; we discover the unwelcome freedom to act in such a way as to challenge the imbalance of a death-dealing 'order' that is in fact generating disorder. Bonhoeffer's treatment of this is as tantalizing as anything he ever wrote. He refuses to say that 'breaking' the law, the order of the mandates, then becomes *necessary*, let alone necessarily virtuous – only that (i) the possibility of breaking the law for the sake of preserving the law is *necessarily* to be confronted, (ii) that in the nature of the case this can never become a new generalization, a new law that promises to tell the agent he or she was right, and so (iii) that the readiness to accept guilt is required, and belongs equally to those who decide to abide by the law in an *ultima ratio* scenario (presumably by something like passive or non-violent disobedience) and those who actively resist. In the extreme situation, there is no human power of absolution.

So the two elements permeating Bonhoeffer's ethical thinking connect at this point – the question of what can be imagined, theologically and morally, for the construction of a post-fascist society and the anxiety about the legitimacy of disruptive action in the light of some *ultima ratio*. Say that the extremity of totalitarian claims prompts active resistance, disloyalty to the state, even violence against the unjust order; the only way in which this

88 *Ethics*, pp. 393–4.
89 Ibid., pp. 272–5.

can be set in a meaningful context – but *not* a context that promises innocence or virtue – is by seeing it as a means of restoring the balance of 'mandated' life, so that this mandated life is again free to be what it is supposed to be, the arena of God's involvement in all aspects of human solidarity. The question of active political resistance is bound in with what will ground a restored society, which is not, for Bonhoeffer, abstract democratic principle[90] but the liberation of the full range of human connectedness; the restoration of law-governed society in which people are fully educated about their civic, cultural and familial capacities after a period in which all these have been reduced to or trumped by political compliance. Despite some persistent misreading, Bonhoeffer is not adumbrating a situationalist or even contextualist ethic: his discussion has nothing to do with imagining some overriding moral principle such as agapeic love sometimes subverting conventional ethical rules, nor with a focus on individual benign or pious intention. He is inviting Christians to develop a discernment about what those things are that corrode and destroy human solidarity in its plural and interactive fullness, because the corruption of these solidarities is a blockage of the divine will which works in and through those solidarities, and which is embodied in the unique connectedness established between God and humanity in Christ. Any proposal for a *system* that will spare us the severity and the unavoidable complicity and guilt of the *ultima ratio* thus becomes a strictly Christological error.

To yield to Christ and to recognize that he is the one in whom finite reality is supremely itself requires us to die to our self-constructed identities and to be ready to be identified anew with Christ; so much is clear from the major Christological passages of the *Ethics* drafts, as indeed from the earlier Christology lectures. A situationalist scheme simply replaces one self-constructed and self-justifying identity with another; it is a way of being sure I am right or just – which is for Bonhoeffer the antithesis of faith. In our identification with Christ, in that formation of Christ in us that Bonhoeffer speaks of,[91] we are enabled to and called to be accountable for ourselves in a new way – not as individual selves, not even simply as agents living under the mandates, but as agents who have grasped or, better, been introduced into

90 See the 1941 letter to Paul Lehmann quoted by Clifford Green, ibid., p. 17.
91 Ibid., pp. 96–7.

the full extent of their solidarity by accepting solidarity in and with Christ. In the light of that, I can say that I am now empowered to 'answer for' Jesus: I represent him before the world, I 'stand in' for him as he stands in for all; and by the same token, I 'stand in' for all my human neighbours before Christ. The only way I can be answerable for myself is by taking on this double accountability, for Christ and for others in the presence of Christ.[92]

But it is time to examine more closely what exactly this recurrent language of *Stellvertretung* actually means. Bonhoeffer's insistent and eloquent evocations of radical responsibility and vicarious agency are not easy to condense into an argument, and there are times when the energy and beauty of the rhetoric run well ahead of anything that readily connects with actual decisions or moral strategies. However, there is a clear thread of exposition to be traced. If, as Bonhoeffer asserts, Christ's incarnate identity is *nothing other* than 'standing in' for us,[93] and if this establishes that human life is in its essence a 'standing in' for one another, what is the content of this representative action? It must be more than just a way of underlining the imperative to give priority to the need of the other, and it is certainly not a sentimental injunction to search for objects of benevolence. In this connection, the language of universal or unconditional responsibility might be thought to be dangerously unreal if it means that we are at any moment literally answerable for the well-being of the entire human community, summoned to solve the problems of all. But in the overall context of Bonhoeffer's thought and life, the central point to understand is surely the literal sense of the words used: we are to stand in the place where the other lives, so that we are vulnerable to what the other is vulnerable to; we are to risk what the other risks. So what Bonhoeffer describes as the father's vocation in the family – 'working, providing, intervening, struggling and suffering' – should be read as a cumulative account of what *Stellvertretung* entails. Beginning with the practical labour we are called to perform for the security or well-being of the other, the maintenance of their conditions for living and living well (and so acquiring their own responsibility), we are led to risk and exposure for their sake and ultimately to the risk of sharing directly whatever challenge and pain they confront. Bonhoeffer is not particularly interested in the

92 Ibid., pp. 255–6.
93 Ibid., pp. 258–9.

discussion of how we make up our minds on isolated questions of behaviour: it is in his eyes perfectly all right if most of our behaviour (so far from involving a series of fascinating existential crises) is unreflective, even rather boring, a faithful living under mandate, performing the prosaically obvious duties entailed by our relationships. Ethics is quite properly a boringly predictable affair for most of the time, and we need to be very wary indeed of self-dramatizing. But it does nonetheless matter to have a narrative about these relationships and our functioning within them which makes plain that they will, *if performed in the context of trust in the incarnate Christ*, draw us inexorably towards something of a diagnostic for clashes of duty, acute temptation or whatever. Routine ethical practice unobtrusively, even invisibly, trains us in alertness to the *ultima ratio*. The Christological 'directedness' of our behaviour means that we must learn to ask how we may act so as to relinquish whatever fashions conventions and securities prevent us from standing with another, whatever self-images protect us from seeing the reality of another, whatever generalities block our attention to the particularity of another. This is how ethical discernment embodies the death that the human ego undergoes in the presence of Christ – which is as dominant a note in the *Ethics* as it is in the Christology lectures or indeed in *The Cost of Discipleship*. 'My life is another, a stranger, Jesus Christ', writes Bonhoeffer;[94] and my life cannot become Christ's without a death that is also a total transformation, a 'No' spoken into our own refusal of life and thus a gift of reconciled existence.[95] All my patterns of relation are now rooted in Christ's absolute being-for-the-other; and so they also take on the unlimited character of his standing with and for all. This is *'limited by our creatureliness'*;[96] it is not a global project or manifesto, but a matter of being disposed to see whatever reality actually confronts us without illusion. As such it is the opposite of ideology, the attempt to lay hold of the future by prescribing a right course of action (a course of action free of guilt or complicity or ambivalence) for every situation.[97] 'Representing all', 'being responsible for all', are not injunctions to a new philosophy of life but a description of what

94 Ibid., p. 250.
95 Ibid., p. 251.
96 Ibid., p. 267, italics in the original.
97 Ibid., p. 268.

life in Christ already is. The other person I encounter is *already* the one with whom Christ is in solidarity, and the death I must endure is the death of anything that stops me acknowledging that and acting accordingly.

The key point is the insight that Christ has no 'identity' that is not an embodying of unconditional solidarity with us and of acceptance of our vulnerable, guilty and desperate condition. And just as Calvin and Aquinas alike insist that Christ wins no merit that is for his own advancement but always and only what he can bestow on others, so Bonhoeffer understands the work and identity of Christ as consisting entirely in the functions of representation and responsibility. Christ's unqualified sinlessness is simply the absence in Christ of anything that prevents or delays identification with the guilty and suffering, the absence of any residue of defended, isolated selfhood. He above all others has no territory to defend, nothing that impedes his solidarity; he has no anxiety that an immersion in solidarity will somehow destroy him because his very being is a being-for, a being-in-solidarity. When Christ declares that he is 'life', he is not making an abstract metaphysical claim but announcing that he is '*my* life, our life'.[98] What it is for him to be alive and active is simply for him to be that which brings life to the human world in every corner. Bonhoeffer is far from asserting here some sort of bland universalism (though he has been charged with this); his account of Christ's solidarity is not a guarantee of automatic salvation for all (after all, he famously insisted that it was possible for a believer to 'separate from salvation', as in the case of the Nazi-supporting *Deutsche Christen*), but a statement of how Christ's radical existence as representative and responsible provides the ground of transformation for all without exception if they are willing to accept the invitation to death that is the proclamation of the gospel. And in the concrete moment, that universal ground of solidarity is what I meet when I meet the human other: I am called to stand with and for that other because Christ has already done so, and I cannot as a member of Christ's Body see or relate to the other in any other way. I must see and respond to them as those with whom Christ has chosen to be. Above all, I cannot – any more than Christ himself – seek the consolation of a life of individual meritoriousness or innocence. 'Genuine guiltlessness is demonstrated precisely by entering into community with the guilt of other human

98 Ibid., p. 250.

beings for their sake.'[99] As in the Christology lectures with the Word's challenge to a false, self-constructed and would-be self-sustaining human *logos* at every level, so here: we must see that the 'I' which seeks individual innocence is a fiction and capable only of building fiction upon fiction if it constructs a self-justified image. Even the dignity of 'conscience' has to be overturned and refounded: the believer's conscience is not an autonomous means of discovering where individual integrity lies, in a 'knowing of good and evil' – the deadly aspiration of the first Adam[100] – but the discovery of an integrity that lies only in Christ. And Bonhoeffer boldly draws the analogy with the faithful party member who can say that Adolf Hitler is his conscience (as indeed Hermann Göring had claimed).[101] This is both analogy and polar antithesis, in that *only* the one whose identity was in no sense seeking to absorb, dominate or replace the identity of the other could conceivably be one in whom I could find my unity or integrity. It is true that I cannot give my conscience away to any other agent in the ordinary course of things; but the Christian's integrity is already in the hands of – in the life of – an agent who is simply not 'other' in the routine, competitive sense. I shall find no unity or integrity in an inner life, a spiritual sanctuary in the heart; only in relation with the life that is given to and for me, the life that claims no place over against me, in rivalry or contention with me. And that other-directed life is what I now, as a believer, live by in every approach to every finite other.

For Bonhoeffer, ethics – and especially the extremer reaches of political ethics which he came to inhabit – was bound to be a discourse about transformation: the fundamental transformation of the ego in relation to Christ. For most of the time, political virtue is going to be and should be invisible,

---

99 Ibid., p. 276.

100 Ibid., p. 277, and cf. p. 268: 'Ultimate ignorance of one's own goodness or evil, together with dependence upon grace, is an essential characteristic of responsible historical action.'

101 Ibid., p. 278. Cf. the words put into the mouth of a Nazi nurse in W. F. Hermans' short story, 'Glass': 'We did what the Fuehrer said! Yes, we were unfree, but we are free of remorse – because he was our conscience. Why was he our conscience? Because all the orders came from him! By doing what he said, we could not sin. He bore all our sins' (Joost Zwagerman, ed., *The Penguin Book of Dutch Short Stories*, London: Penguin Random House, 2016, p. 184).

a life lived faithfully under the mandates, prosaically living out the obvious duties and obligations of the relations in which we stand even before we choose. This 'penultimate' realm in which the call and demand of Christ is muted is affirmed nonetheless as real and valuable. It is not an order of prag-matic compromise but a context in which we may steadily learn something of the discernment we shall need when we are faced with the challenge of acting as though we truly believed in a justification found only in Christ.[102] In other words, Bonhoeffer is not laying the foundations for a revolutionary Christian political ethic of the kind so much discussed in the later twen-tieth century; he is as sceptical of overheated radicalism as of pragmatism,[103] and warns of the risks of an apocalyptic negativity towards things as they are or towards inherited social solidarities. He has no interest in an ahis-torical political rationality, ignorant of historical and cultural rootedness. 'Radicalism hates time. Compromise hates eternity', he writes aphoristi-cally; '... Radicalism hates wisdom. Compromise hates simplicity.'[104] But by arguing so insistently for a Christological ethics and politics, he offers what is in fact a profoundly radical proposal about political virtue. The citizen is challenged not to conform to some measurable standard of satisfactory public behaviour but to practise a steady scrutiny of the ongoing habits of a social order in the light of the question of what does and does not stand in the way of solidarity and shared risk. More specifically, the believing citizen is challenged to recognize what it is in the social order that, in the extremest cases, undermines the fabric of solidarity itself – through the exaltation of state over family, or private life over public, or economy over culture, through the reduction of the given variety of social connection to a single order of compliance or whatever it may be. And in the most extreme con-dition of all, the believer has to learn to trust in the unshakeable action-in-solidarity that is the living reality of Christ when there seems no 'justifiable' way through the net of guilt and complicity; to learn to trust the possibility of grace mending acts that go beyond the obviously lawful in challenging the tyranny of a corrupted 'mandate'. Political virtue is reconfigured as the capacity fully to inhabit a world of social mutuality, with the risk that

102 Bonhoeffer, op. cit., pp. 161–70.
103 Ibid., pp. 153–6.
104 Ibid., p. 156.

accompanies it, especially in times of social crisis, and at the same time to understand this as the embodied process that is 'inhabiting' Christ.

Christology for Bonhoeffer is what makes political ethics – like all areas of ethics – a discourse of transformation rather than one more version of self-creation and self-protection. The *Ethics* manuscripts are already well on the way to the theology of the prison letters, with their evocation of the God who in Christ is 'edged out of the world' because he has no place within the world to defend and so is – paradoxically – capable of being everywhere at the centre of the world's life. Radical discipleship is working out what it means to live within this 'non-rivalrous' framework that is the life of Christ; it is not the adoption of a manifesto or a revisionist ethical system. A certain amount has been written on the way in which Bonhoeffer's language was strangely conscripted in the 1960s to reinforce an individualist relativism that is about as far from his concerns as could be; it is essential in understanding him to trace just how the Christological pattern moulds the argument at every point – a Christological pattern which is itself a refinement of the themes of the 1933 Christology lectures with their austere emphasis on the death of the ego in confrontation with Jesus, and the well-known injunctions of *The Cost of Discipleship*. And what gives this its sharpest edge is the way in which Bonhoeffer constantly returns, explicitly and implicitly, to the *ultima ratio* question: what is possible for the believer and/or for the Body of Christ when the penultimate realm of ordinary connection and mutual service, the order that providentially is part of what makes supernatural selflessness possible and intelligible, is being torn up by the rampant denials of created order implicit in fascism or some comparable form of totalizing social power. What is possible when the social order blocks off identification with the other? The Christological imperative, for Bonhoeffer, is that this social order has to be disrupted, its bonds broken, its obligations set aside – not in an apocalyptic denial of traditional connectedness or a revisionist account of what is good or holy, but as a challenge to a lethally poisonous corruption of the conventional forms of obedient solidarity, the degeneration of the interwoven call of the mandates into a demand for compliance with a single unchallengeable power. In the *Ethics* fragments he is still obsessively exploring the grounds and the limits of this: the texts we have are not a self-justification, but they are undoubtedly an effort at self-explanation.

And they have an inevitably provisional character: he is not developing an apologia for tyrannicide, though he is certainly laying the groundwork for a theology of civil disobedience. The point is the way in which he works through the basic Christological model of being-for-the-other with an eye to an environment in which this is increasingly visibly antithetical to the norms of society. There is a good deal of unfinished business around this, to say the least. We might want to ask how, if at all, the model of disobedience to the ordinary conventions of life-under-mandate might apply to the other, non-political mandates, to the life of work or family. There is, for example, a hint that Bonhoeffer was beginning to reflect on how the mandate of the family's life might also become corrupted: he suggests, though very briefly, that Jesus' leaving of his family home is to be read as a 'purification' of obedience to parents by what might seem a breaking of the law,[105] but this is not developed. Equally tantalizing are the reflections on what the 'space' in the world might be of a Church that was systematically unconcerned about preserving its own space for its own sake.[106] They look forward to the 'hidden discipline' of the prison letters, a Church reduced to 'prayer and righteous action' rather than any self-propagating strategy. And as such they raise the large question of what mission and evangelization could mean in such a framework, and prompt thoughts about how a more developed account of the *sacramental* space of the Church's action might clarify things. That sacramental space, traditionally understood as an *eschatological* place, cannot because of its eschatological nature compete with the space of the present communal and political order; it is not the meeting of a dissident cell, projecting a gradual infiltration or takeover of the public space, but the presentation of the world *as it fundamentally is*, stripped by Christ's presence of its territorial and exclusive distortions, of the various ways in which power confines abundance, appropriates the material order for profit and power, and denies solidarity and the admission of shared, universal human hunger for justice and peace. Bonhoeffer's reticence in spelling out a Eucharistic

---

105 Ibid., pp. 278–9 (it is intriguing to compare this with William Blake's provocative argument in *The Everlasting Gospel* about Jesus' transgression of our habitual definitions of chastity, meekness and social virtue; c.f. p. 46, n. 3, above, for reference to discussion of this theme.

106 Ibid., pp. 63–4.

theology – influenced no doubt by his impatience with the importance ascribed to confessional disputes on this subject between Lutheran and Reformed Protestants – might yet be filled out by an understanding of how Eucharistic practice could embody precisely the non-competitive, non-territorial territory of a visible sign of God's future.

Universal responsibility is what is nurtured in such a territory, where the mythology of a fixed ego with boundaries to be defended is gradually dissolved by the grace of a God who takes on without qualification the consequence of the human world's murderous dysfunctions and so makes possible a different kind of perception and agency. If Bonhoeffer struggles – as he unquestionably does – to pin down the content of this, it is largely because he is breaking new ground in connecting the fundamentals of Christology, with all its implications for the very heart of how we speak of God's own nature and agency, with the world of moral habit as well as moral decision. His originality is marked. He 'descants', as we might say, on themes in Barth and others, just as in his Christology overall he creatively reconfigures the major historic debates of Protestant orthodoxy. The notion of universal responsibility itself clearly owes a great deal to Dostoevsky, whose work Bonhoeffer read with enthusiasm (this important imaginative and intellectual debt still awaits a full-scale scholarly treatment). *The Brothers Karamazov* – a text Bonhoeffer had been drawing upon for theological reflection since his earliest days as a pastor in Barcelona – underlines the theme of responsibility for all in two significant places, first in the materials for a 'Life of the Elder Zossima' which make up the bulk of Book Six of the novel, and then in the fourth chapter of Book Eleven ('A Hymn and a Secret') in which Mitya Karamazov describes his spiritual rebirth after he is falsely accused of his father's murder. In both places, the word Dostoevsky actually uses (the Russian verb *vinit'* and its cognates) means either something like being guilty *for* all, or being guilty *in relation to* all – that is, either 'guilty of everyone's sins' or 'guilty of sin towards everyone or everything'. Whichever meaning predominates, the sense is, it seems, close to Bonhoeffer's protest against aspirations to final justification or innocence. Not only are we summoned to take responsibility, we are summoned to accept the solidarity in guilt that this entails. Tracing these Dostoevskian roots for the concept may help us to distinguish what Bonhoeffer is saying from a simple but ambitious moral universalism, a duty to contribute to the solution of everyone's problems, which is surely one aspect of what Bonhoeffer is implicitly repudiating when he insists on the finitude of the agent and the contingent limits of responsibility, all that makes it 'creaturely and humble' rather than apocalyptically hubristic.[107] Accepting 'responsibility' is accepting both complicity and present and future accountability: if I am complicit, then my transfigured agency, assimilated by grace to Christ's agency, can equally be 'complicit' in transforming the entire situation. But once again, the distinctive element is in Bonhoeffer's Christological anchorage of the theme. He can elsewhere (in his remarkable Barcelona lecture on 'Jesus Christ and the Essence of Christianity') deploy the Dostoevskian figure of Christ silent before the Inquisitor,[108] and the 1933 Christology lectures allude in passing[109] to the supposed Christological significance (for most recent Dostoevsky commentators, a much more complex issue than Bonhoeffer recognizes) of Prince Myshkin in *The Idiot*; but Dostoevsky himself does not directly make the connection that Bonhoeffer elaborates, except insofar as the Christ of the Inquisitor parable is arraigned as guilty of failing to secure human happiness because of the unconditionality of his summons to freedom. What Bonhoeffer contributes (already hinted at in the Barcelona lecture) is the grounding of universal answerability in the wholly undefended humanity of Jesus, his willingness to be in company of children, outcasts, people with no status or claim. It is in this that we see most clearly the *difference* of God, the God revealed in Jesus, the God who makes no competitive claim but equally requires that we make no claim, so that there is 'an empty space in [us] into which [God] can move.'[110]

Bonhoeffer outlines a Christological ethic not primarily in terms of an 'external' imitation of Christ but as the outworking of a transformation of human agency into the kind of life that is uninterruptedly embodied in

---

107 Ibid., p. 269.
108 *The Bonhoeffer Reader*, pp. 64–5.
109 Ibid., p. 268.
110 From the Barcelona lecture, ibid., p. 67.

Jesus – the consistent refusal of a place to defend and the allied readiness to stand in the other's place for their good or their rescue. For him that refusal of a place to defend involves – at least – a scepticism about the possibility of a self-assessed righteousness by either conservative or radical criteria. He is not overthrowing the authority of what we have called 'routine' obligation and the order of mutual indebtedness; we habitually and prosaically owe each other fidelity in marriage, obedience (or, better, law-governed responsibility) in politics, and commitment and dependability in work of all kinds. But the transformative element is that in Christ we should be learning how to discern what destroys this order and when and how the disciple may resist the spurious rationality of a false orderliness, without any given guarantee of getting the right answers. The disciple is transformed into a Christlike figure in the sense of being thrown simply on the will of God to be with the world in its ambiguity and its suffering, that divine will which is uniquely embodied in Jesus. I have not in this book looked in detail at the prison letters, where all this is further developed, unsystematically but profoundly, but I hope that this brief overview of some of the major themes in the 1933 lectures and the *Ethics* fragments will have helped to clarify some of the most important continuities in Bonhoeffer's theology in general and his Christology in particular, and to locate them against the background of long-running and continuing debates within Protestant theology. There are large areas of unfinished business, as we have noted – especially with the integration of Christology into a more explicit Trinitarian schema; but the more we study Bonhoeffer's thought, the more intense some of those continuities appear; the more he comes into focus as a major contributor to the exegesis of a Christology both profoundly 'classical' and startlingly fresh.

And when it comes to the meditations of his last years in prison, he has some unforgettable summaries of his insights on the non-competitive relation of Creator and creature as Christ literally embodies it. Reflecting in 1943 on his reading of Hebrew Scripture, he writes: 'It is only when one knows the unutterability of the name of God that one can utter the name of Jesus Christ; it is only when one loves life and the earth so much that without them everything seems to be over that one may believe in the Resurrection and a new world.' Grasp once and for all that God is never 'available' as an object for speculation divorced from love and discipleship, and it is possible to undertake, in fear and trembling, the enterprise of speaking about Christ.

And, more powerfully still, in 1944, thinking through what is entailed by God's being-for-the-other: 'Before God and with God we live without God. God lets himself be pushed out of the world on to the cross. He is weak and powerless in the world, and that is precisely the way, the only way, in which he is with us and helps us ... not by virtue of his omnipotence, but by virtue of his suffering.'[111] Christology – the doctrine of the God whose self-communication is a humiliated human being, suffering because he cannot and will not defend himself in the terms the untruthful world understands – *means* the human act of commitment to the world in its truth, without the obsession of self-justification; 'taking seriously, not our own sufferings, but those of God in the world – watching with Christ in Gethesemane.'[112] And, as we shall see in the next and final chapter, it is Gethsemane and Calvary that provide the clue to an account of created reality itself in relation to its maker; recognizing a God who has been 'pushed out of the world' is not to be faced with a shocking anomaly, but with the revelation of *how things are with the world* if God is indeed the God whose life is fully enacted by Jesus of Nazareth.

111 *Letters and Papers from Prison*, pp. 360–1.
112 Ibid., p. 370.

Conclusion: Christ, the Heart of Creation: The Tension in Metaphysics and Theology

1.

Christological speculation begins from the fact that Jesus of Nazareth was seen and understood as acting in the place or role of Israel's God. That is to say, he was seen as bringing about the kind of change associated with God in his own tradition – the creation of a people, the acting-out of covenanted faithfulness even in the face of betrayal (thus the raising of Jesus from death is to be understood as a restoration or reaffirmation of the covenantal relationship, in continuity with the Exodus or the return from Babylonian exile), the reintegration of lost or strayed children of Abraham into the covenant community through forgiveness and reaffirmation of their status, the delivery of ultimate judgement about the destiny of human individuals (whether on the Last Day or, as in the Fourth Gospel, in every event of encounter). In addition to this, he was seen not only as modelling a particular style of prayer but as actively *animating* it: the Spirit which is released into the community of those associated with him, the community that can be described as his spiritual progeny (see Chapter 2), makes it possible for members of the community to take up Jesus' role and his place before the God of Israel. What happens in his human life can happen in their lives. And what happens in him is both prayer to the God he addresses as 'Abba' and the exercise of his liberty to forgive and to integrate strangers or strays into the people of God. Ultimately, the identity of Jesus and of his community is bound up with the promise of a new communal belonging which is open to all – to those who have been marginal or outcast by the standards of the religious authorities of the day – but a principle that is increasingly interpreted as involving those outside the limits of historic Israel. And so both Jesus and his community are understood as having the responsibility of 'advocating' for the harmony and well-being of the entire human family, once Jesus himself by his death and rising has established a decisive reconnection between God's faithful love and the human world in all its need and confusion. These themes are seldom if ever laid out systematically in the New Testament, but they represent the convergent ideas and images of a spread of very diverse writers; and throughout this book, this has been understood to be the background set of assumptions that has animated the development of Christology.

The challenge and paradox in this picture is of course the simultaneous affirmation of prayerful dependence and divine initiative as equally characterizing the identity of Jesus. As Christological discourse evolved over the first three centuries or so, the options gradually clarified so as to make it clear that a compromise over the unconditionality of divine initiative in Jesus could not be sustained without damage to the concept of God (i.e. by postulating, like Arius, 'secondary' divine agents or something similar), and that a compromise over the contingent and dependent character of his human activity could not be sustained without damage to the basic conviction that Jesus acts as an advocate *for those whose experience he shares*. The *first* step in resolving this is the Nicene doctrine that when we use the word 'God' for the source of all things and for the eternal response to that outpouring as it is finally embodied in Jesus, we mean exactly the same kind of life. The *homoousion* of Nicaea thus allows us to imagine that there is what might be called an analogue of 'createdness' within the divine life – that is, a form of living the divine life in the mode of reception and response, which is no less truly divine (possessed of unconditional freedom) than its source. Its embodied reality in Jesus thus has the exact *effect* of divinity within the finite world: it 'creates out of nothing', in the sense that it overcomes the consistent push towards dissolution and death in which humanity is trapped. It restores the divine image in creation and binds human persons in a holy community. It mends the breach between God and finite agents through the free bestowal of mercy and the restoration of access to God in prayer. The *second* step is to begin to explore what might then be said about how to understand and speak about the 'embodiment' of this dimension of divine life in a single finite inhabitant of the universe. The necessity of conserving the two poles of the original discourse – dependence and liberty – means that it is not possible to 'locate' God as an agent among others within the finite order, since that would imply an *interdependence* of limited agencies: grammatically (so to speak) God cannot be intelligibly represented in this way. But what this in fact means is that any embodiment of divine agency within the finite world must be in the form of genuinely finite action. This may seem at first blush a contradictory idea; but the point is that we cannot imagine God directly acting in the world as one agent among others, so that any claim for the presence of divine action must be a claim about activity that is strictly 'coincident' with an uninterrupted finite action, whose effects are such that it cannot adequately be spoken of *exclusively* in terms of finite action. The post-Chalcedonian model of the composite hypostasis of the eternal Word offers a structure which allows us to say that God is literally and personally acting within the world but does so only in the sense that this particular finite agent acts in such unbroken alignment with the Word's way of being God (in contemplative dependence, unrestricted response, unbroken and unconditional filial love and self-giving) that the effect of this action is completely continuous with the effect of divine action in Israel's history and ultimately with the divine liberty in the act of creation itself.

We touched on the idea of a sort of 'analogue of createdness' within the divine life. There are hints in the writers of the patristic period, notably in Athanasius, that the eternal generation of the Word is indeed a sort of eternal type and ground of the bringing into being of a finite world; and the Word as the eternal form of dependence is likewise the ground and the optimal form of all dependent finite reality. Creation's relation to God, in other words, is grounded in the Son's relation to the Father. And since the Son's relation to the Father is not that of one thing to another thing but an unimaginably intimate existence in the other, a non-duality that is not a simple identity, we are steered towards a similar model of the relation between Creator and creation. They are not two items that could conceivably be partnered in any list, added to each other, but a relational complex in which one cannot be spoken of without the other. The difference which makes this an *analogy*, not a pair of parallel instances, is that this relational complex in the case of Father and Son is eternal, entirely reciprocal, and not conceivable as the result of an act of self-determination, whereas in the case of creation it has a beginning, it must be thought of as a free act of divine determination, and is asymmetrical: God would be God without the world. Yet – and this is presumably Bonhoeffer's point in some of the texts examined in the last chapter – God has so acted as to make himself not conceivable or speakable outside this relation. There is no route around or behind the divine determination to be Creator, to be the God of this world. The relation between Creator and creation is in one significant sense like that of the eternal hypostasis of the Word to the human substance that is Jesus, as this is described both by the Byzantines and by Aquinas: the Word is what it is independently of any created state of affairs, and the created state of affairs that is Jesus' life depends wholly upon this prior and unified action. But if we want to speak of the Word in action, the Word as it has irreversibly defined itself in relation to our finite minds, we speak of Jesus above all else; we understand the unity of that action of the Word as embracing the event of Jesus, and of that event as being itself the divine word and act that enables our word – including our theology – and our acts of witness.

Hence the conclusion that there is no 'alterity' – no sense of 'one and then another alongside' – between Creator and creation, between Word and humanity in Jesus; just as there is no 'one and then another' in the relation between Father and Son. In neither context can we talk about items that could be *added together*. But this implies also that creation is most fully itself when it is aligned with, sharing in the kind of dependency which the Son has towards the Father: the fully responsive and radically liberating dependence that is the filial relation in the divine life is the ground of all created dependence on the Creator, and so the logic of creation includes a natural trajectory towards this kind of life-giving responsiveness. If this is the goal of creation as such, creation must include the possibility of finite creatures who are endowed with love and intelligence after the image of the Son and who are therefore capable of responding to the Creator with something of the conscious joy and generosity which would reflect in finite terms the character of the Son's self-giving to the Father. The focal point, the 'gathering point', of the created order is thus this finite love and intelligence, which we recognize as distinctively present in humanity (as far as we can know; we have no knowledge of what other instances there may be in the universe of love and intelligence, and human intelligence itself is grounded in the long continuities of animate life and its evolution, not something parachuted in to the created order and independent of it). From our point of view in the universe as we experience it, creation is at its optimal level of action and well-being when finite love and intelligence are in accord with the uncreated love and intelligence that the Word eternally exercises. This is the sense in which Jesus Christ is at the heart of creation – or the apex of creation, depending on our basic imagery – as the one in whom the movement or energy of eternal filial love and understanding is fully active in and as finite substance and agency. If we take a broadly Thomist viewpoint, this represents the restoration of a lost or occluded capacity in humanity, the capacity to be a mediatorial presence in creation, a priestly vocation to nurture the harmony and God-relatedness of the finite order overall and to articulate its deepest meaning in terms of divine gift and divine beauty. Sin creates its own 'lineage' of deprivation and distortion, so that the new beginning which is the event of Jesus Christ has itself to establish a new lineage, a new kinship, as we have called it. And, as the Maximian vision of the universe affirms, this healing of humanity unlocks the possibility of a universal reconciliation, the reconciliation figured in the sacramental life of the Body of Christ.

Thus we can say about creation that it is itself when most fully and consciously aligned with the divine act of self-giving; and simultaneously we must say that this divine act can work for the perfection and reconciliation of creation only in its perfect 'absence' from creation as a distinct agency among others, and so only in and through a particular created agency that is capable of healing relation with the entire complex of created act; a finite active substance that is freed from the ordinary limitations of relatedness because of its entire absorption in the freedom of the infinite. Divine agency is always 'in and beyond' the finite, to borrow a favourite phrase from the

Jesuit metaphysician and theologian Erich Przywara, whose work we shall return to in more depth later on in this chapter. As he argues,[1] there can be no halfway house between Creator and creature to bridge some sort of gap; the whole language of gap or distance between finite and infinite is a radically misplaced way of talking. What we look for is rather a point of 'gathering', mediation, interpretation, in which the diversity of the finite resolves into some kind of coherence. In one sense and at one level, we can rightly see the human being itself as a mediating presence, a 'middle' in creation, where meanings are drawn together, because it is the full animation of the material by the intelligent, capable of relating to the rest of finite reality in more than material ways; it occupies a border, it stands at an 'intersection' where both differentiation and connectedness are at work. Does this mean that a freer spiritual or immaterial agency would be a still more effective 'middle' – the created intellectual stability of the angelic world, between God's unchanging goodness and the unstable reality of human will? But once again we must beware of treating any part of the finite order as capable of performing this radical task of making complete sense of creation: finite spirit remains part of the finite ensemble, itself needing to be made sense of and to be held in the unity-in-multiplicity that is creation as a whole. Ultimately God alone, Przywara argues, can be the 'middle', 'the one in whom alone all multiplicity and all correlated antitheses are one'.[2]

From the created point of view (the only one we can occupy, needless to say), the best we can say unaided about God is that God is that *in* which everything finds coherence and *on* which all acts converge (material or immaterial), in the sense of working towards their fullest level of intelligible connectedness and their place in a consistent universal structure. But we are not left only with what unaided finite discourse can say: whatever we

---

1   Erich Przywara, *Analogia Entis: Metaphysics: Original Structure and Universal Rhythm*, trans. John R. Betz and David Bentley Hart, Grand Rapids, MI: Eerdmans, 2014 (henceforth AE), pp. 294–5. The book is divided into two sections, the first representing the original German *Analogia Entis* of 1932 and a series of related essays covering what was to have been a second volume; the original book and the later essays were first brought together in the standard German edition of 1962 (*Analogia Entis I. Metaphysik. Ur-Struktur und All-Rhythmus*, Einsiedeln: Johannes Verlag).

2   Ibid., p. 299.

may deduce in retrospect about this abstract recognition of 'the divine' as that which holds finite reality as one, the actual realization of this is what is revealed in the historical mediator, Jesus Christ, who 'appears as *the* reality of the way in which God-the-middle takes up the All: as the "infinity that assumes" (*infinita virtus assumentis*) he is the unifying head of everything from the invisible to the visible'.[3] Przywara is here interpreting a very dense discussion by Aquinas[4] of the Headship of Christ, which we have repeatedly seen to be a key concept in the maturation of Christological language. But he gives a very distinctive emphasis to how this requires precisely the divine assumption of a finite reality that is as different as we could imagine from the ideas we entertain of the divine as an indefinitely magnified reflection of what we understand as power or freedom. In other words, it is as the unfree, the mortal, the failing and suffering, that God realizes the centrality, the focal and magnetic significance of the divine in the created world. Only in the incarnate Word as revealed in the crucified Christ is it possible to have both direct openness to infinite activity and an unarguable sign of the fact that God is that which is 'always greater', *semper maior*. This, Przywara affirms, is the heart of the doctrine of analogy – no similarity without an always greater difference; so the Christ who reveals what the analogical relation of finite and infinite actually and abidingly is must be 'man wholly circumscribed in his humanity, in whose humanity there is nothing visible, audible, scrutable, or tangible, that would immediately suggest divinity'.[5] Revelation means that we are enabled to recognize not only that God in general terms is the focus, the ground of the 'rhythm', of finite reality, but that this is realizable only when God acts in *and as* the unequivocally finite, not in some sort of exalted and insulated finitude that 'looks more like' divine liberty as we might be tempted to imagine it. And insofar as the believer who lives in Christ now embodies this unique divine self-relation with the created world, Christian identity, *das Christliche*, is the goal and fulfilment of all creaturely process.[6]

3   Ibid., p. 301.
4   ST III.8.
5   Przywara, op. cit., p. 424.
6   Ibid., p. 345.

2.

Christology is a key to the 'logic of creation' because Christ appears as the *perfectly creaturely*: the unlimited, unconditioned reality of the divine Word animates within creation the active, energetic interweaving of intelligible life that makes finite reality a *universe*, not a chaos; and that interweaving is focused upon the life in which the Word is uninterruptedly active as the determining form of a human identity, realizing what humanity itself is called to be. Finite life 'in itself' would be simply the bare reality of process, change and becoming: but it is never simply 'in itself'. It is always related to the infinite cohesive agency that is the Word, which gives finite existence a *history* of responding to the gift of infinite love and invitation. Finite reality never just – as we might say – lies around simply existing; it is, in its variegated response to the gift of the Word's continuing and living engagement with it, always related to the infinite and thus always caught up in *analogy*: that is to say, it is always capable of being understood in terms of greater or lesser alignment with the infinite movement of God to God that is the giving of life between Father, Son and Spirit, the giving *from* each of these 'moments' in God *to* all in the divine circulation of life. Temporal existence is indeed 'the moving image of eternity', but of an eternity that is always a plurality in unity, a plurality of reciprocal gift. Thus, where the relation between God and God is most fully embodied within creation, we can see created reality as such in its proper light, as the analogue of that inner-Trinitarian movement. This is why, in embodying the Word's relation to the Father, in embodying what is the hypostatic distinctiveness of the Word within the Trinity, Jesus embodies also the maximal and optimal relation of creature to Creator.

And, as we have seen repeatedly in this discussion, this would make no sense if the embodiment of the Word were anything other than an unbroken finite identity, a genuinely created sequence of agency. We might turn back to the opening pages of this discussion and recall Farrer's insistence on what would have to be entailed in the very concept of a supernatural act as an act 'absolutely continuous with [...] natural activity'.[7] If this were not the case, it would simply not be the finite agent's act at all. The supernatural

---

7   Robert MacSwain, *Scripture, Metaphysics and Poetry* (above, Chapter 1, n. 1), p. 35.

is not something inserted into the natural and breaking its integrity; it is never 'cut off from its natural base'. Its distinctiveness is not in some sort of 'territorial' difference from finite acts and substances, but is simply to do with the degree to which the unconditioned is allowed to transform the finite from within. Thus the supernatural is neither an exalted version of the finite – the finite with certain constraints removed – nor a reality along-side the finite. Its difference is absolute – which is why it is possible for the infinite to be present in and as the finite, since (Farrer again) it is never the case, as with discrete finite substances, that more of one entails less of the other. In thus informing, subtending, permeating the finite, the infinite Word shows once and for all equally the non-*duality* of God and the world and the non-*identity* of God and the world. But the infinite Word is free to do this because the Word's eternal nature is defined by a relationship of non-duality and non-identity with the Father. It is this eternal relation that is imaged by the relation of Creator and creature, so that we can look for ana-logical connections between them – not in the sense that the world offers phenomena to our view that ' resemble' God, but that the world's non-dual relation to its maker appears in the world in more and less transparent modes, with the hypostatic union providing the ultimate and optimal cri-terion of discernment for this, as well as the point that gives meaning and coherence to all other manifestations of the relation. In association with the Word incarnate, redeemed humanity is set free to respond to its primordial vocation, to become (as Bonhoeffer would have it) answerable for creation's good order and preservation through the exercise of supernatural charity in respect both of other humans and of other creatures in general. The human agent incorporated in the Word has the responsibility of serving and con-serving the good and articulating and working with the intelligibility and beauty of creation in a way unique to humanity. So far from the doctrine of Christ's restoration of human dignity being a way of bestowing arbi-trary powers of control upon humans, it grounds a vision of humanity as itself meaningless or dysfunctional independently of its work in and for the well-being of creation, since this restored dignity is precisely a restoration *in* the Word in whom all things cohere (Col. 1.17). And in the light of this, we must recognize that the affirmation of the 'cosmic' role of Christ the Word and the historical specificity of the incarnate life belong inseparably together. It is the Christ who can – in virtue of his non-dual relation to the

Father – inform and shape the finite identity which is Jesus who can also be understood as the universally present and active 'logic' of the created order, the unbroken system of finite agencies interacting in a universe.

God cannot be (in the ordinary sense) identical with any subject in the world or any system of subjects or substances in the world because God cannot intelligibly be thought of as one among interacting, reacting, composite agencies. The pattern of such agencies that makes up the world is what it is, not God in disguise but a truly coherent intelligible system. If we are to hold to the doctrine that creation is a free or gratuitous bestowal of life, not a necessity for God, we must hold to the integrity of the system of finite causes and interactions. And thus, in such a world, God can act only from the centre of finite life, not as an intruder; otherwise the divine act dissolves the integrity of what is made. The classical doctrine of the Incarnation is, in short, a way of declaring what the terms 'Creator' and 'creation' have to mean if they are not to be reduced to a description of some sort of relation between two solid, limited subjects.

The idea that Christology tells us who and what God is in this respect is explored in a forbiddingly complex and highly original discussion by Przywara in an essay of 1958, 'Between Metaphysics and Christianity',[8] which builds upon his earlier discussion, already referred to, in the original (1932) text of *Analogia Entis*. He begins by attempting to interpret the 'meta' in 'metaphysics'. The metaphysical is, he argues, any discourse that opens on to what is *beneath, behind, above* or *within* the immediate field of perception or analysis – these four terms being taken as the range of meanings for the 'meta' prefix. Thus metaphysics is never a matter of something *to which* an argument concludes: it is to do with what is presupposed

---

8   Przywara, op. cit., pp. 520–36. The earlier material from the 1930s already quite explicitly lays the foundations for not only a Christological framing of the metaphysical discussion, but specifically for a theology of the cross; see, for example, pp. 179–82, 267–8, 294. Przywara's whole scheme is radically misunderstood if this Christological context is ignored; see John R. Betz's admirable introduction to the translation of *Analogia Entis*, pp. 110–12, and also his 'After Barth: A New Introduction to Erich Przywara's *Analogia Entis*', pp. 35–87 in Thomas Joseph White, OP, ed., *The Analogy of Being: Invention of the Antichrist or the Wisdom of God?*, Grand Rapids, MI: Eerdmans, 2011, especially pp. 84–6. See also in the same volume Kenneth Oakes, 'The Cross and the *Analogia Entis* in Erich Przywara', pp. 147–71.

as the ground of any discourse; it is the proper exercise of *intellectus*, intellection understood as 'reading [from] within the interior of things',[9] and of *ratio*, reason understood as the calculating of connections. But such a 'meta' can never appear as an object; it is a formal category such that the difficulty of bringing it into focus is (though Przywara does not use this image) like the difficulty of seeing one's own eye. What makes the 'meta' visible is a *method* in thinking/speaking.[10] In the process of the most intimate investigation of the finite – the *phusika* of the universe which we perceive – we cannot escape the question of what grounds these finite substances 'above' and' below' (i.e. the conditions of their active existence both in relation to what elements constitute them and in relation to the wholes of which they are a part). And in seeking to understand and articulate the most comprehensive account of finite substances in their fullest possible context, we cannot escape the particularity of these substances as precisely those things that the global context makes possible. To use a very different philosophical vocabulary, 'holistic' and 'reductionist' accounts of natural process and agency merge into each other in a conceptual Moebius strip (the American physicist and philosopher Douglas Hofstadter offers a number of teasing visuals to illustrate this point in the course of his discussion of holism and reductionism[11]): we cannot absorb one level of description into another without remainder because that which we are talking about is always inseparably both – the system that allows the particular substance to be intelligible, the particular substance that gives actuality to the systemic pattern. But what we can have no language for is the relation between the two: we can only articulate the *rhythm*, the reciprocal movement back and forth between the two (a key concept for Przywara[12]). And in speaking in the pattern of this rhythm, we express the 'meta' as method; we express an 'analogy of method' in which we state the formal truth of an analogy of being. That is, our speech

---

9 Przywara, op. cit., p. 524.

10 Ibid., pp. 525–7.

11 See Douglas R. Hofstadter and Daniel C. Dennett, eds, *The Mind's I: Fantasies and Reflections on Self and Soul*, New York: Basic Books, 1981, pp. 149–91, especially 160, 191.

12 Przywara, op. cit., pp. 139 (on 'oscillating unity'), 208, 264–6, 484–5, among many other passages.

moves between two poles: we drive down towards the 'smallest' or the most abstract intelligible elements of any substance, from the biological to the chemical, the physical and the mathematical; we drive outwards towards the comprehensive, 'ecological' picture, the system of interlocking agencies that is the universe. In this movement, we demonstrate that we cannot arrive at a final ontological statement that privileges either the particular or the general, and we cannot produce a *concept* of the relation between them: what *is* is the complex of difference-in-continuity that shapes the way we speak. Philosophies that try to establish either an *a priori* or an *a posteriori* starting point (in transcendent regulative generalities or in empirical finite interactions between clearly demarcated individual substances, such that one level of reality can be straightforwardly derived or deduced from the other) are actually trying to find a single principle of pure self-identity – that which is just itself and unfolds in a 'linear' fashion.[13] It is a doomed enterprise, since all substances are as they are in continuity and difference. The 'transcendent' is always 'transcendent as immanent', the finite *physika* are incapable of being spoken about without reference to the ultimate context that makes them thinkable (and thus makes them perceivable in the proper sense; forget the myth of 'innocent', uninterpreted or unmediated sense-perceptions).

But there is another level to the discussion. The purely formal account of 'metaphysical' analogy as we have just been summarizing it is not the whole story. It establishes that 'ordinary' perception of the world we inhabit is always analogical in the sense of showing us a world in which participatory relations always hold between particulars and forms, but in which neither can be said to be the origin of the other or the level to which the other ultimately reduces. What then must we say about the *entire* system of the universe, considered *as* a universe, as some sort of intelligible unity? This is the level of what Przywara calls the 'theological "meta"':[14] this designates a relation of difference more radical than any we can imagine, the groundedness of all finite relations in that from which they are absolutely different, the infinite. The infinite *meta* is a ground which (unlike the *meta* that prevails between levels of finite reality) escapes from any reciprocity of intelligibility

13 Ibid., p. 526.
14 Ibid., pp. 526–7.

(it is what it is independently of what is generated by it). The finite pattern of analogical relation pushes us outwards from the particular *physika* to ever-richer levels of intelligibility, levels not only of material organization and intelligible complexity but of spiritual and imaginative complexity, the aesthetic and the ethical. Metaphysics is 'polymorphous', says Przywara,[15] in the sense that within any specific discipline or discourse it is whatever presses 'outwards' and 'inwards' to the less obvious levels that make the object of the discourse meaningful. Various modern philosophies seek to stop this pressure outwards and inwards by identifying the metaphysically ultimate with a specific level of reality – knowledge (Descartes), morals (Kant), Art (Schelling), sexuality (Baader), the immanent rhythm of history (Hegel). But all these are bound to undermine themselves to the degree that they settle with a variety of *finite* categories or principles or acts posited as final and determinative for finite existence: the *meta* becomes, after all, another item in the list of substances, rather than that which always eludes being identified as an object for thought.[16] Observing and obeying the rhythm of thought as it has been set out in Przywara's argument so far means denying any identification with some specific level of the finite ensemble and launching into a further deep. Hence this 'polymorphous' character of metaphysics: it is always a context-specific denial of whatever pressures there are to stop the search for the final ground of intelligibility, in full awareness of the paradox that this final ground is not to be identified or thought in the way any *thing* is thought. This is where 'analogy as method' really comes into its own: we indicate the analogical relation of all things to God by this steady habit of denial that we have reached a conceptual answer or identified a scheme that would allow us to see either the finite deriving from the infinite in a kind of succession (first there was infinity, then there was finitude) or the particular deriving from the general (first there were forms, then there were particulars). Any such formulation would be a surrender to what he calls 'linearity', an implicitly univocal approach to being, and to the relation between God's Being and finite *esse* and substance – i.e. a model of being in

15 Ibid., pp. 527–8.
16 I.e., the unconditionally other or transcendent becomes no more than the most elevated or comprehensive item in an ontological list instead of eluding capture as *any* kind of item, and so expressible only in the very *method* of thinking.

which we simply understood radically different understandings of what it is to exist as if they were the same, as if God, intelligible forms, and specific finite objects were just diverse examples of 'existing things'. Accepting the necessity for analogical thinking means recognizing that these terms do not identify items that can be added to each other.

Przywara's stress on method means that *how* we think and speak is bound up absolutely with *what* we think and speak. The whole of his *Analogia Entis* is a prolonged examination of this connection, dismantling the idea both of a pure, detached subjectivity and of a set of fixed objects for the mind to register and describe. What we know is both the *So* and the *Da* of the contents of the universe: they are thus and not otherwise, a unified and continuous pattern of agency; they are here rather than there, which means they are actual only in relation to myself as knower and to the immediate circumstances of their becoming and subsisting. The thinking of reality thus moves constantly between the 'dissolution' of a given object into its components and the deepening grasp of the form that allows it to be thought as *a* subject in the first place; and this tension, which constitutes intellectual activity itself, sets up the regulative notion – out of the corner of the eye, so to speak, never delivering an object for the finite mind – of what reality might be when known in its final truth as an aspect of God's self-knowledge. The fact of metaphysical restlessness, the irreducible and inevitable oscillation between 'thus' and 'that', between form and phenomenon, is what creates the intellectual space in which we intuit an unsurpassable perspective, the Creator's knowing of creation as utterly not-God, yet utterly grounded in divine self-knowing and self-loving, the free but intelligibly self-consistent life that is made possible by the fact that the infinite is as it is – Trinitarian plurality and mutuality.[17]

What emerges from Przywara's account is that the enterprise of metaphysics is not a single discipline or discourse; it is whatever within a particular discourse shows in its method, its intellectual oscillations, what opens

---

17 This is finely drawn out by David Bentley Hart in his essay ('The Destiny of Christian Metaphysics: Reflections on the *Analogia Entis*) in White, *The Analogy of Being*, pp. 395–410, especially pp. 406–7. Cf. his own more extended discussion of the theme in Part 2, Chapter 1, of his major work, *The Beauty of the Infinite: The Aesthetics of Christian Truth*, Grand Rapids, MI: Eerdmans, 2003, especially pp. 241–2, 247–9.

up between the poles of *So* and *Da*, and thus points to a depth in which the coherence of any specific object of thought, and of the thought world as a whole, is grounded – a transcendental unity, if you want to use that language, but never over and above what is presented for thought, and so never an additional item for thought. Our intellectual activity in respect of this can only show this depth by the way it operates, not by displaying a transcendental object – which would in any event be a nonsense, as it would have to be subject to the same method of thought as anything else. All of this is part of Przywara's heroically resourceful attempt to restate aspects of Aquinas's ontology, even Aquinas's so-called Five Ways to the affirmation of the divine as real. And its importance for Christology, especially in the light of the whole argument of this book, is that it allows us to understand how and why we can see Christ as answering the question of what God is (*quid sit Deus?*).[18] The metaphysical argument so far has clarified the sense in which the method of self-aware intellectual activity leads us to what I earlier called the space in which a recognition of God, but not a concept of God, can occur; it is the sheerly *formal* aspect of discourse about God, and as such it points to a God who is necessarily incomprehensible, whose reality can never be an object for thought. This, says Przywara, is the 'natural' knowledge of God which grace takes for granted; it is a *mise en abîme*, a method that repeatedly denies the divinity of any formulation we can come up with; Przywara refers us to Augustine as well as Aquinas here, notably to Augustine's language about being able to say what God is *not* but never what God is. But – and here is Przywara's most important contribution to the theological discussion – so far from this being opposed to a doctrine of incarnational revelation, *it is the only principle that enables us to make sense of such an idea*. Formally speaking, 'what is ultimate in "what God is"', says Przywara, 'is "what God is not"'. Metaphysics leads again and again to the ultimate 'poverty' of this formal necessity of denying any determinate concept of the divine and being reduced to a sort of gesturing towards the generative mystery.[19]

But this is where Christology makes a surprising and crucial entrance into the argument. The fact is that, while we are decisively turned back from

18 Przywara, op. cit., p. 530.
19 Ibid., pp. 531–2.

any attempt at conceptualizing the divine, we are not simply silent about God. Christian Scripture presents Christ as 'icon' or 'mirror' of the Father, Jesus himself is represented as saying that in him the Father is to be seen (John 14.9), and so we speak of God and claim to 'see' God in Jesus. God is understood as having articulated a divine answer to the question, *quid sit Deus?* But to make that answer our own in human speech involves, in Przywara's pregnant formulation, 'a participatory re-enactment and comprehension of the "theology of God himself" (in his "self-expression in Christ") as the "Christological theology of God himself"'.[20] Just as in metaphysics, what displays the transcendent is the mode of our speaking out of the tension between transcendent and immanent, so here what shows Christ as the answer to the question of 'what' God is must be our enactment of the Trinitarian life, the birth of our confession of and discipleship to Christ out of our acknowledgement of the mystery of the Father. But this in turn means that we cannot speak about Christ as the answer to the *quid* question as if his identity in the world were simply the identity of God introduced as an item of discourse into a world that would have to be interrupted in order for God to come in – pure 'Godness' standing alongside the phenomena of the world in the form of a humanity transformed out of the shape and conditions of ordinary humanity. Equally, as Przywara argues, the 'form of God', in Paul's phrase in Philippians 2, is not divine glory breaking through the life of a mere human individual. Both the 'Alexandrian' and the 'Antiochene' extremes are ruled out by the fundamental shape of the argument. The God whose *quid* is revealed in Christ is the God who is strictly un-speakable by finite beings but who speaks himself in and as an entirely finite subject, wholly flesh and blood, mortal and vulnerable. This is why we can never speak of the nature of God as an object in anything like the ordinary way: we speak because God has given us (literally) a Word: God has invited us into the life that is his self-expression. And since that self-expression is an act of radical selflessness, the unconstrained gift of life in Jesus Christ, it can be expressed only – ultimately – in the theological enacting of that life, not in the words of a self observing a phenomenon.[21]

---

20 Ibid.

21 The resonance with Bonhoeffer is marked, and Przywara can even write in a latish book, *In und Gegen. Stellungnahmen zur Zeit*, Nurnberg, Glock und Lutz, 1955, p. 275, with

Thus the reality of the incarnate Christ is the 'paradox of paradoxes', says Przywara.[22] We have to clear our minds of what may seem to be an obvious way of proceeding – imagining that there is a human life so flawlessly ideal (according to our expectations) that we can conclude that it embodies the divine. This would still give us a sort of 'linear' connection between a supposed finite perfection and the perfection of the infinite; which would imply a continuity between finite and infinite as between two comparable kinds of life or being. As we have seen repeatedly in this book, this is the most fundamental mistake Christology can make, a mistake that effectively dissolves the unique and decisive contribution of Christological language to the understanding of the 'logic of creation'. But Przywara is also careful to identify and warn against the opposite error. The human story of Christ is not a sort of arbitrary occasion for recognizing the authority of divine transcendence, revealed in the paradoxical act of proclaiming the crucified as the Lord. Przywara does not spell it out, but an educated guess would be that he is thinking here of Bultmann's theology, in which the bare proclamation of the authority of Christ crucified is what is essentially meant by the credal confession of Christ's Godhead.[23] This would leave us with another kind of linearity and mutual exclusivity: God is shown to be 'beyond even his own human form' in the sense that the paradox of the proclamation projects us into a 'beyond' where God lives, leaving behind the conditions of this historical and material world. So, to the extent that this presupposes that to come to God we have to dissolve and/or abandon the finite world itself as void of meaning, this strategy is still trapped in the model of a competitive relation between the two orders, so that union with the divine is simply, undialectically, a negation of the created.

---

explicit indebtedness to Luther, of the impossibility of seeking as an object for thought a 'naked' God, stripped of the humanity assumed in Jesus.

22 Ibid., pp. 533–4.

23 See, for example, Bultmann's essay, 'The Christological Confession of the World Council of Churches', in his *Essays Philosophical and Theological*, London: SCM Press, 1955, pp. 273–90, especially p. 284: 'The divinity or deity of Christ is revealed in the occurrence in which we are given a place by the fact that the message of the gospel rings out' in such a way that we can say 'God is encountered in him and only in him' (sc. the crucified Christ).

But 'God in Christ is something above and beyond even "paradox"'.[24] The proper proclamation of the Lordship of the crucified is more than a rhetorical shock; it is an affirmation of the transforming *coincidence* of finite and infinite in the detail of this finite life, including and especially its humiliation and powerlessness, in an 'ultimate realism' which insists that the unprotected historical fleshliness of the incarnate Word is the appropriate embodiment of the selflessness of the divine. The absolute simultaneity, as we might say, of the Word and the crucified means that it is indeed possible to affirm that *quid sit Deus* is here answered. What God *is* is self-gift made specific and historically real in the scandal and folly of Christ's expulsion from the covenanted human community. In the very fact that Jesus abandons all claim to holiness and perfection in the religious and political terms of his contemporary world, the divine freedom is made plain. And in that making-concrete of divine freedom and love, through the shedding of blood on the cross, the Headship of Christ in creation – and most signally in the human world – is made known and made effective. This is where God's glory is to be discerned, the glory which is the suffusing of all things by the outpouring of divine Wisdom. The action of the Word in Jesus is not, therefore, something for which the particular human *event* of Jesus is simply accidental, simply the 'occasion' for a kind of timeless proclamation or summons to the human hearer. It is a genuinely transformative act, penetrating and pervading the whole reality of finite vulnerability; and through the living out of this in life and death it extends its transformative reach to those who are associated with Jesus in his Mystical Body – which, as Przywara reminds us, is therefore called to the same exposure and the same saving folly of self-forgetfulness. It is a striking parallel with Bonhoeffer's account of the Church's calling to costly solidarity, the renouncing of coercive power and of the battle for a 'place' in the world on the world's terms.

Przywara's target, again and again, is what he calls 'linear' accounts of the relation between finite and infinite and between formal and material, universal and particular. God repeats God's self non-identically in the Trinity; God repeats God in another kind of non-duality, in and as the finite creation which lives from the divine Word and Wisdom; creation repeats God in the analogical tension between abiding intelligible form and diverse

---

24 Przywara, op. cit., p. 534.

historical specificity. Not one of these relationships allows a deduction of one term from the other: they are different levels of a single ontological fact, 'non-dual non-identity' – which is eternally and unchangeably at the root of all being in the form of the Word's and the Spirit's relation to the Father. And the unique shape of non-dual non-identity that is the union of divine and human in Christ is therefore nothing to do with recognizing a humanity that is 'like' divinity. There is no such thing; there is only a humanity which establishes itself as the locus of divinity through the whole complex of action and possibility into which the would-be theological thinker has to be inducted as a sharer in the gift of relating to the Source of all as a daughter or son. We can go further (Przywara does in his 'Metaphysics and Christianity' paper). We cannot say that Jesus 'knows as God knows' if what we mean by this is that Jesus' knowledge of himself or his Father is a miraculously elevated or superhuman knowledge detached from the conditions of a finite subjectivity which learns and questions and is bound up with the life of feeling and instinct. The aspiration to this non-human knowledge was the primal human sin. On the contrary, Jesus knows the Father in the depths of his abandonment on the cross, and we grasp him as image and manifestation of God precisely 'in the unresolved and irresoluble *Mysterium Crucis*'.[25] As he had argued in a much earlier (1939) essay,[26] the radical humiliation of Jesus in his humanity signals the divine repudiation of any project of becoming 'like God' in the Adamic way, trying to acquire divine powers that are unfairly withheld from humans by a self-protecting deity anxious about his unique coercive authority. So the creature tempted to seek 'likeness' to God is shown that the true and divinely meaningful and free creaturely destiny is to be here on earth.[27] 'The patience of resting in the ordinary' is what the crucified Christ proclaims and makes possible, not as a form of passivity but as the way to release in finite reality the absolute self-dispossession of God's love.

And for Przywara, God alone is free to reveal to us that divinity is precisely not that elevated state of supernaturalized humanity that we so often imagine, the possession of a set of powers that magnify human capacity so

25 Ibid., p. 535.
26 'Philosophies of Essence and Existence', ibid., pp. 317–47.
27 Ibid., p. 346.

that it can transcend the limits of time and the body. *God is not humanity freed from frustration.* The divine life is what it is; the eternal and necessarily existing ground of all, a life that is simply the conscious everlasting generativity we can only call love. 'What is specifically Christian is the making visible of the invisible God in *"the form of a man like any other"* (Phil. 2.7); over against the drive of the world of original sin to be "like God", the God who alone is "wholly God" appears as "wholly man".' Or, more accurately, it is the making visible of the utter difference of God in the form of a slave: 'he who alone is unlimited in form and being (essence and existence) appears in the patience of the longsuffering of the most extreme limitation – in the "deformed" form of the crucified slave'.[28] And this in turn means that the invisible God is to be recognized in a 'deformed' Church, always dying to itself, its power and triumph, in witness to the 'redemptive patience of God'.[29] The categories of patience and service become the way in which the tragic tension between ethical effort and mystical participation is resolved: what is participated is divine patience; divine patience, acceptance of limit, is the door which opens on to radical transformation. Once again, Przywara's vision and Bonhoeffer's converge in an affirmation of the 'ordinary', the persistent labour of truly 'creaturely' work for God's will or God's Kingdom, in opposition to both pietist resignation and apocalyptic self-dramatizing. What is Christian is what is properly creaturely – 'the factical inner *"fulfilment"* of creaturely becoming'.[30]

Przywara's analysis is dense and many-layered, but what is clear here is the sense in which we can rightly say that Jesus answers the question, 'What is God?' The uncompromising embrace in the life of Jesus of the ordinary and the limited, to the point of complete powerlessness before the weight of human injustice and violence, exhibits the divine will – the divine passion, we could analogically say, God's 'wanting-to-be' – as wholly other than any finite assertion of one being against other beings. All that we do to protect ourselves against the consequences of our finitude – against our involvement with each other, the materiality of our lives and our indebtedness to our material environment, our mortality, our need to learn and change – is

28 Ibid., pp. 346–7.
29 Ibid., p. 347.
30 Ibid., p. 345.

put radically in question by this divine embrace of the ordinary. And in this we may understand that it is our denial of all this that puts us at odds with our Creator and thus with ourselves and our world, to such an extent that only the Creator can restore us to being creatures. Here is the heart of Przywara's argument; and it is the heart of the entire tradition of reflection on Christology that we have been tracing in this book. The real and deepest paradox is that only the Creator can exhibit fully what it is to be a creature. To recognize God in Christ is not to conclude that Jesus' exceptional human qualities point us to a still more exceptional kind of life, a few notches higher on the scale, which we can call divine. Nor is it to identify glimpses of 'the transcendent' framed by a human life, rays of divine light breaking through a great prophetic career. It is – as the writers we have studied repeatedly insist – to see an entire human identity as an unbroken embodiment of divine life; not 'resembling' it but enacting it. This is why – to go back for a moment to the discussion at the beginning of Chapter 1.1 – it is a mistake to imagine the origins of Christology lying in some sort of analysis of the character or quality of Jesus' human attainment, a judgement of universal ethical or spiritual superiority; insofar as we can even begin to imagine the roots of the confession of Jesus as the bearer of divine identity and liberty, it is in the context of considering the effect of his entire identity as an historical agent, the things that are made possible because of his existence in the world. The heart of the matter is the claim that this specific 'performance' of finitude or creatureliness is to be identified as the self-disclosure of the infinite, an answer to the *quid sit Deus?* question. It discloses the 'supreme inconceivability' of God as such:[31] that is, it shows that God, as the reality which does not ever have to defend itself against any 'other', is not susceptible of description as any kind of determinate subject. At the same time, it turns inside out any negative theology that is no more than a programmatic denial of qualities or predicates, since the negative is brought into focus only in and through the scandal of the cross of Jesus. Przywara navigates between a conceptual Scylla and Charybdis: on the one hand, a dialectic or contradiction *within* God, between wrath and love, darkness and light, Father and Son (a theme going back in modern times to the theosophy of Böhme and his followers); on the other, a negativity which

31 Ibid., p. 535.

is simply the projection over the conceptual horizon of finite qualities into a philosophical Absolute. The tension he puts at the centre of his scheme is the 'unresolved and irresoluble' reality of the humiliated and executed Christ: *this* is what God does, this is God's enactment of what it is to be God in the terms of finite, 'speakable' action in the world. And if this claim is true, God's completely unique difference from creation is affirmed; and thus immediately creation's integrity is likewise affirmed.

Analogy in general has been characterized by Przywara as the 'in and beyond' relation of two terms: one term can be thought of in terms of the other, not in any sense that would suggest an ultimate identification beyond superficial differences, but in a way that recognizes the irreducibly 'layered' character of finite reality and the ultimate layering that grounds the finite in the infinite. Thus, x is as it is, can be understood for what it is and spoken about as what it is, because it presupposes the y that is formative of it, but to which its particularity cannot be reduced. Each particular finite substance demands to be understood and so to be seen as the embodiment of form, but it is never the case that to speak of its form is to identify it completely. Every particular, because it demands to be understood, is more than its own raw particularity; every vehicle of formal understanding allows particulars to be seen in relation to other particulars and to a connecting rhythm within all of them. Analogical discourse denies both nominalism and reductionism ('x is nothing but y').

And this applies in Christology in the sense that the humiliated, abused and slaughtered body of Jesus in its scandalous particularity makes a shockingly urgent appeal to be understood (since if it is *not* to be understood, it is no more than a contradiction, the record of a fatal disjunction between divine meaning and human violence and catastrophe). To understand it, Przywara is claiming, is to see that the extreme tension between the paradoxical assertion of the divine in Christ and the actuality of the cross is the ultimate clarification of what analogy implies: the ultimate level of the 'meta' in metaphysics. That which is above and beyond every similarity or continuity, that which is definitively beyond every category of description, the infinite itself, speaks itself or embodies itself *only* in that which makes no claim to similarity or continuity – the finite, but more especially the mortal, and still more especially the abandoned and despised mortal. This is where we can discern the link between the theological metaphysics which delivers us into the unknowable divine darkness, that which is simply *not* anything we can name or recognize as belonging to our world of things that can be spoken and conceived, and the event of the cross in its 'scandal and foolish madness' enacted for the sake of our healing, our reconciliation to the infinite and to our own finitude.[32]

3.

Nothing in the world that claims to be 'Godlike' can be so in any straightforward sense, given that God is infinite and beyond all categorization; yet we speak of God. This is the central theological paradox. That we are enabled or even entitled to speak of God cannot be grounded in any kind of 'let-out clause' about God's infinity – God is beyond speech, *but* is still sufficiently like creation for us to project qualities on to him. No buts; our authority to speak must rest upon something more radically theological, and our Christological discourse is the key to this. We are enabled to speak of

32 Przywara wrote at a time when issues of gender in relation to Christology were hardly ever raised. But his discussion of the sense in which the humanity of Jesus does and does not tell us 'what God is' or 'what God is like' offers an important resource for responding to the challenge raised by some more recent theologians about how the masculinity of the incarnate Christ enshrines male privilege ('If God is male, the male is God', in Mary Daly's much-quoted aphorism). Przywara's insistence on the ever-greater unlikeness which analogy points to means that any claim that 'maleness' was 'more like' the divine than 'femaleness' (Przywara's prodigality with scare quotes is catching) would be immensely problematic, even if there were an answer to how these gendered essences could be defined. It is an area where his greatest and most creative disciple, Hans Urs von Balthasar, developed in a significantly different direction; see, for example, the exemplary essay by Lucy Gardner and David Moss, 'Something Like Time, Something Like the Sexes', in Lucy Gardner, David Moss, Ben Quash and Graham Ward, *Balthasar at the End of Modernity*, Edinburgh: T&T Clark, 1999, pp. 69–137. On Balthasar's Christology in general, see Mark A. McIntosh, *Christology From Within: Spirituality and the Incarnation in Hans Urs von Balthasar*, Notre Dame and London: University of Notre Dame Press, 1996, and, more schematically, 'Christology', in Edward T. Oakes, SJ, and David Moss, eds, *The Cambridge Companion to Hans Urs von Balthasar*, Cambridge: Cambridge University Press, 2004, pp. 24–36. McIntosh shows clearly how Balthasar uses his understanding of 'mission' as a way of approaching the identity of Christ and bridging between divine and human personhood.

God as God is (not merely as God is not, as the inaccessible Other) because of what is made actual in the fleshly reality of Jesus, the divine act which establishes the community of thanksgiving and service speaking God's praise and addressing God as *Abba*. But this divine act is recognizable not because it 'resembles' any divinity of our imagination but because it *creates* a new people in a renewed world. It shows itself divine by utterly refusing what we might be tempted to regard as signs of divinity; by enacting itself ultimately in the emptying of power, the humiliation and the immobilization of the cross. And the resurrection is not a triumphant instance and epiphany of divine power so much as the bare fact of the impossibility of defeating and extinguishing the divine presence in Jesus: *as* the incarnate and crucified, he lives. But the implication of all this is the theme that has preoccupied us throughout this book: the life and well-being of the creation cannot be found in the disruption of the finite world by some insertion of the infinite into it, even if we could make logical sense of this. Christ as finite, as creature, guarantees the integrity of the created order, even though the infinite resource that flows from the eternal union of the Word with the Father makes new the possibilities of that created world. The finite – and more specifically the mortal and suffering – Jesus, in releasing into the world the act of the Creator, in new forms of relation and possibility, makes clear once and for all that creation's wholeness and fulfilment are realized neither by the unfolding of merely immanent possibilities nor by the violent interruption of divine agency supplanting created reality, but by the bringing into being within creation of the relatedness of the Word to the Father which is the eternal ground of all finite existence.

This book began with a discussion of some of Austin Farrer's theological insights. It is intriguing to discover that one of Farrer's early publications was a substantial review of Przywara's *Polarity*, translated by the Cambridge scholar, A. C. Bouquet, who had published a few months earlier an impressively thorough digest of the book (as an article in the same periodical in which Farrer's review appeared).[33] Bouquet in this digest had summarized one of Przywara's key arguments in a way that makes very clear how close the

---

33 Austin Farrer, review of *Polarity* by P. Erich Przywara (trans. A. C. Bouquet, Oxford: Oxford University Press), *Theology* XXX.186, 1935, pp. 361–3; A. C. Bouquet, 'A German Catholic Philosophy of Religion', *Theology* XXIX.174, December

Jesuit's view is to what Farrer later developed: 'Because the whole creation is wholly "out of Deity", there is no dilemma in origin between Divine Act and Creaturely Act, as between two equally authorized and independent entities standing over against each other, but all true independence ("Eigen") in the creature is "from God hitherward", so that the apparent dilemma is the mystery of God the Creator, the Self-Existent Being Himself.'[34] And he has already drawn out the implication of this in a passage that strikingly anticipates the Farrer of *The Glass of Vision*: 'the form of the orthodox Christian solution to all these problems (of natural and supernatural, of grace and free-will, of inspiration and incarnation, of discovery and revelation, of mysticism and theophany) ... is ever the same – i.e. neither the fusion of the antitheses, nor the annihilation of one by the other, but the mystery of their tension', and the Chalcedonian formulation is the pre-eminent statement of this solution.[35] Farrer himself, who mentions Bouquet's summary with appreciation, highlights the same point in different terms: 'we cannot get the "allness" of God and the "someness" of the creature into one picture: that is the inevitable infirmity of the creaturely mind to which precisely the doctrine of *analogia entis* reconciles us. We have here neither a conflict disruptive of reality nor a contradiction destructive of theology.'[36] Theological activity cannot escape tension and alternation between the poles of its reference, except at the price of subsuming God and creature under one heading, which would be the ultimate absurdity in thinking both about God and about creatures, destroying the integrity and intelligibility of both terms.

Does this, though (Farrer asks in his review), mean that our theological reflection is bound to an ever-swinging dialectical pendulum, a process in which no position is ultimately to be *judged*? This would mean that theology could never rise beyond the level of reflection on the processes of religious consciousness, and could not truly be held answerable to some revealed criterion of truth and adequacy. And Farrer responds on Przywara's

---

1934, pp. 327–48. I am very grateful to Professor Robert MacSwain for drawing my attention to Farrer's review.

34 Bouquet, art. cit., p. 347.
35 Ibid., p. 339.
36 Farrer, art. cit., p. 362.

behalf: 'religious awareness' is always something allied to revelation, not an independent ascent to Heaven, but it is also importantly true that 'this act of God towards the creature is not everywhere the same',[37] in the sense that there are genuinely different metaphysical relations established by the historical fact of revelation in Christ – by the unique embodiment in finite life of the infinite creative love of the Word. To paraphrase Farrer's brief discussion, it seems to be a matter of what happens when the (always God-activated) 'religious consciousness', which – as we saw in the last section – delivers certain formal apprehensions of the infinite in its mystery and ineffability, is transformed into *filial* consciousness. Because of what is done and suffered in the life of Jesus, an awareness of radical dependence, of the 'in-and-beyond' of the absolute divine difference which confronts us, becomes an awareness of living in the presence of the God addressed by Jesus as Father; life in the Spirit of Jesus, acting in attunement with his eternal agency and so receiving his identity as one's own in the Body that is his continuing presence in the finite world. We are thus – Farrer concludes his review – able to affirm both the unity of all human God-relatedness or God-directedness and the radically new and different character of what is done in Jesus. To discover ourselves as adopted children of the eternal Father is not something alien to our nature as dependent beings, haunted by a recognition of the analogical openness of our connections with beings and Being; it is to acknowledge and inhabit that eternal relatedness which is the ultimate 'in-and-beyond', the relation of Father and Son, the non-dual, non-identical relation in which all finite relation is grounded.

So we are brought back to the insight with which we began: Christology is the context in which we think about the unavoidable tensions between all those various forms of apparent duality that we have to reckon with in theology; and it is also the context that points us to the resolution which is the Trinitarian life, not as a conceptual answer to the problem but as a living of the tension in gratitude and trust. In this framework, the tension – Przywara's *Spannung*[38] – is not something that tears apart but something

37 Ibid., p. 363.
38 See, for example, Przywara, op. cit, pp. 122–4, 148–52. For a very brief summary, see also Rowan Williams, 'Dialectic and Analogy: A Theological Legacy', pp. 274–92 in Nicholas Boyle, Liz Disley and Nicholas Adams, eds, *The Impact of Idealism: The Legacy*

that stably anchors a rhythm like that of breathing or heartbeat. It is a contradiction only if we seek to arrest the rhythm, and 'freeze' one moment of it. But this does not mean that we have no conceptual work to do. Theology will consistently need to dismantle such 'frozen' version of metaphysical tension, and to reshape its language in order to clarify the underlying vision of what we have been calling the non-dual, non-identical grammar of divine relation and thus of divine relatedness to what is not divine, infinite relation to the finite. And if we follow though the argument we have traced in various writers on Christology through the centuries, this reshaping of language happens in the actual life of the Christian community as it reflects on its creatureliness, in prayer and sacrament, and in its negotiating of its role and responsibility in human society. It is striking that both Bonhoeffer and Przywara see the primary Christian calling in the modern age as a recovery of apostolic *reticence* – not a nervous self-consciousness about professing faith in public but in a sense the exact opposite, a confidence that God's active indwelling does not need to be insisted upon either with exaggerated aesthetic gestures or with anxious political aggressiveness. In a paper of 1957 on Christian aesthetics, Przywara muses on how contemporary Christian art and architecture may have to recognize the 'exhaustion' of all those styles and registers in which it seems to be implied that God is to be represented in the extreme projection of earthly splendour, beauty and opulence or elaboration,[39] and to break through – or back – to the primal realities of incarnate simplicity, even anonymity, to the humility of 'ordinary, communally shared private rooms' as reflected in the most undistinguished and practical village church.[40] Przywara is not arguing for a self-conscious puritan aesthetic as such, nor is he simply dismissing the 'glories' of Byzantine or Gothic or Baroque renderings of the Christian vision. But he is clear that what most integrally embodies the original gift of the gospel and the glory of the crucified is an art that does not look for *mastery* but begins by acknowledging the priority of childlike responsiveness;

---

of Post-Kantian Thought, Vol. IV: *Religion*, Cambridge: Cambridge University Press, 2013, pp. 285–6.

39 The essay is 'Beautiful, Sacred, Christian', Przywara, op. cit., pp. 537–55; see especially pp. 551–2.

40 Ibid., p. 555.

somewhere in the skill needed for this we learn to distinguish the merely beautiful from the holy, the transparent. No less than Bonhoeffer, Przywara sees the integrity of the Church of the future as lying in its 'prosaic' character and style. Neither man (and we might remember the wealth of cultural and artistic resource which underlies and pervades their thought) would mean by this a denial of the imagination, a reductive philistinism about sacred representation. Both are simply looking for what *now*, under the hyper-scrutiny of a cultural world nervous of rhetorical abundance and illiterate about symbolism in general, might be the gestures that could make connections alive once more, and expose us to the central paradoxes of the analogical understanding – in and beyond; like this, yet immeasurably more and other than this.

This essay of Przywara's appropriately rounds off a consideration of his Christology, since it demonstrates how his analysis of finite and infinite in Christ acts as a foundation not only for metaphysics but also for aesthetics; and, allied to Bonhoeffer's more direct exploration of the ethical and political implications of Christology, it reinforces the emerging picture which this book has tried to outline. As the quotation from Austin Farrer with which we began implies, the leading themes of Christian theology are closely interwoven, and a healthy 'ecology' of doctrine depends on certain connections being made and understood. Pivotal in this process is the affirmation of the full divinity and full humanity of the Saviour – a doctrine which can be maintained coherently only in the light of a careful clarification of the relation between finite and infinite act. Once that clarification has been made, the theology of grace and sacramental life comes into better focus; but also the whole question of how the Church lives and acts in the world is opened up at a new depth. This in turn carries with it implications about what we might call the 'style' or 'register' of the Church's self-presentation in art and architecture as well as in the political sphere. The faithful living out of the *tropos* of the incarnate Christ is the challenge that faces us in all these areas, and what it entails (so Bonhoeffer and Przywara alike insist) is the patient embrace of finitude, the refusal of defensive anxiety about the Church's privilege or influence, the recognition and valuing of the unspectacular, in life and art, as the site where we may expect the paradoxical radiance of the infinite to become visible. Christian ethics is not about dramatic and solitary choices for individual good or evil but the steady building of a culture of durable mutuality and compassion. Christian aesthetics is not about genius-driven or near-magical transmutations of this world into some imagined semblance of divine glory and abundance, but the gift of unlocking in the most ordinary setting or object the 'grace of sense' that allows it to be seen with (to use the word again) durable, attentive love.

And Christian metaphysics? Przywara's work clearly understands the role of Christology in developing a schematic and consistent view of analogy, depending on the recognition that whatever comes into intellectual focus in our human understanding is always already implicated in relations that make its life more than a single and containable phenomenon but something opening out on to an unlimited horizon of connection.[41] But in those pages (unusually complicated even by Przywara's standards) where he lays out the different senses of the 'meta' involved in the metaphysical enterprise, perhaps the most original and important point is what he has to say about *method*. What is most straightforwardly 'metaphysical' is the way in which reality is approached, represented and spoken of; the metaphysical is, we could say, a *mode of conducting ourselves* in respect of finite reality, not simply a specialist division of our professional philosophical language. To render this in the very different language of Wittgenstein, metaphysical perspectives have to *show* themselves, not just be talked about. And Przywara's fascination with the model of 'tension', *Spannung*, 'the swaying of the intra-creaturely, the in-between-God-and-the-creaturely, and the intra-divine itself',[42] reflects an implied conviction that metaphysics at its most authentic cannot be a subject in itself, but must always be the context and 'colouring' of various kinds of human discourse. As we noted earlier, it shows itself in language about assorted areas of human activity or culture when these are understood and represented as 'more than themselves', as analogically implicated.

That in turn has consequences for how we think about theology itself. Przywara can write that the 'formal content' of a theology beginning from the incorporation of the believer into the filial relatedness of the Word to the Father is *'participation in God's nature and person'*;[43] and the 'formal

---

41 Above, pp. 228–232.
42 Przywara, op. cit., p. 314.
43 Ibid., p. 366, italics in original.

act' is *gnōsis*, the spiritual knowledge that, in Przywara's bold formulation, 'co-enacts' God's life.[44] God's unveiling of God is the heart and foundation of theology, and this entails visible sharing in the mission of God in the world, in the Church's kenotic identification with God's will for the healing of creatures. Consciously echoing Augustine, Przywara insists that union with the immaterial and transcendent God can only occur in union with the suffering, struggling, compromised body/Body on earth, living out God's descent into the depths.[45] Thus what he has to say about method in metaphysics is paralleled by a prescription for theology: authentic theology *shows itself*, in self-forgetting and self-dispossessing practice. The theology that we write and discuss has no substance independently of this formal content, this knowledge of how to 'enact Christ' in the world. And it is because of this that Przywara resists[46] a reading of St John of the Cross's spiritual teaching which simply identifies the 'night of spirit' with the negation of the creaturely. Put like this, it can suggest yet another form of the competitive ontological model which we struggle to escape from – more world, less God, and vice versa. But St John properly read – giving priority to the poems rather than the commentaries on them – characterizes the night as participation in the act of Christ the Word. The darkness of our prayer is not the result of a straightforward gap between what we can know as creatures and the unknowable depths of God, the infinite dissimilarity between finite and infinite; it is our assimilation into the infinite's self-unveiling in the dark places of the finite world, in the wordless helplessness of the cross. And because it is in this way an entry deeper and deeper into the centre of God's activity, it is a journey into the 'excess' of divine light, the overflowing of God's absolute abundance, which is itself nothing else than

44 Ibid., p. 367.

45 Ibid., p. 368.

46 Ibid., pp. 607–12, in a discussion of the use of St John by Edith Stein and Simone Weil, gently critical of Stein's written essays in metaphysics and of what seems her embrace of John as a 'religious essentialist' for whom the goodness and integrity of creation are not fully in focus, while acknowledging that her martyrdom, as a life-giving offering for her people and her Church, resolves her embrace of John's dark night into luminosity and a transfiguration of finite existence. This essay is a powerful statement of *Spannung* once again, the tension between Stein's essentialist and Weil's existentialist readings and partial misreadings of John of the Cross.

agape directed towards the life and joy of the other – in the divine life and in the relation of divine to non-divine life.[47]

So an analysis of the Christological tradition illuminates the 'grammar' of God in the sense that it establishes the mode in which God may be spoken and known: in the dereliction of the cross, and therefore, for us as believers, in the radical dispossession summed up so austerely by Bonhoeffer as 'prayer and righteous action in the human world', in the taking of human responsibility for human justice and flourishing and in the labour of a prayer that moves in and out of words and images, recognizing the fundamental dialectic that emerges in reflection on the Christian narrative – the unfathomable nature of the God who cannot be contained in any concept or picture, and the simultaneously realized fact that this unfathomability is the freedom of unrestricted love, the act that generates the life of the other. 'Such a Strength as makes his guest', as George Herbert put it;[48] it is the infinity of divine energy that means it is free to live in what is other and to welcome its other, not to be threatened by it.

But the working out of this also has clear implications for ecclesiology. As we have argued, the central themes of classical Christology are closely bound up with the doctrine of Christ's Headship: that is, to acknowledge the divine life of the Word at work in Jesus is the foundation for thinking of the community of believers as bound together with him in a relation that is unlike any other. Because the life of the Word is – in virtue of being infinite and divine – different from the life of a bounded finite ego, it creates relations that are not just those of individual to individual. The Word lives in and through those affiliated with Jesus, and as a result, their lives are also linked to one another in a way that is not simply that of individual to individual, but in a comprehensive pattern of interdependence – the common life of the Body as Paul describes it. If the incarnate Word creates community in this unique way, every individual united with the Word becomes a point in a network of mutually defining and conditioning subjects in such a way that no individual's temporal or eternal well-being can be isolated from that of all others. Without the basic recognition of who the ultimate agent is in the life of Jesus of Nazareth, this would make no sense; the

---

47 Ibid., p. 612.
48 Herbert, 'The Call' ('Come, my Way, my Truth, my Life').

Church would inevitably become an association of finite individuals with common convictions. And whatever the eccentricities of the contemporary Church might at times suggest, the language and sacramental practice of the Church continues to take for granted something much more solid than this, anchored in what is said about the identity of Christ as defined and activated by the Word.

Christology, in short, is 'done' by the Church; it is done in the practice of a community that understands itself to be the Body of Christ, a group of persons living and acting from the conviction that human community is most fully realized in the unconditional mutuality which is represented by the language of organic interdependence. Christology is done in the practice of lives that embrace their finitude and materiality without fear, lives that enact the divine self-identification with those who endure loss, pain and contempt. Christology is done in a practice of prayer and worship that does not approach God as a distant and distinct individual with a will to which mine must conform – as if in a finite relation of slave to master – but acts out of the recognition of adoptive filiation and the intimacy that flows from this. It is done when we see that the doing of God's will 'in earth as in Heaven' means that the eternal will of God is for the life of the world – that God is 'satisfied' when our flourishing is secured.[49] Christology in this vein is the impetus for both the stillness and expectancy of prayer and the risk of action on behalf of the neglected or oppressed other; and it is, as for Bonhoeffer, the rationale for resistance to any human system that tries to overstep the bounds of finitude and to create permanent systems of absolute human power.

And at the core of all this is the focal historic insight that God and humanity are not rival presences in the phenomenon of Jesus Christ. Classical Christological teaching declares that we may believe this because of what happens in Jesus of Nazareth. Our general metaphysical language about how the finite enacts the infinite by being itself is crystallized once and for all in the event of the new creation in which finite humanity is so activated by the divine that we see not only that general relation in its formal terms but something more. We see that the infinite realizes itself in loving self-gift for

---

49 Cf. Julian of Norwich, in Chapter xxii of her *Revelations of Divine Love*, where Christ says, 'If thou art apaide, I am apaide.'

the sake of the healing and remaking of the finite; that this finite life that is Jesus' enacts the infinite in such a way that its loving agency permeates and transfigures the lives of those touched by it, and so transfigures the meanings of the entire material world. As theology labours over its terminology, what comes into focus is that the life of the infinite is eternally relation and gift – not a bare limitlessness, but the endlessness of a mutual outpouring of life and bliss; so that the infinite Word taking flesh embodies itself as a source and agent of undefended and unconstrained welcome in our world, opening up access to its own relation to its infinite Source.

This book is dedicated to the memory of Austin Farrer, the theologian with whom we began our exploration: at the end of his first great essay on these matters, *Finite and Infinite*, he states both carefully and starkly what his discussion has and has not done. It has clarified the grammar of a finite/infinite relation that is not one of mutual exclusion but one in which the finite expresses the infinite in its finite forms; but it does not say whether that relation has any discernible moral quality. 'The man [*sic*] expresses it in being a man, and the microbe in being a microbe and killing the man, and the God of rational theology, we may conclude if we like, is equally but no more than equally concerned on both sides.'[50] What remains to be established is whether the relation of God to finite human agency is purposive and healing. If the agency of God can be identified within the finite order in a way that is oriented to this, the entire schema of infinite and finite act is transformed, because the infinite's self-representation and self-veiling in the finite becomes an act of *love*, a uniquely radical love without any self-directed aims. In an eloquent closing paragraph, Farrer points us forward to what more the Christian must say:

> As I wrote this, the German armies were occupying Paris, after a campaign prodigal of blood and human distress. Rational theology will not tell us whether this has or has not been an unqualified and irretrievable disaster to mankind and especially to the men who died. It is another matter if we believe that God Incarnate also died and rose from the dead.[51]

---

50 Austin Farrer, *Finite and Infinite: A Philosophical Essay*, London: Dacre Press, 1953 (second edition), p. 299.

51 Ibid., p. 300.

Yet it is not a matter of metaphysics delivering half of the picture and revelation the other half. The language here might tempt us to such a conclusion, but the older Farrer was to qualify it in several ways. Przywara's schema
offers a corrective. The 'in-and-beyond' of his analysis already implies that
what we encounter in any finite substance is a kind of *excess*, an overflow of
connectedness and so of possible meaning, which cannot be detached from
a sense of life and of participation in abundance; and we have seen that he
also insists on the inseparability of the true, the good and the beautiful in
his account of metaphysical perception. But for him it is the tension created
by the paradox of Jesus that eventually mandates a new level of metaphysical
precision. It is not, then, that we begin with a neutral account of finite and
infinite upon which the relation of divine and human in Jesus is projected.
The *Spannung* of genuinely metaphysical and thus of analogical thinking is
born out of our observing *how* a range of actual human discourses operate;
and if one of the actual human discourses around is that of the Church's
faith in Jesus as Lord and God, combined with the practices we have noted
as constituting the fundamental 'statements' of Christology, what we have is
a uniquely metaphysically rich language growing out of this particular discourse in such a way that it illuminates and reorganizes all the rest. The primary datum is not a doctrine of Being worked through in detail and applied
to Christ, but rather a clarifying of what we need to say to make sense of
recognizing Christ as the agent of divine acts – which inexorably leads us to
certain affirmations about what finite being itself must be in relation to its
infinite source.

'God the Son on earth is a fullness of holy life within the limit of mortality; it is for him to be, and for theologians endlessly and never suffi-
ciently, to define.'[52] But one of the lessons these chapters have suggested we
need to learn is that this definition is bound up with the incarnate reality
of the body of believers and their interaction with the world; bound up
with living the Christological tension of entering into the deepest unity

---

52   Austin Farrer, 'Very God and Very Man', in *Interpretation and Belief*, ed. Charles Conti,
London: SPCK, 1976, pp. 126–37, quotation from p. 136. This essay is perhaps
the most luminously clear statement of a contemporary orthodox Christology to be
found in modern theological writing in English, and worth more than many far longer
expositions.

with God's endless life through a sacrificially attentive engagement with the matter of this world. Theological discussion – not to mention devotional exhortation – has not always been faithful to this; it has succumbed to the temptation to project onto God the forms of otherness or difference that characterize the finite world, by treating the divine Persons as if they were individuals like us, by treating the Incarnation as an episode in divine life, by treating the divine nature as a set of detached predicates that characterize divine individuals, and so on. It is easy to mythologize the confession of Jesus as God, or to treat it as an identity statement of the most problematic kind. But the established grammar of speaking about Jesus and the Word Jesus incarnates pulls theology back repeatedly from these oversimplifications, insisting that only in the full recognition of divinity and humanity unqualified and unchanged in Jesus can we say what we need to about the absolute and radical character of divine gift and about the abiding and non-negotiable goodness of the finite order. Creation is healed and restored to itself not by a supplement or an interruption but by an opening into its own depths of connection with the creative act. Christ is that event of opening, revealing the Creator as the guarantor of creation's integrity, the point upon which finite form converges in beauty. And that becomes visible only when the Word speaks in and as a human identity that is past all doubt subject to the vulnerability of finitude, not only mortal but at the mercy of human violence in its most arrogant and naked forms. The Logos in whom all things hold together, the divine Wisdom which orders all things from end to end of creation, 'utters' the whole of this fleshly, suffering life as its self-definition. The Word appears in the form of a slave because only so can God's freedom from every form of earthly authority be shown; and only so, therefore, can the rootedness in God of creation's order and coherence be shown. And the Body of Christ in turn seeks to show the logic of creation in its prayerful scepticism about its own wholeness or success or resourcefulness and its attempt to let itself be shaped by the act of self-sharing that is its own foundational reality.

'I have really done no more than define and explain a few of the things which the Christian Church teaches and believes', says Farrer at the end of his brief essay on 'Jesus, God and Man'.[53] I am not even sure of having

53 Ibid., p. 137.

defined or explained; but perhaps these pages will serve to prompt some at least to look harder and longer at the classical shape of incarnational teaching, and to see how it is in this light that we see light on the entire creaturely landscape which we inhabit, and which we are called in and with Christ to transform.

Appendix: Concluding (Untheological?) Postscript: Wittgenstein, Kierkegaard and Chalcedon

1.

We have looked briefly above at the impact of Kierkegaard on Bonhoeffer's distinctive Christological rhetoric; but Bonhoeffer was not the only great twentieth-century mind to discover in Kierkegaard a stimulus to thinking about Jesus. Ripples from the turbulent waters of Christological controversy can be discerned in unlikely places, and in this excursus I want to look briefly at one such unlikely location for Christological debate, the notebooks of Ludwig Wittgenstein, and to outline how his characteristic concerns about the language of ethics and his personal reading of Kierkegaard combine to shape a gnomic and highly suggestive series of comments on the Gospels and their central figure, comments which may throw some light of the entire discussion followed in this book and where and how the challenges of Christology are to be encountered now.

But we need to begin some way back before we examine Wittgenstein's wrestling with theology. Understanding how he approached *ethics* in the earlier part of his career will give some sense of the perspectives he brought later on to a reading of the

New Testament. Some modern discussions of Wittgenstein and ethics note the paradox that, while he has very little to say explicitly about what are traditionally thought of as ethical questions, there is a strong and pervasive assumption being made about the ethical character of his entire philosophical enterprise.[1] The brief but significant 'Lecture on Ethics' which he delivered in 1929 helps to clarify some aspects of this tension.[2] Ethical utterances are not, he insists, statements of fact: 'no state of affairs has, in itself, what I would like to call the coercive power of an absolute judge'. That is to say, an ethical judgement ('such and such an action is unequivocally good') cannot be the outcome of either a series of empirical/deductive steps or a chain of logical reasoning. Ethical utterance, Wittgenstein argues, belongs in the same territory as the experience of wonder at the existence of the world or of the sense of absolute security beyond all contingent possibility of hurt or failure. Both these experiences are different in kind from others which are described in a seductively similar vocabulary: I wonder at this phenomenon or set of phenomena (it could be otherwise, I have never seen anything like this before); I feel safe here (in a way I do not feel safe there). If I wonder at the world, it is not because I have never seen anything like it; it is not a thing in a series of things, a new bit of information. If I feel absolutely secure, it is not because this situation makes me feel more comfortable than that; this is not one state of affairs in a succession of possible states of affairs in which I feel varying degrees of safety. And so as soon as we try to find appropriate words for such sensations, or, better, such dispositions towards our environment, we are likely to talk nonsense. Ethical judgement is the same kind of nonsense: an action is not good because something in the world makes it so, and to speak of its goodness is not to add anything to the sum total of

---

1   The literature on Wittgenstein's ethics is still a bit patchy, but it is worth noting in this connection James C. Edwards, *Ethics Without Philosophy: Wittgenstein and the Moral Life*, Gainesville, FL: University Press of Florida, 1985, and J. Jeremy Wisnewski, *Wittgenstein and Ethical Inquiry: A Defence of Ethics as Clarification*, London and New York: Continuum, 2007. Sabina Lovibond, *Realism and Imagination in Ethics*, London: Blackwell, 1983, remains perhaps the most creative engagement with ethical issues from a broadly Wittgensteinian point of view in recent decades.

2   There is now a critical edition of this text with notes and comments in Ludwig Wittgenstein, *Lecture on Ethics*, ed. E. Zamuner, E. V. Di Lascio and D. K. Levy, Chichester: Wiley/Blackwell, 2014.

facts. Thus it is not a judgement which has the 'necessary' force of a conclusion in argument, a demonstration that a course of action is unconditionally required in order to fulfil the definitional requirements of the terms being used. Judgements of relative value have the form, 'If this is the goal you propose, this must be the way to attain it': 'if you want to go to X by the shortest route, this is the way you must take'.

In contrast, nothing *makes* ethical judgements true, and they do not have the conditional structure possessed by the kind of utterance just quoted (if this is what you want, this is how to get it). In that regard, we could say that they have another sort of 'necessity' which is significantly different from logical necessity, in that they cannot be understood as *products* of any sequence of events. In 1929, still more or less committed to the thought world of the *Tractatus*, Wittgenstein provocatively concludes that all systematized ethical and religious discourse must be 'nonsense' – not in the reductive sense such a word would have in the mouth of a straightforward logical positivist, but in a far more complex manner. It represents the human desire to go beyond language itself; that is itself a fact, and as such cannot have 'absolute value'. But all this means is that there is no way of so describing the fact of this obstinate anomaly in human speech as *either* to make it an argument for a particular judgement of value *or* to give grounds for prohibiting it as something that should not be said. Wittgenstein remarks that he is 'tempted to say' that 'the existence of language itself' is the only adequate expression of the sense of the miraculous (or, presumably, the sense of impregnable spiritual security or of unconditional moral summons); if this is the case, then once again we cannot argue or describe systematically, since 'language itself' is not a subject that can be spoken about – except 'nonsensically'. But the 1929 lecture shows us Wittgenstein already on the edge of a different kind of analysis: having said very plainly in the lecture that direct speech about ethics or religion is bound to deal in 'similes', and that a simile can be recognized as such when we are able to say what it's a simile *for*, he presents an intriguingly different (but not wholly discontinuous) approach in the lectures on aesthetics in the late 1930s, as well as in his notes from the 1930s and various reported conversations. The aesthetics lectures begin by addressing the question of the '*discontent*' we experience in viewing certain phenomena, including artefacts: we feel uncomfortable with what we see (hear, etc.) and identify a 'cause' for that discomfort – but only in a very unusual sense of 'cause'. We are looking not for a fact or set of facts that will explain why I feel uncomfortable, but for what Wittgenstein seems to have called a 'direction' of feeling in our response: '*that's* where it doesn't work'. He compares it with the processes around composition, looking for the 'right' word or phrase, and even with the question of what makes a joke work. And in speaking about a work of art, we look for comparisons until we find one that 'clicks' or fits, even though we know that this is a very blunt-edged metaphor: what we are really saying is that we are satisfied, we recognize something. In a lecture 'belonging to a course of lectures on description', he returns to the same point: 'You say of a certain phrase of music that it draws a conclusion, "Though I couldn't say for my life why it is a 'therefore'!" '[3] It is hard to imagine that Wittgenstein did not have in mind the famous '*Muss es sein? Es muss sein!*' in Beethoven's notes on his String Quartet no. 16: the way the music unfolds displays an inevitability, a move towards resolution that feels natural or organic, connected without force, argument or strain with all that has preceded it. Later, in a note from 1947, Wittgenstein strongly repudiates the idea that this means no more than that we find the transition *angenehm*, 'pleasant': we want to exclaim 'Of course', he says.[4] That is, what we seek to say is not that there is a psychological explanation of why the transition seems good to us; that we feel 'satisfied', to use the word he favours earlier, is not at all an observation of the fact that we are emotionally pleased.

This illustrates something of what Wittgenstein is feeling towards in the 1929 lecture: there are judgements that we can intelligibly call 'necessary', while being clear that they are not *necessitated*: they do not come at the end of a chain of evidence or argument such that we can say that this or that stage of argument or this or that state of affairs makes it inevitable that this conclusion has to be accepted. The later notes suggest that we convey how such judgements work not by locating them within a scheme of causal relations but by directing someone's attention towards a very variegated practice: a person will come to understand music (and so to understand why

---

3   Ludwig Wittgenstein, *Lectures and Conversations on Aesthetics, Psychology and Religious Belief*, ed. Cyril Barrett, Oxford: Blackwell, 1970, p. 237 (henceforth LC).

4   Ludwig Wittgenstein, *Culture and Value*, ed. G. H. Von Wright in collaboration with Heikki Nyman, trans. Peter Winch, Oxford: Blackwell, 1980 (henceforth CV), p. 57.

some musical transitions seem 'necessary') by attending to the conventions of sequencing and harmony in a particular musical tradition, by observing the gestures and facial expressions of performers, by reflecting on the images a musician may use to describe musical activity. Why music works like *this* is something we can only clarify by accumulating instances of what we recognize as music; why this 'has' to follow from that we can clarify only as we attend to someone who navigates musical practice and shows signs we should in other circumstances see as characteristic of a response to constraint or obligation. There are obvious parallels with the treatment of rule-following in the *Philosophical Investigations*: we could point, for example, to PI #490 on how I know that such and such a line of thinking brought me to this particular action. 'Well, it is a particular picture: for example, of a calculation leading to a further experiment in an experimental investigation. It looks like this – and now I could describe an example.'[5] And all this is a move on from the lecture on ethics to the extent that Wittgenstein is no longer confident that the use of a simile is vacuous if we cannot specify what we should want to say in 'plain' language. If the only real representation of the miraculousness of the world is language itself, this later development seems to say that 'language itself' is already diverse and metaphorically charged in a number of ways that cannot be reduced to or translated into a speech that is free from simile and image and indeed physical gesture – bearing in mind that the issue of the logical form of communicative physical gesture was (anecdotally at least) one of the worries that moved Wittgenstein on from the philosophy of the *Tractatus*. It remains true for him that an ethical judgement cannot add any new fact to the world, and that the recognition of the world as miraculous is not the deposit of an argument, let alone an assessment of probabilities. And the 1940s' discussions in Wittgenstein's *Vermischte Bemerkungen* notebooks (translated as *Culture and Value*)[6] imply that the form of an ethical education may be the description of a series of events in such a way that the learner recognizes what to do next, how (in the language of the *Philosophical Investigations*) a person may intelligibly 'follow' the acts being displayed or described: 'then *that* would be the right

5   Ludwig Wittgenstein, *Philosophical Investigations* trans. G. E. M. Anscombe (third edition), Oxford: Blackwell, 2001 (henceforth PI), p. 116.
6   See above, n. 4.

thing to do next'. And in a related sense, the awareness of an imperative of a certain kind can itself be a claim about how things irreducibly and necessarily are: 'The utterance of a command, such as "Don't be resentful!", may be like the affirmation of a truth' – or, to translate more exactly, 'A command ... can be articulated as the affirmation of a truth.'[7] The boundary between a narration and a sense of what is imperative is being deliberately blurred here, not in a way that represents any reversal or qualification by Wittgenstein of his early disjunction between ethical judgement and statements of fact but so as to make the point that the mode in which fact is spoken of tells us what kind of comprehensive ontological claim is being made – and such a claim *cannot* be made in the form of any claim as to specific extra states of affairs in the universe.

2.

This rapid tour of Wittgenstein's thinking about ethics and aesthetics is designed to locate more precisely the way in which he reflects on both theology in general and the foundational texts of Christian belief in particular. The *Culture and Value* notebooks contain a cluster of entries on the Gospels and related matters, in which Wittgenstein compares the style of the Gospels to a 'mediocre' stage set for a drama: the staging does not distract from the actual drama. It is important that there is no way in which the literary excellence of the gospel narrative can be deployed as a covert or overt *argument* for taking the content with appropriate seriousness.[8] Equally, the claim articulated by the Gospels, the claim on our faith or obedience, cannot be dependent on the historical accuracy of the texts: 'The historical accounts in the Gospels might, historically speaking, be demonstrably false and yet belief would lose nothing by this.'[9] And this does not mean that their truth is a matter of reason or logic – nor, presumably (though Wittgenstein does not quite say this in so many words), that it is a matter of some eternal 'message' symbolized or encoded in the narrative. The point throughout is that there is nothing in or about the Gospels that would

7   CV, p. 61.
8   CV, p. 31.
9   Ibid., p. 32.

persuade us of their claim *in any terms not intrinsic to their own language.*
They offer no information to justify what they say, and it is a category mistake to try and quarry their historical basis to reinforce the claims made; all
this would do is to establish or otherwise certain facts in the world, certain
bits of information. As Wittgenstein puts it, 'Christianity ... offers us a (historical) narrative and says: now believe!'[10] – that is, not 'Believe that this is
a true historical narrative!', but 'Believe that your life can and must change!'

'It is *love* that believes the Resurrection.'[11] What Wittgenstein is asserting
is that religious conviction belongs precisely with ethical and aesthetic
judgement in being, grammatically speaking, a transition between narrative
and judgement that is 'necessary' in the terms of the process of a certain
kind of discourse, yet not explicable as something *caused* by that process.
Hence Wittgenstein's provocative remark that it would not matter if the
gospel records were 'false': if the story of Jesus (including the Resurrection)
were a fiction, the relationship between narrative and judgement would
be unaltered because historical certainty is not the basis of the judgement
that follows, the judgement which we call faith or obedience and which
changes my life's conditions. It is worth noting that this is something of
a loose end in Wittgenstein's reflection, and not in any obvious way consistent with his comments on the impossibility of thinking that Christ's
body is 'dead and decomposed' while having hope or confidence in Christ.[12]
If the gospel narrative is what we usually mean by a fiction, it is presumably a *deliberate* fiction; and if it is a deliberate fiction designed to produce
faith, what is produced cannot be faith but only a capitulation to some
other individual's purpose of persuasion. Even if we were to say that it is
not a deliberate fiction but a series of half-conscious misrepresentations
or distorted traditions, we should have to imagine a process whereby the
narrative was constructed in response to various historical conditions; and
this takes us back to Wittgenstein's basic problem – here as in the ethical

10 Ibid.
11 Ibid., p. 33.
12 'What inclines even me to believe in Christ's Resurrection? It is as though I play with
    the thought, – If he did not rise from the dead, then he decomposed in the grave like
    any other man. *He is dead and decomposed.* In that case he is a teacher like any other and
    can no longer *help*' (ibid., p. 33).

and aesthetic sphere – of the relation between contingent fact and absolute significance. To put the point as Wittgenstein does in terms of the 'falsity' of the narrative allows us – awkwardly, in terms of Wittgenstein's basic argument – a kind of space into which we can slip to view the narrative independently of its actual relation to the believing hearer; so to consider this perspective is already to deny the 'necessity' of the response. Faith does not guarantee the historical accuracy of the text; equally, lack of faith is not the same as scepticism about the history.[13] In that sense, we can say that historical accuracy is immaterial to faith; but this is not the same as saying that faith exists in direct and deliberate *contradiction* to historical veracity ('alternative facts', to borrow the singular language of an American political communicator ...). Considering the text as an imperative is a distinct kind of discourse, where assent or refusal is not determined by a judgement of historical fact. An inability to believe cannot be dealt with by reinforcing historical claims. All we know is that the story is told, as a story about events in this world, in such a way as to lead up to the imperative: believe!

Consequently Wittgenstein's aporia is – as he expresses it in the note on belief in the Resurrection – that in order to believe and to be changed, you must *already* have been changed; you must already 'no longer rest your weight on the earth but suspend yourself from heaven'.[14] He implies strongly here and elsewhere that there is, in effect, no way in which religious commitment could be 'learned', no possibility of induction into faith. This relates to his statement[15] that no one can truthfully speak of herself in terms of absolute self-disgust – either this is the mark of (or the beginning of)

---

13 Wittgenstein's approach to these issues had a substantial impact on Hans Frei, whose book, *The Identity of Jesus Christ: The Hermeneutical Bases of Dogmatic Theology*, Minneapolis: Fortress Press, 1975 (enlarged edition, Eugene, OR: Wipf and Stock, 1985), argues for just such a position. The meaning of the text is what it narrates, not its correspondence with otherwise-establishable 'fact'. But this does not mean that historical claims are irrelevant or that historical scepticism is mandated: if the narrative works in a certain way, the believer understands that the required response is belief – not conviction about historical probabilities or possibilities, but commitment to the text's presenting meaning as a true depiction of the reality which reader and text alike inhabit.

14 CV, p. 33.

15 Ibid., p. 32.

madness, or it heralds radical change. Thus, to speak *at all* of the imperative embodied in the gospel story is to move away from any kind of simply
descriptive language; it impels us into a frame of, or mode of, discourse
where stating the truth is inseparable from obeying an imperative. The transition from narrative to judgement in respect of the gospel leaves no room
for an account in third-person terms of what the story might mean to a
hypothetical hearer: I either hear or do not hear, I either respond or do not
respond. When the Wittgenstein of 1937 objects to the language of St Paul,
as opposed to that of the Gospels,[16] it is because he reads it as attempting
such a third-person account. This makes Paul's writings *schäumlich* – not
simply 'frothy', as the published translation has it, but literally 'scummy',
what you see on standing water rather than flowing. And Paul's discussion
of predestination is a cardinal instance of a sort of category mistake:[17] it
cannot be understood in an authentically 'religious' way – or if it can, it can
only be by someone who has learned to read it quite differently. Later on,
according to Con Drury, Wittgenstein had second thoughts on this, and
allowed that Gospels and Epistles witnessed to 'the same religion;[18] but in
the context of the earlier notebooks it is not difficult to see why he turns
away from what he thinks is the Pauline approach. He reads Paul as trying
to imagine God's purposes in a sort of narrative of divine agency; and this
is obviously another attempt to slip away from responding to an imperative
into the realm of description. If I were to venture a guess as to why the later
Wittgenstein changed his mind, I suspect that he had come to see that his
own analysis of impotence to respond in the face of the gospel narrative,
his recognition that you would already have to have changed in order to
respond, might correspond to Paul's anguished arguments in Romans about
both his personal awareness of imprisonment ('Wretched man that I am!' in
Romans 7) and about the 'resistance' of Israel to Christ (9–11).

   'The way you use the word "God" does not show *whom* you mean –
but, rather, what you mean';[19] similarly, and famously, in #373 of the

16   Ibid., pp. 30, 32.
17   Ibid., p. 32.
18   Rush Rhees, ed., *Recollections of Wittgenstein*, Oxford and New York: Oxford University
     Press, 1984, p. 165.
19   CV, p. 50.

Investigations, 'Grammar tells what kind of object anything is. (Theology as grammar.)'[20] There is a way of speaking about God which clearly cannot be speaking about *God*, in Wittgenstein's eyes: he notes[21] that stories of the Greek gods of Olympus allow us to frame the question, 'What would it be like if they existed?' – i.e. what difference would it make to the world if it happened to have these agents within it? We cannot ask what difference it would make if the world 'contained' God, any more than we can ask what difference it makes in the world that we perceive it and describe it in terms of colour. We are proposing a comprehensive scheme of perception and of 'reading' the facts of the world, not speculating about what the world might or might not contain.[22] Thus the grammar of belief in the Resurrection, say, is manifest in narratives of how a person's life is radically and comprehensively altered by belief in the Resurrection. 'It looks like this', in the language of the *Investigations*. Just as 'God' does not pick out an agent or an individual among others, in the way a proper name does, so 'resurrection' does not pick out a specific event in chronicled history – which does not mean that the Resurrection of Jesus is without any historical correlate, so to speak, but that no account of it in terms of information is adequate. Like belief in God overall, believing in the Resurrection is positing a 'system of reference', as Wittgenstein puts it in a note of 1947,[23] which I can find my way into only as it is repeatedly portrayed in connection with 'an appeal to conscience' – until the point at which I connect the narrative with what I now recognize I need and want. What it is that brings me to that point of seeing a response as natural, 'necessary' or imperative cannot be systematized or generalized. But, as the discussion so far has spelled out, it is going to be comparable to the varied ways in which I am inducted into a moral or an aesthetic practice,

20 PI, p. 99.

21 CV, p. 82.

22 The point has been made that for an ancient Greek this might not be so straightforward a question. We can imagine after a fashion a world in which certain supernatural agents might or might not be present (do ghosts exist? pixies? dragons?). But what would a Greek of the fifth century BCE have made of this? Or a contemporary educated Hindu, say, for that matter? This does not invalidate the grammatical point about the difference between speaking of the divine and speaking about the contents of the universe, but invites some further refinement of the argument.

23 CV, p. 64.

a system of reference. If the early Wittgenstein is inclined, as we have seen, to characterize ethical and aesthetic judgement as more or less inaccessible for speech, his developing sensitivity to the diversity of speech itself and the beginnings of his analysis of what it is to 'follow' a mode of discourse, a language game, gives him some space to grant that what we could call a process of induction is not unthinkable; we can reflect on how in fact people come to believe, come to occupy a stance, without thereby sacrificing the fundamental point: that this process is not an acquisition of information or the conclusion of an argument.

By now it will be very clear how close Wittgenstein is throughout his reflections in this area to the Kierkegaard of the *Philosophical Fragments*. Kierkegaard's concern is almost precisely the same anxiety about ways of speaking about God that are in fact grammatically incapable of doing what they purport to do. Thus Kierkegaard can argue, in his chapter on 'The Absolute Paradox',[24] that if the human subject comes to know the unknown and unconditional truth that surrounds her, she can only know it as that which is without qualification *different*: the knowing individual is 'untruth', and thus cannot realize for herself the very fact of her untruthfulness. We can be taught about the unconditional, about 'the god', in Kierkegaard's terms, only by what is not ourselves; which implies the recognition of 'sin', the endemic state of self-deceit in which we live. Reason confronts its downfall; if it passionately wills its downfall, desiring not to be untruthful, it confronts its difference from the unconditional not with terror but with faith or love.[25] If we are to be confident that we have not *created* the difference in the terms that suit us, we must be clear that the way in which we are taught the difference is precisely *not* by the god manifesting himself exhibiting a particular kind of worldly difference. It is this which puts the revelation to faith of the divine difference on a different level both to the teaching of a human sage, a Socrates, and to the putative revelation of *a* god, a divine agent intelligible in the same terms as finite agents. The absolutely different god can confront us with our own

---

24 Søren Kierkegaard, *Philosophical Fragments, or a Fragment of Philosophy/Johannes Climacus, or De omnibus dubitandum est*, ed. and trans. Howard V. Hong and Edna K. Hong, Princeton: Princeton University Press, 1985, pp. 37–48.

25 Ibid., pp. 46–8.

untruth only as the anonymous saviour who does not seek to convince us, let alone compel us, to submission, since that would be to abandon his difference in favour of a kind of power or freedom directly competing with our own, different in degree not kind.[26] We might plead for the god to reveal himself in a clearer way, but we should have to be prepared to hear the god reproaching us: 'so you love only the omnipotent one who performs miracles, not him who humbled himself in equality with you'.[27] This has consequences for how we read the gospel narrative. Kierkegaard, in his discussion of the 'contemporary follower' and the 'follower at second hand', insists that the only advantage of the contemporary is in terms of information; but information is not what occasions encounter with truth and acknowledgement of untruthfulness. The god must provide the condition for such recognition, whether for the contemporary or the non-contemporary.[28] And if some immensely powerful contemporary or near-contemporary brought to bear all possible resources of research and testimony to establish a dependable and universally acceptable report of the events around the god's manifestation, this – although producing an *historical* certainty ironically greater even than that of the contemporary – would have nothing to do with faith. If an infallibly comprehensive historical record put before us miraculous events at which we were invited to 'wonder', this would not be the wonder of faith itself.[29] Rather like Wittgenstein speaking of the sense of the world being 'miraculous', the wonder of faith is radically different from finding aspects of the world amazing. The follower, in Kierkegaard's schema, is not amazed at certain events in the life of the incarnate god (and therefore not at others), but wonders at what is done in the entire reality that is the god's incognito in the world, whose effect is the new and converting self-reflection that is the recognition of untruth. If faith requires the veracity of the contemporary's witness as its condition, faith will have as its object not the god but the reliable contemporary.[30]

26 Ibid., pp. 29–33.
27 Ibid., p. 33.
28 E.g., ibid., pp. 65–6.
29 Ibid., pp. 92–3.
30 Ibid., pp. 100–1.

Wittgenstein's general debt to Kierkegaard is regularly acknowledged; but their closeness in this particular connection still needs some further explication. Wittgenstein's throwaway remark about the possible historical falsity of the Gospels as a matter indifferent for belief makes a good deal more sense if read against the background of Kierkegaard's analysis of what the contemporary follower can and cannot claim: Wittgenstein is in his own idiom clearly repeating Kierkegaard's point about what is the *condition* for belief. In his notes in 1937, he explicitly wrestles with Kierkegaard in regard to the eternal consequences of faith: if the consequences are such, why is God not clearer in communicating what has to be said? But if God sets out all this in a riddle or in the form of four not obviously consistent records, is this not because the appropriate form simply *is* a riddle, or a set of 'quite averagely historically plausible' narratives?[31] As Wittgenstein remarked to Drury, 'It is impossible for me to say what form the record of such an event should take.'[32] The excellent discussion of the two philosophers by Genia Schoenbaumsfeld, *A Confusion of the Spheres*,[33] notes that both see the philosophical task as the removal of illusions about the thinking subject, a task which is not achieved by information or by erecting a 'world-view'. Their shared suspicion of metaphysics is a suspicion of any claim to a 'God's eye' view of reality,[34] or of the idea that we can 'think ourselves out of' illusion, untruthfulness.[35] But what is especially interesting is their convergence on the questions we have been examining – the nature of Christology, of faith in Christ as risen, and the role of the gospel witness in generating faith. If Kierkegaard clears the ground for understanding what the grammar of 'God' requires in this connection, Wittgenstein in effect applies the same kind of argument to the whole discourse of value. It is not that he is arguing a textbook disjunction of fact and value, in which 'value' becomes simply a judgement that cannot be backed up by fact: it is rather that he seeks to clarify the grammar of value itself as the result of the wide variety of 'cultural

31 CV, p. 31.
32 Rush Rhees, op. cit., p. 164.
33 Genia Schoenbaumsfeld, *A Confusion of the Spheres: Kierkegaard and Wittgenstein on Philosophy and Religion*, Oxford: Oxford University Press, 2007.
34 Ibid., p. 46.
35 Ibid., pp. 50–1.

inductions' in which human beings engage with each other, in a way for which the mere transfer of information is of limited importance. As he acknowledges with increasing clarity, this means that we are constantly bound up in the exchanging of narratives, continuously being reworked to draw out their 'compelling' aspects, so that we can see why certain transitions are natural within the terms of the discourse. And in this respect at least, Wittgenstein is very far from suggesting that religious language is a special case among discourses: what marks it out is not that it is somehow more inaccessible to fact or 'reason' than other kinds of discourse, but that it insists on the most radical kind of self-dispossession, the recognition of some fundamental lack of truthfulness in our self-perception. Kierkegaard is manifestly a major presence in the background of all he has to say about the error of linking conversion to information.

3.

But there is a further point worth making in relation to these two philosophers and their responses to the Gospels and to the figure of Christ, a point that connects them – surprisingly – to the mainstream of Christian doctrinal reflection. Wittgenstein certainly and Kierkegaard probably would have seen the history of Christological debate and clarification as 'grammatically' odd – as claiming the territory that cannot be claimed, from whose vantage point we can describe the ways of God in the third person. But there is a way of reading the tradition which echoes precisely this central grammatical anxiety of both philosophers. The classical doctrinal definition of the Council of Chalcedon declares that Christ is complete in both divinity and humanity; and much of the monumentally complex argument of the centuries that followed turned upon what was meant by completeness in humanity. In the debates leading up to Chalcedon the point had already been made that it was improper to associate some of Jesus' activities with his divinity and some with his humanity; and by the eighth century, the majority of the Church had agreed that the Chalcedonian Definition entailed the unbroken exercise of *created* activity and will in Christ. In other words, the divine indwelling in Christ, the presence of the eternal Word united with the humanity of Jesus, cannot be conceived or described in terms of anything that looks like a divine 'interruption' of the human narrative.

Kierkegaard's argument that any such interruption would – paradoxically – signal not the omnipotence of God but its opposite is a typically counter-intuitive and teasing version of this. Referring back to his earlier parable[36] of the king who seeks to woo the beggar maid, Kierkegaard explains how the god has, in a crucial sense, less 'freedom' than such a king: 'He cannot betray his identity ... he does not have the possibility of suddenly disclosing that he is, after all, the king – which is no perfection in the king (to have this possibility) but merely manifests his impotence and the impotence of his resolution, that he actually is incapable of becoming what he wanted to become.'[37] For God to interrupt the human life with which he has united himself in order to communicate with humanity is for God to admit defeat, to admit that what is said and done humanly cannot communicate in a manner that transforms and saves. Even more, it undermines the very principle of the god's action in 'descending' to the level of equality with us: *that* is itself the thing that has to be communicated, the freedom of the god to be what he is not for the sake of uniting human beings to the truth they repudiate. All we can say about the visible sign of divinity in the human Jesus is that his mission consumes him; he understands himself as identical with his work.[38] But this is a matter of what can be said of an uninterrupted humanity, not of any epiphany of Godhead. An epiphany would necessarily in this context be an epiphany of something *less* than God: an agency that was not suffi-ciently free or self-sustaining to be wholly itself in the humble and formally anonymous shape of the human ('formally' anonymous in the sense that there is nothing odd or imperfect in the way Jesus satisfies the criteria for being recognized as human).

Connecting this with Wittgenstein's discussion of ethics, we could say that the point made in the shape of Chalcedonian Christology is that the divinity of Christ is not an item of *information* about him. Divinity is not a predicate that can be added to the sum total of what is true of Jesus as human individual ('Jewish, male, brown-eyed, divine ...'). His divinity is thus not something that can figure in any argument about how we should respond to him; and the theologian is not free to use the affirmation of

36 Kierkegaard, op. cit., pp. 26ff.
37 Ibid., p. 55.
38 Ibid., pp. 56–7.

divinity as any sort of explanation of either certain facts in Jesus' life or of the response of faith itself. We have seen how Dietrich Bonhoeffer, whose Christology is arguably more deeply shaped by Kierkegaard's approach than that of any other modern theologian,[39] insisted that – for example – the use of the miraculous elements in the narrative of Jesus to confirm his divinity would be a kind of category mistake; after all, miraculous deeds were the stock in trade of plenty of wandering sages in the classical world.[40] But there is a deeper point to be drawn out. Classical Christology has to be understood as itself part of the process of clarifying the grammar of God. If God acts fully and without restraint in the human life of Jesus yet does not in any way 'break the surface' of that humanity or replace some aspect of it, it is clear that there can be no sense in which finite agency and infinite are in competition with each other. As some have put it, the religious believer does not claim that there are any more facts in the universe than the unbeliever allows; they may disagree about the status of various reports of fact, they may offer radically divergent readings of fact, but *in principle* their difference is not about the presence in the world of some extra agency called divine. The believer will no doubt maintain that there are events and outcomes that would have been radically different in a different kind of universe, one that was *not* permeated by or sustained by divine agency, but cannot claim that belief gives certain access to extra matters of fact within the realm of contingent and finite causes. And, as we have seen, this is precisely Wittgenstein's claim about ethics: the person making an ethical judgement does not have access to extra information that would clinch an argument about what to do; she is simply someone who inhabits a culture in which certain 'moves' have become clear, certain connections have been acknowledged and must be acted upon. As Schoenbaumsfeld explains with admirable clarity, this does not mean that the religious believer or the ethical agent has no beliefs about what is true of the world and is simply adopting a willed set of policies: 'no such thing as a fully fledged understanding of

---

39 Above, pp. 186–91.

40 See, for example, *The Bonhoeffer Reader*, ed. Clifford J. Green and Michael P. DeJonge, Minneapolis: Fortress Press, 2013, p. 311, from Bonhoeffer's 1933 lectures on Christology. The parallels with Wittgenstein's comments are striking.

any domain of discourse is possible without both aspects of understanding [sc. what Schoenbaumsfeld calls "external" and "internal" understanding, doctrinal assertion and personal or "mystical" involvement] being present.'[41] The difficult notion for some philosophers is that of 'beliefs about what is true *of the world*': these are not beliefs about what is true of states of affairs in the world but about how adequately to operate what Wittgenstein calls a 'system of reference' affecting every specific claim about matters of fact (remember Wittgenstein's comparison with the language of colour: we do not ask what would be different if it were not the case that things had colour because things having colour is not a fact among others in the list of actually prevailing states of affairs).

In sum, what Wittgenstein and Kierkegaard have to say about the gospel narrative and about the nature of the grammar of claims about divinity – divinity in general and Christ's in particular – offers a novel and clarifying perspective on some of the features of classical doctrinal language about Christ. Any qualification of the Chalcedonian insistence on the complete-ness of the two 'natures' will in fact compromise the grammar of God: it will imply that God acts in the world by displacing finite agency and thus cannot coexist in the same logical space as finite agency. But if this is the case, then divine agency becomes a rival fact in the universe; and as such it cannot make upon us the unconditional claim that it purports to. Unless religious discourse is of a piece with the judgements of ethics and aesthetics that Wittgenstein analyses, it becomes something that can in principle be refuted by evidence: it has been 'made to be true' by a certain causal process and thus can be made untrue by another process. To recognize this is not to say that religious (or ethical or aesthetic) conviction is beyond challenge; only that such challenge has to be about a global shift in the framing of reference, not the production of a new piece of evidence. Thus the confes-sion of Christ as divine – or simply as risen from the dead – has the form of a proposed global 'reading' of facts; one such fact being the narratives of those who have responded in a certain way, those who have created the cul-ture of faith. To put it in more theological terms, it is a reminder that the acknowledgement of Christ's divinity is inseparable from the reality of the

41 Op. cit., p. 188.

Church. The imperative to which the Church's gathering is a response is the way in which 'the affirmation of a truth' about Christ is encountered. Does this mean that explicit Christological doctrine is an inappropriate exercise? Not necessarily: as we have seen, clarifying the grammar and avoiding reductive, unbalanced or mythologizing ways of talking about God is not a waste of time; we need ways of checking whether it is indeed *God* we are still talking about, and this must apply to what we say about God in Christ. But Wittgenstein would, I think, insist that Christ's divinity is essentially what is affirmed by the practice of repentance, radical change of life or obedience or, most simply, love. And if anyone should be tempted to say, 'Is that all?' it is not difficult to imagine a derisively incredulous reply from the philosopher: '*All?*'

INDEX

A Note on the Author

Rowan Williams is the former Archbishop of Canterbury and the Master of Magdalene College Cambridge. The author of many books from *The Wound of Knowledge* to *On Augustine* he is also a published poet and contributor to the *New Statesman*.